THE RECOVERY OF SPIRIT IN HIGHER EDUCATION

THE RECOVERY OF SPIRIT IN HIGHER EDUCATION

Christian and Jewish Ministries
in Campus Life

Edited by ROBERT RANKIN

*with Myron B. Bloy, Jr., David A. Hubbard,
Parker J. Palmer*

THE SEABURY PRESS NEW YORK

1980
The Seabury Press
815 Second Avenue
New York, N.Y. 10017

Printed in the United States of America

Library of Congress Cataloging in Publication Data

Main entry under title:
The Recovery of spirit in higher education.
1. Universities and colleges—United States—
Religion—Addresses, essays, lectures. 2. Church and
college in the United States—Addresses, essays, lectures.
I. Rankin, Robert, 1915-
LC383.R36   378   80-20770   ISBN 0-8164-0469-0

DEDICATION

This book is dedicated to Jewish, Roman Catholic and Protestant campus ministers in America whose missions, conducted quietly behind the scenes, save the lives of countless students and their mentors— through hope which loosens the bonds of despair and faith which grants new vision.

CONTENTS

PREFACE

For fifty-three years the Danforth Foundation has expended its funds exclusively on education—primarily in efforts to assist in the humanizing of learning. Included in the concerns of the Foundation has been the role of religion in both private and public colleges. Faculty striving to clarify the value-laden issues of education have been supported by the Danforth Foundation through grants, fellowships, and Foundation-sponsored programs.

In early years, a portion of the Foundation funds supported endowments and grants to encourage universities, both public and private, to establish departments of religion, and approximately seven hundred persons have been appointed to study and research fellowships and internships in campus ministry. Other grants supported campus ministry projects in peace studies, ministries with minorities, women in campus ministry, values education, and in efforts to start discussions among evangelical, charismatic, and ecumenical campus ministers. Two major research projects were funded by the Foundation: *The Church, the University, and Social Policy: The Danforth Study of Campus Ministries,* by Kenneth Underwood, 1963–69, and *Church-Sponsored Higher Education in the United States* by Manning Pattillo, Jr. and Donald MacKenzie, completed in 1965. Since 1950, over twelve hundred persons have been directly involved as participants or consultants with the Foundation in programs in support of ministries in higher education including the Danforth Seminary Intern Program and several campus ministry fellowship programs sponsored by the Foundation.

This year, Robert Rankin completes twenty-two years of service to the field of campus ministry as a member of the Danforth Foundation staff. This book is both a tribute to his leadership in the field and a challenge for the future.

The Foundation staff celebrates the contributions of countless persons who have served to enhance the quality of life on college campuses—including the many who have worked with Foundation projects. This volume, prepared by seventeen writers and thirty consultants, attempts to report some of the results of the work the Foundation has accomplished through its campus ministry programs and their vitality and significance. We express appreciation to all who have assisted in these activities in past years. We extend special recognition to the three persons who accepted the responsibility to serve as directors of this project: Myron B. Bloy, Jr., David A. Hubbard, and Parker J. Palmer. They have given generously of their time and have shared with the reader their insight into the role of campus ministry on college and university campuses. To them, the writers and the consultants, the Foundation is grateful.

Gene L. Schwilck
President
The Danforth Foundation

EDITOR'S NOTE

In 1978, I called a meeting of advisors to the Danforth Foundation to ask how I could best use the remaining time, before my retirement in 1980, to enhance ministries in higher education. The Foundation was soon to end its support of campus ministries. After decades of service to these ministries—through grants, fellowships, projects, research, and publications—what should be our last investment?

I did not like the answer they gave me, namely that I should use the time to write a book about my experience with the vocation of campus ministry. When I reminded them that I was an administrator by trade, not a writer, they had the temerity to say that this would not be the first time an administrator had written a book. The point was driven home by one of the advisors, an administrator who had written several excellent books and, to make matters worse, a person who had published partly because in earlier years I had challenged him to do so.

A chronicle of my professional experiences? I could not justify it. But the persistent pressure of those advisors started an investigation which ended in a recommendation to the Foundation that a book should be published in 1980 to observe the three decades of work the Danforth Foundation had invested in ministries in higher education.

Yet the project is biographical in two ways. First, a few personal episodes and reflections which I have recorded and explored in the introductory and concluding chapters helped to shape plans for the project. Second, the design of the book—which brings together persons of widely diverse religious commitments—is typical of the aims I have pursued as a campus minister and as an officer of a foundation.

R.R.

I

Beginnings ROBERT RANKIN

Two Gifts from Two Persons

"Jesus stood right there by the oven, yesterday, and told me not to let those Japs come back from those camps." To the ears of a young, liberal, Protestant parish minister, that unconditional pronouncement by the parishioner I was visiting induced a double shock, one generated by her theology and the other by her politics. In the first place, Jesus couldn't just drop into her house to chat and, in the second, it was unthinkable that he could have uttered such a judgment about the Americans of Japanese descent who were then, in 1942, interned in relocation camps. Yet there she sat, Grandma Fiehman, an unforgettable member of the small Methodist church in California which I served. Certitude of faith induced a stony look in her eyes, unchallenged by her ownership of a garden farm which had competed with farms owned by Japanese Americans, or by concern for the constitutional rights of those people.

It was not my first collision with this colorful member of the first church I served as minister. She considered my wife and me her personal property and thus felt free to visit the parsonage in our absence to examine the books we read or the sermons I prepared. I had been told by my ministerial predecessor that on occasion Grandma, who believed passionately in the inerrancy of the Bible, could be expected to arise in church during the sermon to denounce the heresies uttered by liberal clergy. I prepared for this fearsome event by typing 1 Corinthians 14:34–35 in my pulpit notebook, which I intended to read after I had inquired if she believed in the truth of the Holy Scriptures: "As in all the churches of the saints, the women

should keep silence in the churches . . . they should be subordinate
. . . it is shameful for a woman to speak in church."

No opportunity was given to me to use that strange teaching in
Corinthians since Grandma elected to suffer in silence. Why was I
spared? There were at least two possible explanations. My homilet-
ics were so pallid as to threaten no one. And it is not impossible that
Grandma had inspected my pulpit notebook and knew that if she
interrupted a sermon she would be impaled by Saint Paul, hoist as it
were by her own petard.

Yet even with the protection of the spurious and ambiguous defense of Saint Paul, I must confess that Grandma scared the day-
lights out of me. That apprehension, one which revealed the
vulnerability of my liberal theology, became a basic ingredient in
my spiritual formation.

If Grandma had been the only critical evangelical force at work in
my experience during those days, I could have been propelled into
single-minded, if not bitter, opposition to the fundamentalist-evan-
gelical wing of the church. But she was more than matched by Bill
Hooper, who represented a different breed and became a stronger
evangelical model. It was that edge of strength, I believe, which
converted closed opposition to an open fascination.

Bill Hooper was a rancher whose ruddy, delightful face revealed
his days of work in the sun and whose blue eyes, sparkling under a
thatch of pure white hair, revealed, I believed, his life in the Holy
Spirit. The parish asked him to become superintendent of the Sunday School, and he accepted and handled that responsibility with an
intelligence and spirit unmatched by anyone I have ever known. Bill
listened to Billy Graham and to me, and loved both of us. He
strongly advised me to listen to Billy and read his books, but I doubt
that he ever advised Billy to return the favor. Bill Hooper was a loving man, and the spirit of Christ seemed to beam from him. When
he said "Amen" during a sermon I knew that, despite all of the hom-
iletical frailties of a young parson, I had stumbled into truth or
that I had been grasped by the love of Christ.

I envied Bill Hooper, his difference from me in the quality of his
spirit, his assurance, and the solidarity of his roots in biblical faith,
his concern for other persons and his infectious presence. Bill's gentle power in the congregation, wherein he created confidence among

the people through his capacity to love and to understand, was beautiful to behold. I loved him, and I thank God that this love was stronger than the fear of disaffection and suspicion generated in me by Grandma Fiehman. Through Bill Hooper I began to define a distinction between evangelicals and fundamentalists, and to learn for the first time about the scope and magnitude of the evangelical world. Through him I began to see a new vision of the church's ministry. And, of all things, I was able to feel a first very faint hunch about why Grandma Fiehman hung on to her fundamentalist faith with such fierce tenacity. It is not at all unlikely that in the long run my perception of that terrible strength was more important than any other discovery in those early years.

Another experience in that parish was revelatory. It centered on the Japanese-American civil rights issue which had been dramatized in Grandma Fiehman's vision, and which had evoked vehement criticism among many people on the West Coast and throughout the country. The mayor of our town, the postmaster, the city attorney, and the head of the local American Legion post led an unofficial community coalition to disbar Americans of Japanese descent from United States citizenship. Out of anger inspired by the biblical prophets and by democratic values, and with guts born of nervous bravado, I took on this fearsome foursome from the pulpit and in writing. I composed a long letter to them which began with "But let justice roll down like waters, and righteousness like an everflowing stream" (Am. 5:24). I then moved into the Bill of Rights; shifted to statements of defense of the Japanese-Americans by the former ambassador to Japan, Joseph Grew, and news accounts of the heroism of the Japanese-Americans fighting fascism in Italy; and ended in an attack on the parochial views of those four city fathers. I contended that their ideas could demolish justice for some Americans and threaten the freedom of all.

All of this led to a feisty affair during which I feared I might be handed a one-way ticket out of town. Yet in my fear I had underestimated the power of the church and persons of Bill Hooper's caliber, whose love of Christ required obedience not only to personal evangelism, but to the social responsibilities demanded by the gospel. That little congregation supported me in the struggle against the local principalities and powers, with Bill Hooper in the forefront of the defense. They and he enabled me to grow in certitude and in openness and to learn that evangelical faith could be a powerful force for social justice.

What do these incidents—not unusual in the experience of mainline Protestant clergy in America—have to do with this task of introducing a book on ministries in higher education? In a world boiling with religious and political perils, and with awesome issues facing the church and the university, why bother to mention such seemingly trivial events? They have been recorded because at that time two ideas began to take shape which later affected the plans for this volume: a simple perception about the usefulness of a process of inquiry, and a basic conviction that balance is required in religious faith and ministry.

A PROCESS OF INQUIRY

In that little parish a process of inquiry about the religious faiths of other persons, as well as my own, was initiated. There a process, cultivated in a liberal home and education but which had remained largely mental and abstract, began to change from a condition of thinking to a state of being. The Word became flesh. Problems which had been largely intellectual in character became charged with emotion. Those parish experiences stimulated an inquiry which, after all these years, shows no sign of ending. It required only two years to have some understanding of Bill Hooper and to learn from him, but it has required nearly four decades to begin to understand Grandma Fiehman, to get her on the agenda, and to learn from her.

For one thing, it has taken a long time to understand how fiercely all of us, conservatives and liberals alike, Jews, Catholics, and Protestants alike, require spiritual moorings, something fixed and infallible to depend upon. I have begun to see that it is not enough to say, as liberals are fond of saying, that the Bible should be taken seriously although not literally. The trouble with simply taking the Bible seriously is that we usually don't. Grandma Fiehman was saying, although I doubt that she perceived any fancy nuance in her witness, that it requires the doctrine of inerrancy to produce seriousness. One gets the same impression from a delegate to a Missouri

Synod Lutheran Conference who, in a debate on the authority of the Bible, declared that he not only believed that the whale swallowed Jonah, but claimed that he would believe the Bible even if it reported that Jonah swallowed the whale. That fellow was earnest. He and Grandma Fiehman were driven by desperation into strange theology, and Grandma into dangerous politics and dubious manners as well. Why? They were seized by the conviction that an indescribably precious possession was at stake and must not be lost at any cost.

Now, if I could learn this much from Grandma's fundamentalism, and from the linkage of personal piety and social justice in Bill Hooper's evangelicalism, what could I learn from Jews and Catholics? And what could they learn from us?

Grandma and Bill were the first in the parade of people who, through a succession of evolutionary and revolutionary events, challenged, altered, battered, demolished, and enriched my religious commitment and knowledge. This is what happens to every man and woman who takes religious faith seriously. In my experience it has involved a long and varied succession of people and events, granted through twelve years as a campus minister at Oberlin College and the Claremont Colleges, through a year working for the Rockefeller Brothers Fund, and through twenty-two years as an officer of the Danforth Foundation. That succession of people includes university rabbis, Roman Catholic nuns and priests, Protestant clergy of various kinds—evangelicals, liberals, and humanists—and laity in all three faiths. They include academic and foundation people, teachers, administrators, and trustees who respect religious faith as an ingredient in human growth. They also include others who look upon religion only as an obstacle, as an affront to intelligence, and who regard the profession of campus ministry as an embarrassment, as a contradiction in terms.

It was that succession of experiences which led me, along with many others, to discover in the early 1970s a phenomenon in American religious life: persons, who because of the reality and radicalness of their differences had not imagined that they could join together in any enterprise, were becoming willing not only to work with one another, but to learn from and teach one another. Clearly, major shifts were revealing new needs and offering new hopes. We discovered that there is no conceivable way for the spiritual and moral hunger of the people within the academy to be nourished unless all who are linked by religious faiths find ways to work together.

Something new is happening which we do not fully understand. A wind of the Spirit is rising, a force before and beyond our perception is at work, one which enables us to see new visions and to feel new hopes. That reality enabled a group of people from sharply divergent faith commitments within Judaism, Catholicism, and Protestantism to accept the invitation of the Danforth Foundation to contribute to this book. They were asked to draw upon tested wisdom from their variegated experiences, to explore and interpret the religious phenomena occurring in and around the profession of campus ministry which is placed, sometimes precariously, between the church and the university.

Two convictions guided the project from its beginning. First, we were determined not to indulge in the luxury of reductionism, to reduce down to any one factor, or any few, an explanation for complex religious phenomena. Second, we would not court reductionism's equally retarded ecumenical cousin, settlement on the lowest common denominator. On the contrary, we were determined to honor our differences and to build upon them. We hoped that the interconfessional process we followed would keep us honest and would spur us to offer each other the best thinking of our faith communities. We looked for points of agreement not on the lowest possible level, but on the highest. If, for example, an evangelical built a case about faith's requirements for social justice derived from commitments to the Lordship of Jesus Christ and the authority of the Bible and found, as the exploration proceeded, that it coincided with a claim made by a rabbi derived from talmudic authority, the Jewish experience, and biblical prophecy, we discovered an element we covet: the highest possible denominator. Yet when points of agreement were not found—and that happened frequently and emphatically—we lived with the mystery and power of difference.

The process of inquiry was affected by another longing, one generated primarily from a long-standing personal need of mine. Amidst all the complexity of this book, all the differences among the authors and their varied ideas, I hungered for simplicity—not reductionism, but simplicity. The need for simplicity became particularly poignant during my years in the campus ministry when I was assailed by hosts of conflicting intellectual and ideological claims.

I can recall one especially revelatory time during my years as chaplain of the Claremont Colleges, a moment of professional paranoia familiar I dare say to all campus ministers. It seemed as if all the complexities of the world and all the demands for ministry were aimed precisely at me. I confronted a complicated combination of questions generated by the church, the academy, and the government— a heavy trinity. The church seemed to call upon me for theological perceptions and interpretations about what on earth was going on; the college called for understanding and conduct of the teaching-learning process, plus a sympathetic and informed understanding about the importance of the advancement of learning through research; and the government called for public leadership aimed at the achievement of justice among the oppressed.

As if this were not enough, at the same time I entertained some serious apprehensions about my professional work. It seemed to me that the Claremont Colleges were expecting me to *preach* so convincingly and winsomely that throngs of students, teachers, and administrators would attend College Church; to *teach* so wisely and well that the colleges would face difficulty handling registration for my courses in New Testament; to *counsel* so sensitively and compassionately that long lines of students, hordes, would form outside my office on the Pomona College campus; to *handle* administrative and managerial duties with crisp efficiency and diplomatic tact; and to *smile* grandly in a genuinely relaxed manner while performing this juggling act.

It did not matter at the time that not one of the administrators or professors or students had ever expressed such expectations. In fact they had consistently offered encouragement. But I thought that they expected all that, and I knew that I did; so I believed that my work was doomed to disappoint them and I knew that it frustrated me. It was during such a time that a member of the Pomona College English department, a witty and wonderful man, perceived that wars were being waged within me. He made a comradely but arch comment about slings and arrows shot at, as well as by, campus clergy. There was something healing in this recognition of pain and in his ardently welcomed friendship.

It was also during such a bruising time that I heard an address at Scripps College by a visiting lecturer who attributed the following

statement to Justice Oliver Wendell Holmes: "I do not give a fig for
the simplicity this side of complexity, but I would give my life for
the simplicity on the other side of complexity." It was a revelation
and a turning point. It led me—by what psychological and spiritual
trajectories I do not know—to some healthy conclusions. Our souls
and minds obligate us, just as do the church and the academy, to
move beyond the luxury and the danger of naiveté, the simplicity
this side of encounter with complex reality. We are required by our
moral responsibilities to go beyond oversimplification, to resist "the
sacrifice of complexity . . . a crucial form of the vice of untruthful-
ness."[1] But the longing for simplicity is legitimate if it is aimed toward the simplicity on the other side of tested exploration and
conflict.

Another perception, inspired by Justice Holmes, took the form of
a simple point of personal theology. While perhaps others and I expected too much, God did not. How was I so sure about that? All I
mean is that the talents God has given us reveal something of his
expectations for us. While the colleges may have expected a lot and
while I expected the impossible, God, it seemed to me, did not. I was
called not to do everything but some things, just those which I could
do. I was called to leave to others the hosts of duties that remained
not only in worship, but in teaching, devotional life, administration,
counseling, finance, and all of the rest.

THE NEED FOR BALANCE

It required the genius of Kenneth Underwood to sort out these
questions. From 1963 until his death in 1968, Kenneth Underwood
directed the Danforth Study of Campus Ministries, a large investigation which embraced all of the struggles I had known and many
more.[2] Through an investigative process he called "prophetic inquiry," he led a way through complexity to the simplicity on the
other side. Underwood recognized, as I shall note later, that the
complexities at work in the interstices between the university and
the church, and the persons who worked and lived within them, require different kinds of ministries, four different kinds handled by
different persons, groups, and institutions. Underwood passionately
advocated the cultivation of balanced ministries which together

would respond to varied spiritual and moral needs of the church and the university.

In several personal conversations Kenneth Underwood stressed how important it was for the Danforth Foundation, and for me, to comprehend that he did not expect that the four tasks could ever be handled by any one religious community, let alone one person. His action theory called for a combination of missions and a variety of gifts brought by persons working in coordinated teams in religious communities and educational institutions. In collaboration they could match the complexities of university life and bring to them ministries which offer a healthy balance of spiritual commitment, concern for social justice, talents which would enrich community life, and responsible governance of academic and religious affairs.

My conviction about the need for a multidimensional, balanced ministry also emerged in my experience in that small California parish. I first saw its outline in the link between the spiritual disciplines of the congregation and Christian humanitarian concern for the American-Japanese, in the connection between the power of the gospel and its moral derivatives. I began to understand, although faintly at first, that any one mode of ministry without other modes is dangerous as well as incomplete. It was imperative to affirm the fullness of Bill Hooper's faith: his personal piety, his social conscience, and his commitment to the church community. It was equally imperative to challenge the frightful parochialism of Grandma Fiehman and those four city fathers.

I learned the hard way about the destructiveness of imbalance, the danger of one-dimensional religion, in a jolting experience nine years after I joined the staff of the Danforth Foundation. At that time I gave my strong support to a campus ministry project which turned out to be distorted and dangerously imbalanced. It was programmed for disaster and I should have recognized that, but I did not.

In 1967, the Danforth Foundation received reports about the formation of a student Christian movement among Orthodox, Protestant, and Roman Catholic youth, an effort to establish a new ecumenical and intercollegiate Christian organization. Presumably, it was to be built on the remains of several predecessor movements, including the Student Volunteer Movement, the Student YMCA and YWCA, and the National Student Christian Federation, which was the latest of several attempts to reorganize mainline Protestant intercollegiate life. The new effort was called the University Christian Movement and it would, I believed, draw strength and momentum from the spiritual and moral forces at work in the Orthodox, Roman Catholic, and Protestant faith communities.

It looked like a bold and beneficial venture. The Student Young Men's Christian Association, in which I had been active as an undergraduate at the State University of Iowa and which I had served professionally at Oberlin College; the student Young Women's Christian Association; the Student Volunteer Movement, which had challenged young people to enter foreign missions; and the World Student Christian Federation were all losing strength. The new coalition seemed exciting not only because it brought Orthodox, Roman Catholic, and Protestant students together for the first time, but also because it seemed to contain the promise of reviving and building upon those older noble movements.

Thus, when leaders of the University Christian Movement approached the Danforth Foundation for funds to support their first national conference, I responded with enthusiasm. The prospect of slowing, if not stopping, the evaporation of enthusiasm and commitment in the older groups was immensely stimulating. I seized upon the UCM proposal as a means of encouraging the birth of something new, built on the best of the old—a liberal's dream! Although my colleagues on the staff of the Foundation did not share all my enthusiasm for the proposal and some trustees believed the national conference would be a waste of time and money, I advocated a grant. It was reluctantly approved, and fifty thousand dollars were committed to support the first national conference of the UCM to be held in Cleveland that winter: "Process '67."

In 1968, the officials of the University Christian Movement voted the organization out of existence and it sank out of sight, vanished from the scene without a trace, its death ending a long succession of national student Christian conferences sponsored by mainline Protestant movements. This created a huge vacuum in American student religious life, a tragic loss. Since those last rites I have remarked on occasion that, at my urging, the Danforth Foundation had furnished the UCM with sufficient funds to purchase a fifty-thousand-dollar gun with which they committed suicide. The reservations and hunches of the staff and the resistance of the trustees had been correct. My hope had been sadly and naively wrong, a victim of imbalanced judgment based upon simplicity this side of complexity.

What had happened to cause UCM's demise? For one thing, it occurred during a time when people, young and old, seemed to enjoy destroying things—an unlovely product of the Vietnam War. The UCM was vulnerable, easy prey to an anger at everything that dominated the mood of American youth. For another, the University Christian Movement was imbalanced. Neither Bill Hooper nor Grandma Fiehman was there. "Process '67" relied on one form of ministry for its direction and motivation, the mode of Christian social action concerned for justice. Its death certificate was signed by its indifference to other modes of ministry.

An interpretation of "Process '67" by Davis S. Wiley of the University of Wisconsin and Jackson W. Carroll of Emory University, distributed in 1971, furnished documentation for this claim.[3] In a thorough and respectful analysis, Wiley and Carroll noted that the Cleveland conference was dominated by "peace symbols, calls for political action of the liberal and radical varieties . . . political graffiti . . . a profusion of McCarthy and Kennedy buttons, and strobe lights at the conference-sponsored rock dances." The conference program was organized around "Depth Education Groups" on subjects such as "Violence in American Life," "the Growing Threat of U.S. Militarism," "Latin American Politics," "New Life Style," "White Power and Ghetto Exploitation," and "the Marxist-Christian Dialogue." A service of worship featured the burning of draft cards.

What was the glue that held the University Christian Movement together? Cohesion was not, as I had permitted myself to hope, created by ecumenical depths drawn from Orthodox, Roman Catholic, and Protestant spirituality, contemplation, and action. Although the UCM involved Christian students and clergy from those three faiths, the main ingredients of the glue were political dissidence, anger against inequities in racial relations, the threat of militarism, and oppression at home and abroad. Its glue was moral conscience, but a morality with few roots into spiritual disciplines and into continuing communities of faith. It is significant that, as Jackson and Carroll reported, "in preparing for 'Process '67,' the traditional Student Volunteer Movement Quadrennial channels of recruiting participants were bypassed." Moreover, many of the campus ministers who worked with the Cleveland conference "were without constituencies."

Looking back, it now seems clear to me that many of the people involved in the UCM had, with the best of intentions but with the worst of politics, detached themselves from the primary sources of their political and financial as well as spiritual power. They had broken away from their basic constituencies: the churches and the previous student Christian movements. The UCM had pulled its roots out of the soil which had sustained its predecessors.

It is interesting to see that the Student Young Men's Christian Association and the Student Young Women's Christian Association, together with the Student Christian Movement, are now returning to the national scene. For example, the Student YMCA has recently conducted consultations about the re-formation of a national movement. These meetings, one of which I attended in 1978, draw strength primarily from well-established local university associations which refused to evaporate as a result of the demise of the University Christian Movement. It will be fascinating to see if the intercollegiate Y, which has a long history among campus ministry communities in America, having begun at the University of Michigan and the University of Virginia in 1858, will return to national strength. An international conference of the World Student Christian Federation will take place in the summer of 1981 at Berkeley, California. Whether the Federation can and will seize the moment to enable rebirth to happen is also a fascinating question.

In 1979, twelve years after the Cleveland UCM conference, I attended an altogether different kind of student Christian conference: "Urbana '79," the triennial missions conference sponsored by the Inter-Varsity Christian Fellowship (IVCF), the largest evangelical parachurch organization in the United States. It was a remarkable event not only in its immense size—seventeen thousand people—and its superb organization, but in its spirit. No explanation on the basis of the tidal wave of conservatism moving through American religious and political life, nor the organizational excellence of the preparation and leadership of the conference, can account for that spirit. To understand "Urbana '79" one is driven to theological and spiritual conclusions. The spiritual commitment to Jesus Christ on the part of the students, faculty, and missionaries in attendance and their personal reliance on the power and truth of the Bible were driving forces which must not be underestimated. Moreover, the conference, in my view, was nourished by a theological system and was held within an evangelical society, both of which in their ways are as powerful, and are as variegated in form, as is the Roman Catholic church.

Yet there was a fundamental flaw in "Urbana '79," caused by the almost total absence in the major addresses of the form of ministry which, in its overwhelming abundance in Cleveland in 1967, suffocated the University Christian Movement. The basic mistake was the same: imbalance. The prophetic call for social justice, for systemic criticism of national priorities which create injustice, was almost silent in Urbana. The seventeen thousand people in attendance needed desperately to hear the evangelical witness of Professor Ronald Sider as articulated in his chapter in this book. They needed to hear the declaration in 1976 by Reverend Davie Napier—Old Testament scholar, seminary president, and campus minister—that

any talk or practice of evangelism . . . that avoids identity with and care for the hungry, the poor and powerless; any claim to the propagation of "Good News" that is not also "good news to the poor"; any alleged commitment to the Gospel of Jesus Christ unaccompanied by a fully responsible and informed participation in the life of this very powerful nation at the level of public policy—any such evangelism is, in true biblical understanding, truncated and distorted if not fradulent.[4]

There was a major exception to the silence at Urbana, in a small but critically important series of workshops on "the Gospel and Social Concern." There the call to piety and the call to justice were proclaimed with equal seriousness. The students who attended— about three hundred at the session I observed—were there because the Bible told them to come. The social responsibilities related to hunger, poverty, bigotry and violence were repeatedly answered with biblical references which, when cited, put an end to doubt about what those students were called to do. Questions were also raised by those students about systemic problems arising from international, political, and economic forces which cause cruelty and bigotry. I doubt that one of those approximately three hundred students at the workshop I visited would have questioned for a moment the truth of Davie Napier's claim, nor the claims of Ronald

Sider about the heretical neglect of social responsibilities of many evangelicals.

Yet those students represented only a small minority of the seventeen thousand attending the Urbana conference. It is tragic that the convention planners failed to proclaim this basic and neglected message in the plenary sessions so that all of the participants in "Urbana '79" could hear this disturbing word of God. It could have recalled them to the balanced heritage of eighteenth- and nineteenth-century evangelicalism which took this biblical mandate seriously and spearheaded reform in many areas of social and economic injustice. While some veteran observers of IVCF whom I interviewed agreed with that assessment, they insisted that the proportion of evangelical students who are responsive to the call for social justice, the so-called "new evangelicals," is increasing.

There was another related flaw at Urbana, namely its predominantly white, middle-class constituency. Despite powerful criticisms by black evangelicals regarding insufficient minority participation and leadership at previous triennial meetings—the kinds of concerns reported by Eric Payne in this book—and despite a concerted effort on the part of the Inter-Varsity staff to increase the number of minority persons, "Urbana '79" remained on the whole a white, middle-class meeting.

In fairness, three observations should be made. At the time of "Urbana '79," the approximately three hundred full-time field staff members of IVCF contained twenty blacks and ten Asians, ten percent of the professionals. The students participating at "Urbana '79" were in large part products of American Protestantism and reflected the class and racial constituencies of the churches. Finally, it must be confessed that the track record of IVCF in minority participation is much better than this book's. A consultant to the Danforth Campus Ministry Project, the Reverend Richard Hicks, formerly director of Ministries to Blacks in Higher Education, laid it on the line when he wrote that "the Black church from its very beginning has been in the forefront of the struggle for human justice" and that "more Black writers would have added a perspective to the present book which is missing."

"Urbana '79" and "Process '67" symbolized sea changes in American religious life, for understandable reasons. Both contained assurances. Both possessed frightening flaws. Urbana was starved

for the form of ministry which had glutted the Cleveland conference. "Process '67" needed spiritual roots. Both compel us to consider the drastic importance of the fullness of faith, of prophetic
inquiry informed by many disciplines, and of a healthy balance of
ministries.

As reported earlier, it required the remarkable combination of the
intelligence and faith of Kenneth Underwood's research to spell out
the need for balance in ministry in higher education. His research,
published in 1969, two years after the Cleveland UCM conference,
demonstrated the need for four modalities of ministry: those of the
pastor, the priest, the prophet, and the king. In Underwood's view,
and in his interpreters' analysis, these four modalities were "fore-
shadowed in the Old Testament [and are] fully embodied in Jesus
Christ and are historically normative for the Christian community."[5]
As described by Underwood and by the commissioners of the study,
the pastoral role provides care for persons; the priestly function
proclaims the faith and conducts the sacraments; the prophetic ministry is concerned for justice and lifts up the challenge for social and
economic changes required to assure humane values in society; and
the kingly role relates to responsibility for the governance of faith,
that is, the political function of ministry to fulfill the requirements of
pastoral, priestly, and prophetic ministries.

William Kolb, the chairman of the Commission of the Danforth
Study of Campus Ministries, together with his colleagues, stressed
the wholeness and the unity of those modalities in *New Wine,* an interpretation of Underwood's work:

It is Underwood's claim that although different individuals may carry out
these roles in varying degrees, the roles cannot be separated in the total
ministry of the church without grave distortion of that ministry. He believed that at the present time the prophetic and governing ministries
have been neglected, and that this neglect has led to the failure to care for
human beings and to shape the social order to the ends of justice and hu-
maneness, as well as to severe distortions of the priestly and pastoral
modes of ministry. For Underwood there had to be an unbreakable unity
of the modes of ministry . . .[6]

THE DESIGN OF THE STUDY

The two factors—the process of inquiry and the commitment to
balanced ministries—contributed to the plans for this book. Also,

there was a need and an opportunity to review the present conditions and future prospects of campus ministry based upon information gleaned from years of work by the Danforth Foundation in support of the profession. The Foundation had administered grants, fellowship and internship programs, projects, research, publications, and had served as a think tank in the field. The Foundation—which works independently from churches and academic institutions, but which had supported both—was in an advantageous position to explore the opportunities and obstacles in ministries in higher education.

From that base of experience—with Jews, Roman Catholics, and Protestant evangelicals and liberals—we have sought in this book to explore three elements of faith and ministry which we regarded as indispensable: spirituality, action, and community. As we proceeded we discovered that those three elements were inseparable. For example, Parker Palmer, in his introduction to the second section of this book, notes that we need to learn not to ask how to relate these dimensions of faith, but rather "how to overcome the habit of seeing them as separate." I came to perceive an ancient truth afresh: to know God is to do justice, and the knowing and the doing require and create community.

A consultant to the project, Reverend Ralph G. Dunlop, formerly chaplain of Northwestern University, emphasized this point when asked for criticisms in the early stages of the project's planning. Dunlop noted that we are "talking about Biblical faith, which includes conversion to faith, trust in the Lord God, and care of souls in the gathered community since the world and all people are the parish. The work for social justice comes directly out of that care of souls. It is, then, almost a single task, both with regard to constituency and to the Biblical call from which we take our cues, to which we respond and by which we may be faithful. It is thus truly, literally a catholic task and a catholic community."

This volume, then, seeks to look carefully at one small sector of our common life—the religious events happening within our colleges and universities and the religious communities which have been formed within them. It tries to bring knowledge and commitment from four different faith communities to bear upon three different views of the vocation of campus ministry, at the intersection of the church and the university. How do spiritual life, contemplative life and action, and communal life inform us about our present conditions and our future needs and hopes? To these questions we bring, in each of the three major parts of the book, first an interpretation written by the director of the section in which he introduces the reader to the essayists, followed then by the essays by writers from the four faith communities in the following order: Jewish, Roman Catholic, Protestant evangelical and Protestant liberal.

It needs to be noted that the present book differs from the Underwood study not only in method, but in scope. Kenneth Underwood's distinguished effort examined the large world of the church and the university and sought to grapple with social policies which would release the humanizing and saving energies in each which, through prophetic inquiry, would illumine their work and the problems of the society in which they move. This book looks at a much smaller target: the religious phenomena in higher education and the ministries required to understand them. Yet it seeks to amplify ways through which mature and durable faith may be nurtured among men and women who live and work in academic institutions.

In understanding this task we have looked to religious and lay leaders in higher education to help us all find moorings in a turbulent world and sanity in a society which seems bent toward insanity. We seek durable directions in a world which seems determined to destroy itself.

We attempt this, knowing that America faces a crisis in belief which springs from religious as well as political and economic frailty. We do so also knowing that religion accounts for the worst as well as the best in our culture. Yes, it stands for personal and corporate response to spiritual power and commitment to social justice. In its idolatrous forms, however, it also accounts for arrogance in high places and personal and corporate collapse into greed and fanaticism.

COLLEAGUES AND CONSULTANTS

This book was designed in 1977–78 with the leadership of three persons. The Reverend Myron B. Bloy, Jr., then president of the National Institute for Campus Ministries, is editor of the NICM *Journal* and chaplain and professor at Sweet Briar College, and for two decades has been an advisor to the Danforth Foundation. The

Reverend Dr. David A. Hubbard is president of Fuller Theological Seminary. Beginning in 1974, he helped to lead programs, sponsored by the Danforth Foundation and the Lilly Endowment and administered by the National Institute for Campus Ministries, to encourage conversations among Protestant evangelical and liberal campus ministers and charismatic and other Roman Catholic clergy. Dr. Parker J. Palmer is dean of studies at Pendle Hill, the Quaker Study Center, and in 1973–74 directed an evaluation of the Danforth Foundation's Underwood Fellowship Program for campus ministers. His pioneering work in the examination of the life and work of Thomas Merton has brought fresh insight into Catholic-Protestant relationships.

Through individual and group discussions with these three persons the purposes of the inquiry were determined, namely to examine the religious phenomena occurring in the academic world and in the vocation of campus ministry. We first agreed on the three essential factors in academic ministries which must be examined. Second, we agreed that the task could not be handled responsibly without the participation of Jews, Roman Catholics, and Protestant evangelicals and liberals. Finally, these three persons agreed to serve as editors and interpreters of the three areas of inquiry and to assist in the selection of qualified persons to write the chapters, three persons from each of the four faith constituencies.

The directors, writers, and consultants appointed to work on the book were selected because they bring passion as well as intelligence and faith to their work. Their work is rooted not in a narrow parochialism. Rather, their strength derives from depth and containment of power. While their separate experiences and different commitments were linked in a common task and by respect for one another, those links were never soldered together. They remained faithful to their different commitments and found strength and illumination in those differences, in the creative tension in which they are held.

They are diverse not only in religious commitment, but in their ages and in their years of professional experience. Many bring decades of accomplishment to their contributions, others shorter but well-established careers, and some only a few years of professional work. We see an advantage in this combination of tested long-range labor and the freshness of new experience.

We deliberately chose persons of strong, unapologetic religious commitment. Moreover, we urged them to think and to write on their own, freely, out of their personal beliefs. The chapters, and their interpretations, reveal without apology or restraint the faiths of the writers and their respect for one another. They have been encouraged to write in different styles: in reflections about their careers, in meditation, in studies of individuals, and of academic and religious communities.

We know that these tasks are heavy. Yet in handling them we hope that we have avoided lugubrious attitudes. We trust that the joy of working together, and the celebration of the tasks, have become antidotes to excessive solemnity.

From the beginning, three officers of the Danforth Foundation furnished indispensable counsel. Dr. Gene L. Schwilck, president of the Foundation, gave his full support to the enterprise and worked actively in each stage of its development and funding. Dr. John B. Ervin and Dr. Warren Bryan Martin served with me as staff members of the Committee on Campus Ministry, participated in all of the major decisions of the project, and furnished invaluable and steady criticism. Two secretaries of the Danforth Foundation, Ms. Barbara Campbell and Mrs. Mattylee Ebersbach, were indispensable to the effort. The generous investment of their skills and of themselves repeatedly exceeded vocational requirements.

Rabbi James Diamond, director of the Hillel Foundation in St. Louis, a recipient of the Underwood Fellowship in 1975, consented to assist the editor and served not only as a counselor on questions affecting the university rabbinate, but as advisor and critic throughout the preparation of the entire project. His wisdom, companionship, professional excellence, and wit were invested unsparingly.

Thirty men and women have contributed generously to the book in editorial contributions and criticisms, in preparation of special research reports, and in planning and administering conferences to report the findings of the book to academic and religious organizations. Their names appear in the appendix; each of them has served the project faithfully and their efforts are appreciated beyond the telling.

There was one more counselor. Without the constant support, intelligence, and compassionate criticism of Martha R. Rankin, and her remarkable tolerance for curmudgeonly behavior, my part in this process would have evaporated years ago.

NOTES

1. Alasdair MacIntyre, "Power and Industry Morality," *Saturday Review,* November 24, 1979, p. 36.
2. Kenneth Underwood, *The Church, the University, and Social Policy,* 2 vols. (Middletown, Conn.: Wesleyan University Press, 1969).
3. Jackson W. Carroll and David S. Wiley, *Process 67 and the University Christian Movement,* unpublished report, 1971.
4. Davie Napier, "Prophetic Evangelism," *AD Magazine,* March 1976, p. 32.
5. *New Wine, A report of the Commission on the Danforth Study of Campus Ministries,* The Danforth Foundation, St. Louis, Missouri, 1969, p. 9.
6. Ibid.

II

The Discovery and Nurture of the Spirit

THE DISCOVERY AND NURTURE OF THE SPIRIT
An Interpretation

David Allan Hubbard

INTRODUCTION

My dad's face was awash with joy as he unfurled the crimson and gold blanket. He had just returned from an alumni meeting at the University of Southern California, with the blanket as his prize for being the Trojan who had journeyed farthest to attend the conclave. Fifty years had passed since he had matriculated as a freshman in 1902, and those decades of further education, ministry, and parenthood had only enhanced his loyalty to USC.

My father's smile that day was a glowing definition of *alma mater*. Had it been captured on film as vividly as it is etched in my memory, it could have been the lead photo in a campaign brochure for the university. It trapped the very essence of campus spirit. Its recollection is a relentless reminder of what a place and an experience of higher education can mean to those nurtured by them.

Even analyzing that smile to discover its reasons cannot dim its radiance. Its glow was fired by a host of irreplaceable experiences: a lifelong appreciation of history kindled by his major professors; a contagious enthusiasm for athletics sparked by his years as a two-miler; a winsome gift for leadership encouraged by his place in student government; substantial skills in communication sharpened by his weekly journeys to Buena Park as student preacher; an unyielding dedication to the service of Christ deepened by his participation in the YMCA and Student Volunteer Movement.

That alumni reunion, that Trojan blanket, that incendiary smile all pointed to one thing: the power of an educational institution to seize and shape the spirits of its young. The university counts on that. It knows its clientele—their impressionable age, their first detachment from home, their openness to be nurtured, their quest for identity. And the whole crew—from the football coach, through the chemistry professor, to the alumni director—all count on the time-honored combination: impressionable spirits and the institution's ability to discover and nurture them.

My father's smile, then, can be translated into a mandate for campus ministry. If our colleges and universities can so indelibly stamp their logo on their graduates, if their hegemony over the lives of their daughters and sons is so dominant, then active, effective, vital ministry is utterly essential.

Without it, campus definitions of spirituality—whether by design or default—will be inadequate. And with predictable results: though part of its avowed mission is to criticize the institutions and ideologies of the day, its mood is often uncritically idolatrous; though one of its stated aims is the liberation of the human spirit through knowledge, its actual achievement is often the degradation of that spirit through an abject arrogance that misses the glory of creatureliness under God.

Secular, materialistic, or humanistic definitions of the human condition advertise more than they can deliver. A friend of mine, a Russian physicist who sought asylum in Canada and then became a Christian believer, put it succinctly: "My reading of Hegel and the Bible, exercises discouraged in Russia, convinced me of one great truth: matter cannot create being; being must create matter." The spiritual, then, is a product of spirit.

Those who believe in a biblical approach to creation perceive this and credit the creative contributions of the human spirit to the Holy Spirit. Spirit grounded in Spirit is their definition of spirituality. That definition, in part at least, is the credential of their ministry on our campuses. Their commitment to biblical approaches to spirituality both qualifies and requires them to participate in the nurture for which educational institutions were established.

Why and how some representatives of the biblical traditions seek to do this is the theme of this section. As preparation for their thoughts, I shall attempt to do three things: to sketch in some detail the biblical themes that inform our understanding of spirituality; to test the similarities and differences of the four traditions as they describe and experience their spirituality; to venture some contributions that Hebrew-Christian insights of spirituality can bring to campus ministry.

THE SPIRIT AND THE PEOPLE OF GOD

The work of the Spirit was a central motif throughout the Hebrew-Christian Scriptures and became an essential article in the early Christian creeds. Even a hasty glance at the evidence will suggest how inseparably linked to the work of the Spirit are the mighty works of God and the covenant life of his people.

1. *In the Tanak* (the acronym—based on the initial Hebrew letters of the words for law, prophets, and writings—which Jews use to describe the Hebrew Bible), the Spirit of God does the powerful works of God in ways often marked by mystery. Those twin nuances of power and mystery derived not only from the ways in which Yahweh worked, but also from the fact that the word for spirit, *ruach*, was also the word for wind and breath—whose activities are fraught with mystery and power.

A sample list of the Spirit's deeds will illustrate how powerfully and mysteriously he carries out the divine work, bringing order from chaos at creation (Gen. 1:2), infusing all living creatures with life-giving breath (Gen. 6:17, 7:15), withdrawing that breath when life has run its term (Ps. 104:29), equipping leaders like Samson (Jg. 14:6), Saul (1 Sam. 11:6), and some of the judges (Jg. 3:10, 6:34, 11:29) for works of liberation and deliverance, binding persons to Yahweh in faith and fellowship (Ps. 51:11), speaking mightily through prophets like Micah (Mic. 3:8), and especially Ezekiel (Ezek. 2:2, 3:24, 11:5), anointing Messiah for the tasks of the new age (Is. 11:2), and enlisting young and old, male and female, slave and free to catch and declare the divine word in the messianic era (Jl. 2:28–29; cf. Is. 32:15).

In sum, the Spirit is an agent of Yahweh—an extension of his person, if you will—carrying out Yahweh's work of creation, providence, liberation, redemption, and restoration with all of Yahweh's ability to achieve his will and to surprise us as he does. Given our creatureliness—and the university is nothing but a creature despite its vaunted claims and aspirations—such power is an utter necessity if the work to be done is truly Yahweh's. Given God's majesty—and the men and women of academia are yet his subjects whether or not they recognize it—such mystery should fill us with constant awe at the contrast between Yahweh's excellences and our human limitations.

The word to Zerubbabel is also Yahweh's word to us as we, too, build temples, whether for worship or learning: "Not by might, nor by power, but by my Spirit, says the Lord of hosts" (Zech. 4:6).

2. *In the writings of the Apostles of Jesus,* the Spirit of God carries even further those deeds of mystery and power as he heralds and effects the new age—the kingdom of God. In the life and ministry of Jesus, in the birth and mission of the church, in the recording and interpreting of the whole Christ-event, the Spirit is given a stellar role.

At the major turning points in this section of holy history, he is on the scene signaling divine intervention in Jesus' virgin birth (Mt. 1:18–25; Lk. 1:35); baptizing the Messiah for ministry in fulfillment of Isaiah's prophecy (Mk. 1:8; Mt. 3:11; Lk. 3:16; Jn. 1:32–33); empowering the fledgling church for worldwide witness (Acts 1:8); strengthening believers, just as Jesus would have done, to understand their faith and to withstand persecution (Jn. 14:18–31, 15:18–27); bequeathing gifts for effective service (Rom. 12:3–8; 1 Cor. 12, 14; Eph. 4:11–16; 1 Pet. 4:10–11); transforming persons with the fruit of love, joy, and peace—the qualities of the new life (Gal. 5:22–23); guaranteeing the full achievement of all God's purposes, especially the redemption of his people (Eph. 1:11–14).

In short, for the New Testament writers, the Holy Spirit is the presence of the Father and the Son moving with the church to the ends of the earth and the close of the age, enabling the church to be the people of God in love, righteousness, and wisdom. Where the Spirit is, the new age is present. Where his voice is heeded, where his power is trusted, the Lord's prayer is being fulfilled: God's name is hallowed; God's will is achieved; God's kingdom is present.

3. *The earliest confessions of the church* grasped the centrality of the Spirit's work and celebrated it with passionate affirmation. Let the Apostles' Creed serve as example. In the faith of the church—holy, universal, and apostolic—the Spirit implements the divine task of restoration, carrying out the renewal on which the Creator insists, completing the redemption for which the Savior died and rose again, effecting the full renewal which cancels and transcends the damages of the human fall. In the trinitarian structure of the

Creed, the Spirit is mentioned third after the Father and the Son. The intent of this is not to establish rank—as though the Father were a general, the Son a colonel, the Spirit a major—but to outline the chronology (or kairology!) of the activities of the Godhead: the Father's place as Creator, the Son's as Redeemer, the Spirit's as Enabler.

Significant for our understanding of spirituality in campus ministry are the words that follow our confession of belief in the Holy Spirit. The series of pointed phrases that push the Creed to its climax is a summary of the Spirit's work. He (I use the pronoun not to suggest gender but personhood in my trinitarian tradition) forms the church—setting it apart from all worldly institutions in its holiness, planting it in every culture in its catholicity, and joining every member of it to every other member in its communion; he offers the forgiveness of sins within the fellowship of that church to all who repent and believe in Jesus as Son of God and Savior; he grants the power of resurrection at the end and the gift of eternal life—life in loving fellowship with God and his people—along the way. The fall is reversed, the curse is lifted—and all by the Spirit, who restores community, frees from guilt, conquers death, and plants love at life's center.

This rehearsal of the major themes of our biblical and churchly traditions is not a mere academic exercise. Its purpose is patent and practical: to show how historically based, how specifically expressed, and how theologically grounded our Jewish and Christian understandings of spirituality are. Though definitions may differ slightly in shade and nuance, the consensus is clear: the spirituality we talk about and aim for is the work of the Holy Spirit of God, who revealed himself to his people in history and in the Scriptures which interpret that history.

THE SPIRIT AND THE FOUR TRADITIONS

Just how the Spirit is now working on our campuses is harder to discern. The four essays in this section give us a sampling of what some sensitive and informed persons believe about that work. They intend to be suggestive and not exhaustive. They know that the wind of God "blows where it wills, and you hear the sound of it, but you do not know whence it comes or whither it goes" (Jn. 3:8). They know that the tendency to surprise may be the Spirit's most predictable trait.

What our authors say, then, is both personal and parochial—marks of strength not weakness. They describe what has happened to them in places where they are at work. And that perspective gives their essays both authenticity and authority. In seeking to interpret those perspectives, I shall look first at the uncommon insights of each tradition and then at the insights held in common by all four.

1. Heading the list of the *uncommon contributions* which Max Ticktin's essay made to me is the reality of the Holocaust in shaping Jewish spirituality. Though understated—and, therefore, all the more poignant—the description of that unspeakable event on the agony, resolve, and hope of devout Jews must not be underestimated.

There is an "in-spite-of" quality to the Jewish commitment to the life of the spirit, which virtually defies imagining to our Gentile approaches to piety. Nothing in the experience of God's people—not the savagery of the deportations of the populace under Sargon and Nebuchadrezzar, not the desecration of the Temple by Antiochus Epiphanes, not the desolation of Jerusalem at the hands of Titus—can compare with the horror of Hitler's and Stalin's genocide. That any Jew yet believes in prayer, revels in Torah, congregates with other worshipers in the commitment of *kavvanah,* or writes a cordial chapter in a book edited by Christians is itself a testimony to the Spirit's grace. All Gentile understanding of post-Nazi Jewish spirituality must begin with an awareness of this Jewish commitment to life, faith, fellowship, and continuity, a major motivation of which is to deny their enemies a posthumous victory.

Another contribution—foreign to most of us, though my premillennial eschatology has some feeling for it—is the reminder of the importance of the state of Israel to Jewish students and campus ministers. Their definitions not only of devotion but economics, not only of providence but of politics, embrace the real joys and anxieties posed by Israel's existence as a sovereign nation. The Jewish presence on our campuses can serve as a catalyst to keep our Christian approaches to both redemptive history and social justice from evaporating into clouds of mysticism or stagnating in the ponds of provincialism. God has used not only a people, but a land as instruments of revelation.

Ticktin's honest treatment of the difficulties posed to Jewish students by the pluralistic character of American life, so vividly expressed on our campuses, does more than help us understand a Jewish problem. It also reminds us that all vital spirituality for persons whose roots are in the Bible will be an "over-against" experience. Though Christians in our land undoubtedly present a greater threat to Jews than the other way round, yet all true spirituality is in danger of being quenched by the tides of pluralism that wash our educational institutions. Eastern religions, Marxism, hedonism, positivism are only a few of the challenges to the life of the Spirit against which campus pastors seek to fortify their flocks.

Most of all, Max Ticktin's glimpses into his pilgrimage struck me with the down-to-earth practicality of the Spirit's work. It is world affirming without becoming idolatrous; it is serious about devotion to God's service without deadening into morbidity; it is playful without drifting into flippancy. It has the maturity and reflection of an ancient people and the readiness to cope with tomorrow's surprises. It knows the mix of grace and judgment ever to be found in the Lord's dealings with our race, and it seeks to respond to those dealings in every life situation with obedience and joy.

2. Like a painter who conveys life and movement in a few brush strokes or an actor who utters volumes in a gesture, Nancy Malone gives us a sense of her understanding of Roman Catholic spirituality in a few paragraphs. Her description of spirituality as passion dominates the essay.

It is a hedge against either sentimental or casual approaches to the life of the spirit. And it reminds us that what we claim with our words and what we really live for may be two different things. The application to campus life is obvious. Much spiritual witness has been compromised by this discrepancy. As academic people we have claimed to be zealous for the work of God, but our passions have been seduced by other concerns: competition for promotion, drive for prestige, ambition for political influence, even desire for success in campus ministry. What we are willing to suffer for is what we truly believe in; our passions expose our true purposes in life. Nancy Malone's insights coax us to substantial musing on our own spirituality.

The Creator Spirit, who moved upon the waters at history's beginning, and the Incarnate Son, who changed water into wine at its midpoint, are the shapers of her view of spirituality. Their power and presence sanctify all of life. Her sacramental outlook separates her from pantheists, romantics, and hedonists. All of them—and their representatives are vocally present on our campuses—purport to love life, but for the wrong reasons. Nancy Malone's Catholic spirituality does not confuse the life she loves with the God she worships as would pantheism; neither does it assume that life itself is life enriching and life sustaining as would romanticism; nor does it crave life for pleasure but not for mission as would hedonism. Indeed, to see life as the object of the Creator's power, the arena of the Redeemer's love, the sphere of the Sanctifier's grace is to see it without any *isms*. It is that kind of spirituality which offers best promise to rescue our campuses and their populace from the idolization of ideologies, as Nancy Malone intimates in her call to discriminate passion from passion—futile or secondary passion from fruitful or ultimate passion.

If it is true that we become like what we worship, then such discrimination is crucial. For transformation will inevitably take place—transformation of some kind, in some direction. Our passions are shaping and reshaping us stage by stage. Sensible spirituality, then, chooses the means and direction of that transformation. For Catholics that choice is made, above all, in and through the mass. It is there, in the remembering of Christ's life, death, and resurrection, that the transformation begins, the transformation measured by the likeness of the Lord himself:

Now the Lord is the Spirit, and where the Spirit of the Lord is, there is freedom. And we all, with unveiled face, beholding the glory of the Lord, are being changed into his likeness from one degree of glory to another; for this comes from the Lord who is the Spirit. (2 Cor. 3:17–18)

Transformation whose character is freedom, whose progress edges on from stage to stage, whose source is the Spirit's work, whose aim is to be like Christ—can there be a better description of spirituality than that? Can there be anything more needed on the campuses of our land than that freedom, that progress, that power, that purpose? Nancy Malone's essay, by taking us to the heart of Catholic spirituality, pushes us to questions about our own.

3. In Rebecca Manley Pippert's account, we see an evangelical movement beginning to take stock of its weaknesses. This is salutary. Some of the triumphalism which used to hover over Roman Catholic ministries has, of late, transferred to evangelical territory. It looks no better there than it did in its previous habitat. It is good to see it being chased over the horizons to an oblivion which it deserves.

Evangelical exuberance has at times been directly proportional to its superficiality. Perhaps, at this juncture in our history, we will begin to understand both the depths of true spirituality and the humility appropriate to it. Rebecca Pippert has helped the cause with her acknowledgment that evangelical piety has all too often been compromised by otherworldly naiveté, legalistic rigidity, individualistic introspection, glib irreverence, and quietistic escapism from social problems. My own pilgrimage was enriched measurably by Carl F. H. Henry's *The Uneasy Conscience of Modern Fundamentalism* (Wm. B. Eerdmans Publishing Co., 1947), which I read as a college junior. Pippert's chapter may well do that for others.

The growing appreciation of the life of Jesus and the significance of the incarnation among evangelical students may catch by surprise those who gauge our movement from without. After all, one would expect conservative Protestants to revel in the Gospels, track intently the steps of Jesus, and build their faith and life on the reality of his incarnation. But, as with all other aspects of biblical reality, we partially understand and partially distort the truth.

We have used the gospels as moral illustrations or proofs of Christ's divinity without seeing in them the radical demands of the kingdom. We have celebrated Jesus' full deity without adequately grappling with the implications of his true humanity. A change here is taking place—and none too soon. Our view of the faith has been cabined by our inadequate Christology, and our ability to communicate it has been muffled by our failure to grasp its power as story.

In Christology—more than anywhere else—is where the crucial questions lie. If we misinterpret what the Bible means us to understand about Jesus, we will build error into the very heart of our belief system. With the current Roman Catholic tendency to flirt with constructions of Christology akin to those of contemporary Protestant scholars, it is all the more incumbent upon evangelicals to understand and apply the traditional views of Nicea, Chalcedon, and the Reformation. In the shifting sands of speculation about the baffling person of Jesus, these ancient landmarks must not be lightly moved. Rebecca Pippert's observations remind us that, though we have loudly claimed reverence for the uniqueness of Jesus, we have not always backed that claim with sound application.

The emphases on Bible study, prayer, and fellowship as paths to deeper spirituality should come as no surprise to those who know the evangelical movement. Fresh forms of these disciplines are appearing which make them less insular and sectarian and tie them more closely to the main tasks of mission: evangelism and social action.

In both of those tasks—telling the good news and acting out its concern for justice—evangelical talk may have run ahead of evangelical performance. Samuel Shoemaker's laudable desire to stand by the door for easy access to those outside the faith has not always been emulated. We have been as eager as anyone to crowd to the safeness of the center of the room and leave the outsiders to others. The prodding toward and equipment for relational evangelism that Pippert describes is direly needed.

So are very specific programs in social action. Evangelical practice pursues evangelical theory sluggishly and from afar. The convocations and their pronouncements, the literature and its chidings, will soon turn hollow without whole cadres of young people with lavish commitment to implement them. Very few congregations are mobilized for this expression of Christian duty. Dare we hope that conscientious students will develop approaches that will point the way to wider imitation?

4. Edwin Beers's chapter on spirituality in the mainline Protestant denominations rings with encouragement. In the midst of decades of malaise there is a reviving interest in matters of the spirit. The sources of this revival are harder to trace than the revival itself, but Beers's analysis probably captures most of them: a search for spirit in the midst of despair, an absence of human community, an overemphasis on administration and program within the churches, a shortage of the Spirit's fruit in the lives of professing Christians.

What may be even harder to explain is the reasons for the turning of the tide. One would like to think that the churches and campus ministries have been so staunchly committed to spiritual transformation that they have exercised strong initiative in this revival. The evidence points in another direction. Both the counterculture, with its repudiation of the dominance of bureaucracy, technology, and materialism, and the religious resurgence, with its multiple manifestations in Eastern religions, the occult, astrology, and the human potential movement, may have had at least as much influence on the new quest for spirituality as the biblical witness of church and synagogue.

All of this is not to question the Spirit's role. Bringing order from chaos is what he is good at, and he is not bound by humanly imposed limits. More than once in the course of redemption's history he has used worldly lenses to sharpen spiritual vision. The fact that believing people may often follow the trends of culture rather than lead them does not mean that God's Spirit is not setting the pace. The splendor of Israel's tabernacle was fashioned from Egypt's gold.

The campus is a fertile field for the Spirit's most recent harvest, partly because the campus was a prime site for two of the movements that opened the way for spiritual quest in the decade past— the counterculture and the religious resurgence. More than that, as Edwin Beers points out, spiritual concern—a commitment to a life of worship, prayer, Bible study, shared community, and mission— was part and parcel of campus Christian movements since the beginning of the nineteenth century. Indeed, the more narrowly activistic, almost secular, approaches that marked some campus ministries in the sixties are the exception not the rule.

Campus ministry has had ecumenism as one of its characteristics from the beginning. The YMCA, the YWCA, and the Student Volunteer Movement spanned the denominations and brought persons together for worship, study, fellowship, and mission across the whole sweep of Protestant denominations. The Inter-Varsity Christian Fellowship and Campus Crusade for Christ do much the same today. The various brands and labels that segregate Christians elsewhere have never made much sense to the student world.

A happy byproduct of this concern for Christian unity is the influence that one Christian tradition can have on another. Edwin Beers's summary of the contribution which the liturgical, charismatic, and monastic traditions are making to the spiritual nurture of mainline campus ministries is a splendid illustration. That contribution is also a powerful argument for the transdenominational approach of this book and the discussion which preceded it. Each tradition preserves and features aspects of biblical spirituality that may be temporarily bypassed in the other traditions.

Perhaps the most hopeful note we find in Beers's study is the observation that the revived interest in spirituality goes beyond discussion to experimentation. In the fellowship of a host of Christian communities, lives are being changed; commitment is being formed; love, joy, and peace are being nurtured.

As one who has spent most of my ministry within institutions of a conservative evangelical orientation, I rejoice in the new quest within the mainline churches which Beers has depicted. Would that this quest might result in a recapturing of the best of their history! My reasons for holding that hope are personal as well as churchly. It was the ministries of the mainline churches through the YMCA and Student Volunteer Movement that challenged my father as a university student, grounded him in the faith, nurtured his gifts, and summoned him to mission overseas. Those ministries were part of what made USC an *alma mater* indeed and splashed that memorable smile on his face.

In the Introduction, the editor of this volume pointed to the possibility of a "simplicity on the other side of complexity." The *common insights* of our four essayists in this section encourage us to believe that such costly simplicity may be within reach.

The spirituality described for each of the four traditions is *marked by wholeness*. Each essay takes pains to avoid either reducing spirituality to the trivial, by confusing it with its symptoms or external expressions, or confining it to compartments, by connecting it with some aspects of life but not with others.

This quest for wholeness is implict in what Edwin Beers says about the balance between prayer, Bible study, participation in community, and concern for mission which collegians in mainline communions are aiming for. The other writers deal with it even more explicitly. Rebecca Pippert's definition ("not what one *has* but what one *is*") and Nancy Malone's ("your spiritual life is your life") are in substantial agreement. Both move miles beyond the lofty mysticism, narrow piety, world-denying asceticism, or rigid legalism which have so often masqueraded as spirituality in evangelical and Catholic life. Max Ticktin's spiritual aim may define wholeness as sharply as possible: "holding God and the human in one thought at one time."

Both the doctrine of creation and the person of the Creator underlie this emphasis on wholeness. That magnificent picture of a

Creator shaping humankind out of dust and breathing it into personhood with divine breath (Gen. 2:7) is the definitive model of human wholeness. The true aim of biblical spirituality is to recapture that psychosomatic unity and to live out its implications in all of life's dimensions. And that Creator, who graded each stage of creation as good and who continues to nurture the life and guard the order of that creation, calls all who name his name to share his concerns for and do his will in the whole of life, sustained as it is by the Spirit. What can this mean but that the campus is a wonderfully appropriate arena for the practice of spirituality?

For all four essayists in this section this approach to spirituality is *informed by study of the Scriptures.* Though the human spirit bears the stamp of the Creator, it behaves that way with incredible infrequency. Power and direction for change are not just desirable; they are utterly necessary. The Scriptures link such change directly to the knowledge of God. Knowing, loving, fearing, obeying, trusting God (all of which mean essentially the same thing: depending fully on him and maintaining total loyalty to him) is the source of our spirituality—at least as our Jewish and Christian heritages define it. And more than anywhere else this knowledge of God comes through his written word—the record and interpretation of his words and acts. Not that knowing God means merely garnering information about him. A better rendering would be "getting acquainted with him." The God who is person meets us as persons in the teachings and narratives, in the praises and prophecies of the Bible. It is the story of grace and demand, and it is the invitation for us to write our name into that story.

The excitement that Edwin Beers and Rebecca Pippert find in new approaches to Bible study, the vision for a sacramental view of life that Nancy Malone catches as she contemplates the meaning of Jesus' incarnation, death, and resurrection, the sense of delight that grasps Max Ticktin as he immerses himself in Torah—all point to a specific, concrete understanding of spirituality rooted in biblical revelation. For them, in contrast to some psychological or religious approaches to spirituality, the starting point is not the human spirit, but the divine. The path to spirituality is not unmapped; it is carefully charted by the ways of God and the most sensitive of those persons who have followed those ways in love and service. What can this commitment to divine instruction mean but that resources are available to our campuses for spiritual growth which they will search for elsewhere only in vain?

Each writer in this section testifies to a spirituality *enriched by the collegiality of others* in whom the Spirit is working. Words like *fellowship* and *community* lace the pages of this text. Whether in Edwin Beers's glimpse of the "motley gathering in silence and simplicity" at Taizé or in Max Ticktin's tribute to the "special stimulation and beneficent influences coming from Christian colleagues," the impact of life on life, spirit on spirit, is central. The truth of God is not revealed only in words, it is also demonstrated through persons. After all, if the word *person* is too weak to capture the fullness of the God of Abraham or Paul, no lesser word will do any better. God may be larger than our word *person* signals; he will surely be no smaller. What can this mean for campus ministry but that it can only be carried on by persons—not systems or techniques, but persons—whose spirits are so kindled by the life of the Spirit that they brighten and warm the others whom they touch?

Though all the authors write from fierce loyalties to their own traditions, they all confess a spirituality *illuminated by the other traditions*. I find Max Ticktin's accolade particularly moving: "The greatest intellectual and spiritual stimulation (in the university setting) has come from writers and teachers, mostly Protestant. . . ." When we think of the tensions which history, especially the history of the past half century, has caused between Christians and Jews, we judge that statement both charitable and amazing. It is a signpost to the rich possibility of learning in the midst of dissent, of enrichment in the face of disagreement. Where spirituality is our aim, and the knowledge of God our goal, the way must be left open for as much shared learning as our individual convictions can tolerate. Are there any better places than our campuses—with their license to open investigation—to let humility and charity so crown our ministries that we hear each other and grow by that hearing?

The spirituality which these chapters point toward is *open to the burdens* and *the joys of humanity*. The burden of opposing injustice and combating oppression is carried squarely on the shoulders of each writer. The biblical mandate has been duly heard, and especially in its application to inequities on the campuses themselves. Though in the working out of these concerns commitment usually outraces achievement, the concern figures prominently in current definitions of spirituality—and indispensably so.

That concern in these essays bears little resemblance to what was expressed by those grim, angry faces that shouted obscenities from behind the barricades of the sixties. The sense of providence prompts a serenity, not complacency, that those impassioned protestors of the Vietnam era often missed. Perhaps the reason lies in the changed circumstances. I doubt, however, that this is the whole explanation. Rather, the deep social concern expressed by our authors is held in equilibrium by joy. Spirituality and humor, holiness and playfulness, are not semantic opposites in their lexicon. The burden of a world gone wrong is surely felt, but that feeling is walled off from frenzy or despair by the awareness—through the witness of God's Word and Spirit—that God is yet at work and that joyful, not bitter, workers are his best recruits. What can this balance of burden and joy mean but that our campuses are offered a third way between escapist apathy on the one hand and frustrated desperation on the other?

CONCLUSION

The three sections of this book are of a piece—community, contemplation-action, and spirituality. Each is inextricably interwoven with the other. Pull out the strands of any, and the pattern of the other two will unravel.

All three hang on the Spirit's work. God sends the Spirit to work in his people for their mission more than for their comfort. The prophetic expectation of Messiah gives the model:

> *And the Spirit of the Lord shall rest upon him,*
> *the spirit of wisdom and understanding,*
> *the spirit of counsel and might,*
> *the spirit of knowledge and the fear of the*
> *Lord.*
>
> *He shall not judge by what his eyes see,*
> *or decide by what his ears hear;*
> *but with righteousness he shall judge the poor,*
> *and decide with equity for the meek of the*
> *earth;*

(Is. 11:2,3B,4A)

No true justice is possible without the Spirit's guidance.

As to the relationship between spirituality and community, Joel's paradigm must be recounted:

> *And it shall come to pass afterward,*
>   *that I will pour out my spirit on all flesh;*
> *your sons and your daughters shall prophesy,*
>   *your old men shall dream dreams,*
>   *and your young men shall see visions.*
> *Even upon the menservants and maidservants*
>   *in those days, I will pour out my spirit.*
>
> (JL. 2:28–29)

All barriers of sex, age, and status are leveled by the power of the Spirit, and true community becomes a reality. As Christians, we confess our faith in the Holy Spirit and, therefore, in the Holy Catholic church, the communion of saints.

Can any educational institution truly be an *alma mater* without the Spirit's presence? Is not that presence our best hope for distinguished contribution to our campuses? Without such spirituality we merely add intellectual options to the cafeteria menu already being served or we increase the level of secular arrogance which has already reached the flood stage.

But if we live by the Spirit's influence (walking in the Spirit, Paul calls it), we can help to link the campus's passing influence to the permanence of God's work. Where else will we find power to see our people through the ideologial conflicts which make the campus a battlefield of idolatrous forces? Where else will we find grace to bring unity to the various groups of God's followers who have let their differences deteriorate to divisiveness? Where else will we find strength for love, without whose credentials all our alleged righteousness is exposed as fraud? Where else will we find truth for persuasion, knowing as we do that the commands to worship and obey call for a life-shaking yes beyond the power of human will to muster on its own?

I once heard Aldous Huxley, in a public lecture, call for a Pontifex Maximus, a master bridge builder, to forge ties between the diverse and competitive elements in a modern university. Huxley's cry had been heard, millennia before he issued it, by the God whose Spirit brought order from chaos at the beginning and stands ready to keep doing that through people whose lives are open to him.

Alma maters are powerful places. One of them spread a smile of joyous pride on my father's face that retained its glow for half a century. These essays point out ways in which that power can be corrected, channeled, and enhanced by reliance upon the God of learning and nurture. Campus spirit we have always had in abundant measure; campus spirituality we have much to learn about. Max Ticktin, Nancy Malone, Rebecca Pippert, and Edwin Beers know this, and their reflections are a good place to begin.

SERVING WITH A WHOLE HEART
A Jewish Perspective of Campus Ministry

Max D. Ticktin

And now, Solomon my son, know the God of your ancestor and serve Him with a whole heart and as a willing self, for the Lord searches all hearts, understanding every plan and devising. If you seek Him, He will be found by you, but if you forsake Him, He will cast you off forever. Take heed now, for the Lord has chosen you to build a home for the sanctuary. Be strong and do it. (1 Chr. 28:9–10)

ALL OF A PIECE

When, periodically, I have sought to recover a sense of vocation, I have recalled one of my high school teachers. He frequently took time off from teaching us Latin to ask us sixteen and seventeen year olds what we really hoped to make of our lives. Once he turned to what was then a well-known book by a Harvard professor and quoted a passage dealing with the significance of finding in life a balance of four elements: love and prayer were on one axis intersecting with a second axis of work and play.[1] Expanding on all four and on the complementarity in each pair, my teacher struck several chords in me which have reverberated within ever since.

Aside from the substance of his remarks, my teacher became, because of "asides" like this quotation, a model of pedagogy, concerned not only with imparting subject matter, but also with the person of the student and his or her direction in life. Impressionable adolescent that I was, I was compelled to examine and reexamine four familiar words and activities. I began to understand clusters of significance attached to love, prayer, work, and play and to sense the struggle that would be mine to keep the four in balance, to discover the dialectic tensions, and to acknowledge the yearning for a healing of fragments of my being, for a wholeness.

I was given a spiritual challenge. Was I open to an inner searching? Was I open to the possibilities of change and movement? And where would I go, projected ahead by these two intersecting axes, these fiery everturning swords at the gates of Eden?

Then and now, I have come to see that "spirit" is concerned with openness to a call from without that becomes an inner summoning, as well as with an understanding heart, willingness, resolution, faith, and directiveness. And more than all else, I will be a "person of spirit," I have come to believe, when I become "all of a piece" and not "patchwork,"[2] holding God and the human in one thought at one time.

In our epigraph quotation, David—like other biblical teachers— addresses me not with the philosopher's "know thyself," but with a bidding to come and experience in life the intimacy with God that was true of my forebears and to convert that to service in the world. This I am to seek to do with an understanding heart that is undivided and as a person or self that is open, accessible, and willing. I will need to be mindful that the loving God stands in judgment of me, my plans, and devisings, but also that He is there when I seek Him. ("Longing to draw near to thee/With all my heart I pray;/Then going forth to seek thee/Thou meetest me on the way."[3])

In my most reflective moments, I have striven to link faith and willingness to an understanding of my appointment to build a home for God's holy presence in my personal and professional life.

THE ENTERPRISE OF TORAH

As a student, I could not yet find a harmony of the four disparate elements or activities: work, play, prayer, and love. But I could be and was propelled forward with a murky sense of direction and of vocation that came from my dedication to Torah.

Torah, more an enterprise than a book, but with increasing clarity, became the means that enabled me to consider career or life-course, profession or life-affirmation, and vocation or life-calling. From childhood, I had been privileged to have family members and teachers who were positive models of dedication to Torah.

I enjoyed immersing myself in the texts which dealt with manifold interpretations of the Word of God. It was joyous play to enter into the several stages of Jewish history and to be in the company of the actors of a specific age in the everliving Jewish tradition. The discovery of a new insight or of a new nuance of meaning in a tale or in a teaching was a moment of pleasure. The Psalmist expressed my feelings: "I will find play for myself in Your statutes, and I will not forget Your word. . . . Were your Torah not to have been my play, I would have perished in my affliction. . . . I will delight in Your commandments which I have loved" (Ps. 119:16, 47, 92). Torah was my play-object, my source of delight, my consoling ease. And so it has remained.

"To meditate on it day and night" was my work activity. Play led to work and vice versa. But my work then also became teaching Torah diligently. Imparting understanding of a verse, of a Midrash, of an ethical maxim, gave me a sense of worth and purpose. I was a link in the chain of teachers. I could enjoy being a part of another person's growth and self-discovery, and together we worked at transforming a science of deeds to a life of *mitzvot,* divine commandments becoming good deeds.

Torah as worship and love was another matter. But here, too, over the years, as a student and as teacher, I have come to appreciate the possibilities of Torah study as "the offering of the lips" which is the proper replacement for the "rendering of bullocks" which in the ancient ritual service brought Israel and God into close contact (Hos. 14:3). This study can be for me an act of worship, an affirmation of the unique worth of God for my life. And, frequently, this is all the more so in group-learning: "When ten people sit together, occupying themselves with the Torah, the divine presence abides among them."[4] Most remarkable for me is the recognition by an outsider to my tradition of the uniqueness of Torah as worship: "This conception of individual and collective study as a form of divine service has persisted in Judaism through all the ages, and has made not only the learned by profession but men of humble callings in life assiduous students of the Talmud as the pursuit of the highest branch of religious learning and most meritorious of good works."[5]

Worship and divine service point to love and vice versa. Affirming the centrality of God and of His word evokes feelings of devotion, loyalty, and passionate attachment to another human and to the Wholly Other One. Before beginning daily morning prayers, tradition would have me say, "Behold, I accept the positive commandment 'You shall love your fellow-creature as yourself; I am the Lord.' "[6] Accepting myself, I release the power to accept the other, and also to accept the actual and the potential betweenness that links the two of us. And I can become loyally and lovingly attached to this fellow and neighbor and to our relatedness. All this is the way upward to the love of God, of which Torah is an expression. The central subject of the Torah is the covenant love and loyalty of God for Israel and Israel for God. Torah study yields me discernment and insight, but also creative and healing power to love God and human beings. My devotion to Torah leads to a loving attachment to God and to His world. Ideally, Torah becomes acts of loving kindness, devoutness, and piety.

Striving to keep vigorously alive all four facets of myself as a person of Torah, I set out to be a Hillel director, serving Jewish students and faculty. An evolving understanding of myself as such is, in many ways, the result of surviving many crises of faith and commitment. These crucial moments have their origin in the following: my institutional setting; my relationship with the larger Jewish community; my place in the university; my dealings with students; my association with colleagues; my contacts with "seekers."

TEACHER OF TORAH AND *MITZVOT*

In Hillel, my institutional setting, my earliest dominant self-image was that I was a teacher. In formal and nonformal situations, I attempted to be with students and to be present for them. I had been appointed and mandated to teach "Torah and *mitzvot*," but I would be authentic in my leadership of the community only if I were like the master of the Hasidic community. For such a master-teacher "the core of his teaching is this, that he lets his disciple take part in his life and thus grasp the mystery of the action."[7]

There were always instances of overinvolvement in the life and rhythms of the campus. To "recharge the batteries," I had to remember the rabbis' admonition: "Provide yourself a teacher and acquire a fellow-disciple."[8] So spiritual growth depended on my study, on my being sustained by comrades-in-work. At best, this meant over the years renewed efforts to study with colleagues, Jewish and Christian, to attend retreats, to strengthen my professional organizations, to set aside time for browsing in libraries' periodical rooms, to invite "visiting firemen-lecturers" as much for me as for student groups.

But the institution thrust multiple tasks upon me, and in addition to being teacher (in many guises), I also had to be building administrator, programmer, group worker, counselor, cleric, representative of all Jews to the university, emissary of the campus to the larger Jewish community, and much more. Often, I lost my vocational focus. Wearied, frustrated, and fractured, I doubted myself, my wholeheartedness and integrity. I thought of myself as superficial and dilettantish when in touch with faculty and "burned out" when with students.

Centering could and sometimes did return with the nurturing of play and of avocations; or a reviving light might radiate out over all my work from precious moments of prayerful meditation or of healing love. For me, spiritual renewal came most frequently, however, from immersion in the sea of Torah study, preferably with peers and colleagues.

PARTNER IN THE WHOLE COMMUNITY

In addition, my spiritual development was both aided by, and impeded by, my relations with the larger Jewish community.

As a Hillel director, I served an institution established by leaders of the larger American Jewish community and was accountable to them. My mandate was to serve their children, with Hillel to be "a home away from home." The young people did not want Hillel to be too similar to home or the home synagogue, and the faculty members generally considered themselves critical of, and marginal to, the organized Jewish community. I, too, tended to see our Jewish campus community as radically different from the rest of Jewish society.

But, on further reflection, I saw that all of us were in the same larger historical setting in at least three significant ways.

Like all contemporary Jews, we are survivors of the Holocaust of European Jewry and Jewish communities. We share in the memory, in the agonizing questioning, in the guilt. We share also a determination to continue beyond the remembering with defiance of our enemies, with a heightened sense of responsibility for fellow Jews throughout the world, and with a faith in and hope for the eternal people of Israel.

Like other Jews today, we on campus focus also on the Jewish community in the state of Israel. As our kin, they are our concern. Israel, created not only as a haven for survivors, but also as a response to the temptations of liberal societies and universalizing orders seeking to assimilate the Jew into the larger whole, is our joyful inspiration. It is, however, also for all Jews a new spiritual problem. When, in 1948, a part of world Jewry became a modern nation-state, we were set on the center of the stage of world history in ways unknown to us for two millennia. But those in Zion and those in diasporas like American Jewry now must seek to understand what is God's purpose for us in this new era. What is the challenge to each Jew at a time when Jews are given new forms of power—and powerlessness—over against other creatures of God? Like their parents, Jewish students increasingly asseverate a loyalty to Jewish peoplehood, but, concomitantly, they open themselves to the puzzling questions of what is to be done, under God's judgment, either here or there, with the new potential and the new responsibility they have been granted. (See, in this volume, the essay by Arnold J. Wolf.)

Lastly, we share a focus on the significance of our living in this country. America has enabled Jews to establish here a community that lives in freedom, a post-ghetto free and voluntary community placed in an open society. In a setting without precedent in our history, Jews can remain in, be marginal to, or leave the Jewish collectivity. And, as Hillel director, I serve young people who are at the university, itself a major gateway to the open society, at the very time in their lives when they may be first discovering the possibilities of locating themselves or losing themselves in the wider secular or Christian group. They turn to me with these questions (sometimes only partially articulated): "Can I find resources in the Jewish tradition enabling me to remain honestly and affirmatively identified as a Jew? Can I find a Jewish anchorage for my adult identity? Can I do this with integrity while not cutting myself off from non-Jewish friends and society? Can I do this now when I am 'between families'? Can I do this while I am preoccupied with the acquisition of knowledge, skills, and professional educational requirements?"

These are questions of young Jews, but they are expressed in a historical context which is common to all Jews today in the three ways I have indicated.

There are, however, several sharp differences between campus Jews and those in the larger community which have made my ministry uniquely challenging.

First, American Jewry is pluralistic, again in a somewhat unprecedented manner. But the campus is maximally so, and the Hillel director serves students and faculty who present themselves as being primarily one or more of the following: secular, Zionist, Orthodox, Hasidic, Conservative, Reform, Reconstructionist, Havurah. As one who ministers to the whole community, I have been challenged to affirm and endorse each person and each group, while encouraging cooperation among all. Like other Hillel directors, and somewhat unlike other Jewish leaders (only Hillel and the armed forces chaplaincy have legitimated such pluralism), I have sought to be non-judgmental and accepting of all, recognizing that occasionally young people will be seeking to sharpen certain prior identities and occasionally they will be experimenting with, or searching for, new ones. Affirming a wide range of possibilities for those in their community has frequently led to surprising spiritual enrichment and growth for individual leaders and teachers and their families.

From this there follows, as I have observed it over the years, a unique legitimation on campus for experiments in liturgy, in spiritual disciplines, in modes of building subcommunities or fellowships, etc. (See, in this volume, Richard N. Levy's essay.) Much of what I have written here is under the impact of my learning from students in Hillel who have shaped and shared in such experiments. At moments, we have tasted the joys of being in prayer or study groups similar to those of Hasidim described by Buber where

the teacher helps the disciples find themselves, and in hours of desolation the disciples help the teacher find himself again. The teacher kindles the souls of his disciples and they surround him and his life with the flame he has kindled. The disciple asks, and by his manner of asking unconsciously evokes a reply, which his teacher's spirit would not have produced without the stimulus of the question.[9]

Here then is produced a unique group authority, partially dissolving distinctions between teacher and student, albeit in a transient community. Yet models for other forms of community and synagogue have resulted. From the Hillel experience have issued forth alternatives like the small fellowships or *havurot,* some traditional in liturgy and practice and some clearly not. All are characterized by being experimental, not rabbi-centered, and maximally inclusive.

It has been thrilling for me to participate in these Hillel endeavors, and I have had personal satisfaction in helping shape new sociological alternatives that have made me grow and have also presented to the larger community new "ideologies." That greater community, having no central authority or single, unifying theological governance, has substituted what has been an "ideology of belonging," wherein Jews are called upon to express loyalty to the tradition and to the people by affiliating organizationally and participating in tasks, mostly philanthropic. On campus, in contrast, beyond serving students whose needs and interests are mainly those of affiliation and fulfillment of communal tasks, we on Hillel staffs have ventured with some students on voyages of spiritual inquiry, of meditation and prayer discipline, of group study, and of creating new rituals. (Many of the nonsexist ritual forms increasingly practiced in the community-at-large stem from these campus groups.)

COLLEAGUE IN THE UNIVERSITY

It is the university setting itself which has also been a source of much of my spiritual development. The greatest intellectual and spiritual stimulation has come from writers and teachers, mostly Protestant, who over the years were probing "the Crisis of the University" or "the Church, the University, and Social Policy."

With faculty friends, I struggled, from my perspective of religious commitments, to understand how the university could truly become a "community of scholars" and what were personal and institutional responsibilites for professors in such a community.

Teachers and students in the natural and social sciences shared with me their questions about "scientific method," their encounters with principles of certainty and uncertainty, and their search for values with which they might ground and order their knowledge.

For me, there always was a special kinship with those students and teachers in the humanities who spoke of mystery and miracle, as well as of intuition and imagination, in ways similar to my burgeoning understanding of my faith. For them, furthermore, "the absolute of the humanities has humility at its root; its base must be the most complex of human conceptions wedded to the humblest kind of faith. They must be and are the bases of mature religion."[10]

Lastly, a group of deans and directors of student affairs influenced me and were positive models for me. They were persons who successfully balanced administrative responsibility and dedication to order with humane, caring concern for young people.

For all of us, administrators, faculty, and campus ministers, events in the sixties moved too rapidly. Almost imperceptibly, all of us were part of new types of linkage of the university with government, industry and the military, and we were properly challenged by cadres of young instructors and students, fearful for their personal futures and for the future of our society. For some of us that meant that we no longer could pretend to be concerned with individual souls apart from the politics of the university.

There were also years in which inevitably I, like other campus ministers, observed significant changes in the curricular treatment of religion. First, there had been a need to stress the intellectual and educational *respectability* of religious studies. Then, when, in a measure, that battle was won, we witnessed exaggerated efforts to emphasize the *relevance* of such teaching. And, more recently, we have observed a calmer presentation of religious studies in their *relatedness* to other curricular offerings. Over the years, I have grown in my appreciation of the possibilities of complementarity between campus ministry and the teaching of the history and philosophy of religion. There is a need to confront students with advocacy but also with objectivity, with the building of religious community but also with the religious problem as a universal issue. Often it has been students who have been more apt than I or the professor of religious studies to sense the need for both the discovery and analysis of the ultimate questions and for the faith-commitment that is an answer to these ultimate questions.

I have also had a specific Jewish concern in this area. We Jews have taken advantage of that unique gift of America: broad access to higher education. Have we come to the university in large numbers only to serve ourselves, or do we perhaps also serve some higher purpose, significant for the future of the American spirit and society? For over a century, the university has been a distinctive expression of the American dedication to conquer the frontiers of space. Does the Jewish religious tradition, with *its* "frontier theory," namely a concentration on conquering frontiers of time, history, and eternity, have something unique to say about the limits of technological conquest of space? And when, authentic to my tradition, I seek on the Sabbath to sanctify time as "God's gift to the world of space," am I speaking to a greater American need to learn to "surpass civilization," space, and technology?[11] Can that be part of the spiritual meaning of my being, with thousands of Jewish students and professors, at an American university?

PART PEER, PART PARENT

Reflections about the spiritual significance of my being a Hillel director have similarly mounted up within when I have considered the students themselves. Understandably, these considerations were sharpest in the earliest years when I was almost a peer of theirs and latterly when, as a parent, I was able to sense the different perspectives on life of the young and their elders.

> *To be young means to be all on edge,*
> *To be held waiting in a packed lounge,*
> *For a Personal Call from Long Distance,*
> *For the low voice that defines one's future.*
> *The fears we know are of not knowing.*[12]

Each year anew, I discover the wondrous sense of openness of the young, an openness that, despite acknowledged fears of the future and dread of uncertainty, is expressive of their poignant hope and budding expectancy. How can I not learn for myself as I observe students going through *their* passage from past to future?

How, too, can I fail to empathize with them (and also learn from them) as they strive to make sensible decisions about personal careers? Only a few years ago, there was a general consonance between students' career decisions and their ideals of service to society. Recently, disenchanted by state, government, and even by the university, more and more decide in ways that seemingly are self-centered. But are college registration lines to remain "bread lines" for students applying for means of livelihood—and no more than that? How can I find models for them that will broaden and deepen their perceptions of career and vocation?

And, willy-nilly, I am one of those models for them. Often, however, I myself feel that I am "not a town where things live/but a worry/and a weeping of unused wings."[13] Can I at such a time be present for students dreaming of their flying into a blessed future?

From them I have learned more than all else to be honest in my spiritual self-appraisal. Beyond that, I must with patience, care, and openness listen to *their* questions of spirit. These may be inquiries about the transcendent, about "idealism," about human suffering, about social injustice, or even about the potential for friendships and personal relationships to be meaningful and enduring, beyond merely meeting immediate gratification needs.

FELLOW MINISTERS

In the recent past, my own spiritual growth has been linked more and more to that of my associates in campus ministry with special stimulation and beneficent influences coming from Christian colleagues. Though my Jewish students have been aware of this part of my life, only rarely have they opened themselves to similar relationships. Perhaps they reflect a trend within the wider American Jewish community of setting up, or making peace with, barriers between Jews and Christians, barriers that are more social than theological. This is most evident in the leadership of the Jewish community where, by and large, contact with Christian leadership is now restricted to seeking support for the cause of Russian Jews and for the security of the state of Israel. Campus ministers go further. The commonality of the campus setting leads us to search for a highest common denominator, and it turns out to center on our own spiritual health in this calling. We seem able to do this while not ignoring the real, and the imagined, theological and historical demarcation lines, and we have been aided in this endeavor by Danforth Foundation projects and, in the last years, by the National Institute for Campus Ministries, which was established with a generous grant from the Lilly Endowment.

My younger Hillel colleagues have, in addition, been a source of stimulation for me. We have sustained one another in sharing, openheartedly, our fears of being "burned out" in our work, our concerns for financial security for our families, our apprehensions about not finding enough time for family life amidst the pressures of daily tasks, our difficulties in living with so many calendars (campus, Jewish, civil, family), and, not least of all, our embarrassments in not being successful in instituting and cultivating disciplines of meditation, prayer, and study in our own personal schedules.

Together we also agonized in the last few years as Hillel has gone through a major change in governance. For decades, Hillel was funded primarily from a national source, and we were responsible to senior professional colleagues in the national office. Funding has now increasingly come from local sources, and, understandably, new expectations and accountabilities have confronted the Hillel director. These have been radical changes, not always for the worst, but we now see considerable diversity in governance, budgets, and salaries throughout the country. There is also a major modification in the evaluation of Hillel professionals, with local lay persons or professionals associated with local Jewish funding agencies now making the consequential judgments much more frequently than do colleagues in Hillel. Some degree of demoralization has resulted. In middle-size and large Hillel units, less time and talent is spent by staff in teaching and counseling, since institutional management and public interpretation are perceived as higher priorities.

We ought to note one good outcome, however, from these changes in the polity of the Jewish campus ministry: the introduction of multiple staff, and accordingly of more women (some ordained rabbis), and more social-work professionals (men and women). It is too soon, I believe, to make judgments on whether traditional sexist biases will continue, but as more women join these staffs (sometimes in positions of major responsibility), male and female staff members and students are confronted with a variety of *women's* perspectives on vocation, self-appraisal, and spiritual development. My contacts in the last six years with women colleagues (and also with Hillel group-work professionals) have been challenging and have helped make me more honest and effective in working with students.

FRIEND TO SEEKERS

Then, again, my growth in sensitivity to the spirit has been affected by small groups of "seekers." Most Hillel directors serve on campuses with large populations of Jewish students and clearly must concentrate on maintaining those regular activities dictated by the rhythms of the calendar of Sabbaths and holy days. Yet, we are sustained by encounters with those few individuals who "desegregate" themselves and knock on the office door to discuss a personal concern. Most relevant to our immediate interest are two kinds of students.

The first has an articulated need: support, information, and understanding in connection with a rite of passage, like marriage, baby naming, death, or mourning. Psychological support as well as an understanding of Jewish ritual practice are easier for me to furnish than is the appropriate openness to the student's questions on the meaning and direction of his or her life. Yet, in my experience, by being not only counselor and clergy, but also a solicitous listener, I succeed in eliciting these concerns. Going beyond the roles that the situation ascribes to me and carefully attending what I am being told, I must also be ready to risk, where appropriate, permitting the student to enter into *my* spiritual life, *my* spiritual outlook on marriage, or aging, or death.

A second student seeker is, frequently, one who has been alienated by Jewish worship as he or she has seen it and seeks a fresher more intimate approach to prayer. Together, we, this student and I, have learned and relearned at least the following: disciplines of meditation and contemplation *are* to be found in Jewish literature; the contemporary American synagogue has little time or place for such reflection; the individual seeker must locate (and find) a small worship community where private prayer and public worship *can* nurture one another; *kavvanah* (intention or direction in serving God) must be linked to a science of deeds, that is, to a Jewish regimen of practices and good deeds. Together, we have also discovered, or rediscovered, the luminous power of the writings of Kook,[14] Buber, and Heschel, as well as of older traditional texts of piety.

These student seekers and I have sometimes become close friends, traveling long roads together. But an important element of my spiritual journey has here been patience and forbearance, for some of these young people have betaken themselves to places alien to me. A few have joined contemporary Hasidic groups, whose separation, inflexible obedience to authority figures, and sexism I find unacceptable. Others have resigned themselves to drifting from one group or cult to another, usually without a stable base of family or vocation. A small number have even left, or threatened to leave, the body of the Jewish people in their spiritual quest; here, too, my own sensitivity to the life of the spirit has been strengthened in those sorrowful conversations I have had with them or with their bewildered and grieving families.

WORLD-SHAKING WIND

Ultimately, the search for spiritual resources for my personal life has never been separate from my quest to make significant and invigorated my chosen vocation or service. Somehow, for both, the English word *spirit,* with its centuries of meanings rooted in Oriental-Hellenic usage, is inadequate. Thus, I have found it useful to return to the biblical Hebrew vocabulary: *neshamah,* the breath-life infused into Adam by God; *nefesh,* the life and limb of God's creatures—not soul, but whole self or person; *lev,* the human mind with its capacity for discrimination and understanding—not heart, or emotional center, but locus of the uniquely human power to remember and to imagine and to choose; *ruach,* the power hovering over moving waters, the world-shaking wind which is God's agent. If spirit is understood as biblical *ruach,* I can continue meaningfully to use the term. Like God, this is not spirit in contrast to flesh or matter, but spirit as all: breath, life-activator, understanding heart, and divinely animating and moving force. It is God's power within yearning for the transcendent and expressing it.

WHEEL IN THE LORD'S CHARIOT

Whither has spirit so understood taken me thus far—and whither in days to come?

A wheel in the Lord's chariot, I maintain the freedom to move in any direction: "Wherever the spirit impelled them to go, they went—wherever the Spirit impelled them—and the wheels were lifted up beside them, for the spirit of the creature was in the wheels" (Ezek. 1:20).

I glory in that freedom, but I am in agony when it is directionless.

Perhaps I can best illustrate my quest for direction, my "theotropism,"[15] in an ideal progression of the spirit up the ladder (recalling that, in Jacob's dream, God's grace provides angels that descend and ascend at the same time). This ladder of spiritual movement is a grammar of moods, of modes of human discourse, progressing up as follows:

interrogative: What does the Lord require of me? Or, what is life-truth for me?

subjunctive: Even if I don't have the "facts," I would affirm that I am God's creation, beloved, and suitor for His love and in His judgment.

declarative: "Hear, O Israel, the Lord is Our God, the Lord, Alone."

imperative: "Know the God of your ancestor, serving Him with a whole heart and as willing person."

jussive: "It shall come to pass at the end of days . . .
. . . many people shall come, and say:

'Come, let us go up to the mountain of the Lord
     to the house of the God of Jacob;
That He may teach us His ways
     and that we may walk in His paths.' "

Every day I scramble and clamber up and down the first four rungs. I try the fifth occasionally, for example in festival celebrations. But, always, I am sustained by the hopeful vision of that highest rung, and I seek to bring a bit of its fulfillment into life here and now. "A drop of Messianic consummation must be mingled with every hour; otherwise, the hour is godless—despite all piety and devoutness."[16]

NOTES

1 Richard Clarke Cabot, *What Men Live By* (Darby, Penn.: Folcroft, 1914).

2. Martin Buber, *The Way of Man According to the Teachings of Hasidism* (Secaucus, N.J.: Citadel Press, 1966), p. 21.

3. Yehuda Haleyi, *Selected Poems* (Philadelphia: Jewish Publication Society of America, 1974), p. 134.

4. Mishnah Abot (Ethics of the Fathers) 3:7.
5. George Foot Moore (in an address at the University of Cincinnati, sponsored by the Intercollegiate Menorah Association in 1921), *The Menorah Treasury,* ed. by Lee W. Schwartz (Philadelphia: Jewish Pub. Soc., 1958), p. 21.
6. Isaac Luria, see *Authorized Daily Prayer Book,* ed. by Joseph Hertz (New York: Bloch Pub. Co.), p. 2.
7. Martin Buber, *The Origin and Meaning of Hasidism* (New York: Horizon Press, 1972), p. 229.
8. Mishnah Abot (Ethics of the Fathers), 1:6.
9. Martin Buber, *Tales of the Hasidim,* vol. 1 (New York: Schocken, 1947), p. 8.
10. Douglas M. Knight in *Liberal Learning and Religion,* ed. by Amos N. Wilder (Port Washington, N.Y.: Kennikat Press, 1969), p. 97.
11. A. J. Heschel, *The Sabbath* (New York: Farrar, Straus and Giroux, 1975), p. 96ff. and *God in Search of Man* (New York: Farrar, Straus and Giroux, 1972), p. 200ff., 414ff.
12. W. H. Auden, *The Age of Anxiety* (New York: Random, 1947), p. 42.
13. Kenneth Patchen, *Hallelujah Anyway* (New York: New Directions), p. 15.
14. Abraham Isaac Kook, *The Lights of Penitence,* trans. by Ben Zion Bokser, in The Classics of Western Spirituality (New York: Paulist Press, 1978).
15. A. J. Heschel, *God in Search of Man* (New York: Schocken, 1972), p. 416.
16. Martin Buber, *On Judaism,* p. 209 (in the address, *"The Silent Question"*).

ON BEING PASSIONATE
Reflections on Roman Catholic Approaches to Spirituality

Nancy Malone, O.S.U.

THE KEY INTUITION

He said: "Listen, everybody has a spirituality. I may want to be the best goddamn consumer in the world. That's my spirituality."

I said: "Yes." I thought: *I don't get it. He's probably right because he usually is. I can't use it in the chapter because I don't get it.*

He said: "And the trouble with Catholics . . ."

I said: "I know, you're always suspicious of Catholics and spirituality. You always have been."

He said: "The trouble with Catholics is that they get so caught up in techniques. The whole thing becomes a matter of technique."

I said: "Yes, thanks. And thanks for the lunch." I thought: *That was no help at all.*

It was one A.M. a week later. I was awake in a house not my own, reading an old *Time* magazine. The article was about a professor in New Jersey who, with his own press, turns out beautifully printed broadsheets on the jargon that comes out of the administrative offices at his college. It was a delightful piece, not because it offered examples of administrators' linguistic confusion, but because it was so descriptive of the professor's feelings and fulminations.

I thought: *Well, yes, that's something I'm passionate about —language.*

Then I thought: *That's what he means. Spirituality is what you're passionate about.*

Passion: the Passion of Our Lord Jesus Christ. What you are willing to suffer for. Jesus, a passionate man. The harsh sayings, not so much harsh as passionate. "Unless you hate father and mother. . . ." One passion: God, His Father. "You must love the Lord your God with your *whole* heart, *whole* mind, *whole* soul. . . ." Passion: sexual energy. The body—bodily—the incarnation: I like a notion of spirituality that involves the body. *Patior:* To suffer, to allow. Not what one can command, but what is visited upon one. Francis, passionate about poverty; Ignatius, passionate about obedience; Thérèse, passionate about littleness: the grand, traditional Roman Catholic spiritualities. But diminished passion in their followers: techniques and institutionalization. But what if you're passionate about golf? Or about killing Jews? A problem, a real problem.

There it was: the key intuition, given whole, as intuitions are, in a few sleepless hours one night. What follows is an account of where that intuition led me as I attempted to explore, refine, and test it for its validity and truth, and for its usefulness to persons in higher education. The account does not have the character of expository prose in which the author presents the reader with a logical recital of conclusions reached. Rather, I invite the reader into the process of "reflecting with" me: taking each thought as far as it will go; bumping into problems as they arise; entertaining new insights as they occur; following byways if they look interesting; doubling back to pick up a previous thought. The invitation beckons the reader not so much to the discipline of understanding "from the outside," but to the discipline of imagining "from the inside" of the original intuition itself.

DISCRIMINATING PASSION

Spirituality is what one is passionate about. That's a nice description. It makes spirituality interesting. It puts flesh, blood, bones, and sinews on what is too often, or too often perceived as, ethereal and effete. It points to life: "Choose life," says the Lord in Deuteronomy. It passes judgment on those "spiritual" persons who live without passion, who live by rules and regulations or techniques, or following the latest "spiritual" fad and fashion. It presumes something, or someone, outside of oneself to be passionate about; it suggests ecstasy (*ekstasis*) or at least intense interest. It relates spirituality and meaning: life is full of meaning when one is beset by a passion. It presupposes that ministry flows organically from spirituality, that it is not tacked on as an obligation, that the two are not artificially segregated from each other into public and private domains. It could, conceivably, include everyone; by definition, it does not exclude anyone or anything, except persons devoid of passion. It is nice— and it is dangerous: the Jews . . . tattooed numbers . . . smoking ovens.

One might handle the problem by discriminating among the objects of passion. One could say that the object of one's passion has to be worthy, worthy of one's whole self, of ultimate worth. The ultimacy at least puts the object of passion in the ballpark of religion, in the ballpark of religious language. I don't know; maybe golf is a religion for some people, giving ultimate meaning to their lives. And one could discriminate further and say that one's passion cannot be pursued with harm to other human beings. "With your whole heart, your whole mind, your whole soul": that is reserved for God. "And your neighbor as yourself." Do those criteria safeguard the definition of spirituality by limiting its application, by eliminating unworthy objects and harmful acts?

Perhaps, rather, we should keep the definition and allow for "negative spiritualities": killing Jews, Jonestown, lynching "niggers" under a burning cross. God knows, there is passion there—passion run amok—and something perceived by devotees as "religious," as "spiritual." Hatred, after all, is a passion. When it, or any negative passion, possesses the whole self, we have the demonic.

Or perhaps the discriminating clue is in the wholeness of the passionate self, rather than in either the objects of passion or the positive or negative nature of the passion possessing one. It may be fragmented passion that is demonic or something less: the ruthless pursuit of truth without feeling for other people; a passionate indulgence in emotion uninformed by intelligence or undisciplined by will; passionate willfulness without intelligence or emotion; or any combination that is less than whole. That has critical possibilities beyond the category of the demonic. It might have something to say about our worship.

WHOLEHEARTED PASSION

The definition itself needs refining. Not "spirituality is what one is passionate about." But "wherever you find spirituality, you find something, or someone, people are passionate about." That takes care of a lot of bloodless piety. It tests the quality and genuineness of spirituality. But then we haven't yet said what spirituality is. If religion is the realm of ultimate meaning and value, then, as Brother David Steindl-Rast says, spirituality is religion embodied, incarnate, religion informing *all* of life: what one buys, eats, how one studies, deals with other people. To live with that kind of con-centration is to be passionate, is to be a whole self. It is misleading, therefore, to speak, as Catholics are wont to do, of one's "spiritual life." By our description, your spiritual life is your life. Period. The single most distinctive feature of Roman Catholic spirituality, its sacramentality, says that over and over again.

Of course, Jesus, "the pioneer and perfecter of our faith," did not talk about his spiritual life. Or about ultimate meaning and value. Jesus talked about God, about loving God with passion, with "whole heart." And he did. H. Richard Niebuhr, in the section on the excellences of Christ at the beginning of *Christ and Culture*,[1] catalogues the chief virtues claimed by followers of Jesus to be central to his life: Jesus, the man of hope; Jesus, the humble man; Jesus, the radically obedient man; Jesus, the man of faith; Jesus, the loving man.

We could add to the list—Jesus, the revolutionary man; Jesus, the free man—until we have named every theological and spiritual interpretation put on the life of Christ. Niebuhr acknowledges, and so do I, that Jesus possessed all of these excellences—that he was poor, humble, obedient, loving in a supreme way. But, at the center of the life of Christ, in the heart of Jesus, was—is—God, not any virtue as such. He loved God, he obeyed God, he believed in God, he hoped and trusted in God, he was humble before God. Because Jesus' wholehearted passion was God his Father, because Jesus' life was God his Father, he showed himself to be the Son. This relationship was—is—Jesus' spirituality, properly called the Holy Spirit. This is the Spirit sent by the Father and the Son into the hearts of believers in and followers of Jesus. Living by this Spirit, and no less, is Christian spirituality.

The saints knew this. Rather, the saints lived it. We misconstrue them in the same way we do Jesus. We talk of Franciscan spirituality and elaborate rules about poverty. Francis loved the Father and stripped himself naked while calling on His name. We imitate Ignatius in practicing obedience. Ignatius "imitated" Jesus—lived by His spirit—in a wholehearted love of God; and the greatest obstacle to this love was his own willfulness. We follow Thérèse in the "little way," remembering that even picking up pins can be an expression of passionate love for God. We recognize that passion needs discipline, that the torrent needs channeling. We forget that no amount of discipline can ever create passion. It is a problem for the good. It is the perennial problem of the good: "works' righteousness," or, as my friend put it, techniques. And Catholics are still bedeviled by it. Others too, of course, in different ways.

So where are we? These last two sections, "Discriminating Passion" and "Wholehearted Passion," have meant to test the truth and validity of our description of spirituality against the cardinal touchstones of the life of Jesus and the lesser touchstones of the lives of the saints. The description need not be perfectly accurate, nor the definition airtight. What is important is that the reflections glancing off this question illuminate our lives. I am satisfied; it has done that for me. There are still problems, but there are illuminations, too.

LIFE-LOVING PASSION

Here is one illumination, or maybe several, concatenated. What spirituality is about, finally, is the love of life, all of it: my life, life in the world around me, people—as coming from the hand of our Creator and Redeemer and Sanctifier. That takes care of several matters at once. It eliminates fundamentally world-denying "spiritualities." It validates a central insight of Roman Catholic spirituality, its sacramentality: things, persons, sensible impressions—the fragrance of incense, candlelight—as grace-bearing. For this reason, most Catholics, even passionate ones, are not spiritual monomaniacs. A conversation does not have to be explicitly about the Lord Jesus to be holy. A glass of wine with friends can be an implicit Eucharist. The "sunshine on your shoulder" can be soaked in for itself. All life in a sacramental universe is implicitly holy; this does not have to be constantly explicated, just as symbols do not need to be—and often should not be—explained.

TRANSFORMING PASSION

But, of course, we have to be reminded. The Eucharist calls to mind the loveliness of all of life and expresses our gratitude for it. It calls to mind that every meal, every gathering in fellowship, every conversation, every handshake is graceful and an occasion for gratitude to God. In the Eucharist we are reminded, "we remember most of all," that Jesus lived his life and died his death at the hand of his Father, and was grateful for all: "On the night he was *betrayed*, he took bread and gave thanks and praise...." The Eucharist reminds us of the mystery of redemptive suffering (a note not very strongly struck in our present ritual) and of the reality of risen eternal life. Eternal life, which we have always known was a matter of quality not quantity, *is* life loved. The opposite of eternal life is to hate our life and wish it were over.

Or better, the holy, reverenced life, life loved now issues in life loved forever. "Being in love in an unrestricted fashion" is Bernard Lonergan's definition of religious conversion.[2] Spirituality is aimed at conversion, what Rosemary Haughton calls transformation.[3] Being passionate, being in love, being converted or transformed are by definition ways of being that we cannot command at will. They happen to us. Catholics know this and traditionally aim at transformation by what Rosemary Haughton, again, calls formation. Formation is what the "works," the techniques, the institutionalizations are about. It is all of a piece with Catholic notions of natural law, of grace building on nature, of the goodness—flawed and wounded goodness—of the world and humankind. The trouble is Catholics sometimes forget what they are aiming at: transformation.

In an earlier draft of this chapter, I had selected one-on-one (as they say) spiritual direction as being a notable phenomenon in current Roman Catholic spirituality. It fits in here as being another instance of Roman Catholic sacramentality—dealing with God mediately through another human being. Good spiritual direction has all of the characteristics of good counseling or good therapy; it deals with all of one's life, all of one's problems, joys, sorrows, successes, relationships, but in a context of prayer, of one's relationship with God. That underlines my point about one's spiritual life being one's *life*, doesn't it?

And the Spiritual Exercises of St. Ignatius, a very specific form of spiritual direction, underline the character of Christian spirituality as such. Through contemplating (not thinking about, but experientially living through over a long period of time the life, death, and resurrection of Christ), the retreatant is meant to realize (not think or believe, but realize) that the Spirit of Jesus Christ is the Spirit who dwells in her, leads her through the deserts, events, sufferings, deaths, and resurrections of her own life. The exercises confront the retreatant with the choice of whether to follow that Spirit or not. And they conclude, come to think of it, with the *Contemplatio ad Amorem,* a contemplation on love and gratitude for all.

NEIGHBORLY PASSION

I am aware that in our discussion of spirituality so far I have not said much about love of/for people, except in a passing way. For some religious persons the discussion would have begun—and ended—there; for them, it is only in the neighbor that God is encountered. But the deuteronomic commandment quoted by Jesus begins, "Love God with your whole heart," and continues, "and your neighbor as yourself." And the Fourth Gospel changes that on the lips of Jesus to "as I have loved you." There are distinctions here. What are they?

I am in complete agreement with H. Richard Niebuhr in criticizing the liberal Protestant claim that the ethics of Jesus "has two foci, 'God, the Father, and the infinite value of the human soul.' Such statements forget that the double commandment . . . by no means places God and neighbor on a level, as though complete devotion were due to each."[4] I'm also sure that Caryll Houselander's comment about those who think they love God *because* they do not love anyone else is an equally valid critique of another class of "spiritual" persons. No, the two, God and neighbor, do belong together in spirituality. The question is, how?

I think that this might be where ministry comes in. Wholehearted love, adoration, and thanksgiving are due to God alone. It is love expressed in service that is due to our neighbor. Jesus' life makes this clear in one concrete action after another and, symbolically, in the washing of the feet of the disciples at the Last Supper. But Jesus' "love of God and his love of neighbor are two distinct virtues that have no common quality but only a common source":[5] God. Further, in the great key text for service in Matthew 25, it is precisely those things that we *cannot* do to/for God—feeding, clothing, etc.— that we are commanded to do to/for others. And then, to reverse the reference point in the common understanding of the parable, even these acts are done for God. "I tell you solemnly, in so far as you did this to one of the least of these, you did it to me." That is the relationship of "spirituality" and "ministry," as we usually understand those terms. Not the first a fueling station for the second, but, to paraphrase Saint John of the Cross, "at the foot of the mountain, God, along the way, God, at the top of the mountain, God." Our spiritual life is our life. Period.

DEMONSTRATED PASSION

The toughest part of the task is ahead of us: to relate all of this to ministry in higher education. What do these reflections on spirituality have to say to or about that ministry? What light do they throw on it?

To go back to the beginning of our reflections, being passionate about means, at least, being interested in. Being interested in means, at least, knowing about. Knowing about means having learned in one way or another. Education might be thought of as engendering passion for the world about us and ultimately for God.

Passion requires discrimination: intellectual discrimination as to worthy objects, and moral discrimination as to the good or harm visited upon others and ourselves by the pursuit of passion. Education might be thought of as teaching discrimination of judgment.

Being passionate means being a whole self. Probably every college catalogue contains a statement of purpose that has to do with educating the whole person. That has become educational cant. And then the whole person is departmentalized. The head is assigned to the classroom. The emotions and feelings are assigned to student services, dorm life, the counseling office, or the psych department. And the will, if it is attended to at all, is given over to the chaplains and campus ministers, who are supposed to be about right living and social action and concern for others. Rather, it seems to me that good teaching is the best formation that the college as such can offer for the wholeness that is transformation: good teaching begets good learning and both involve the whole person—mind, will, and emotions—of the teacher and the learner.

Bad teaching, whether due to lack of intellectual preparation, engagement of the will, or feeling for the subject and/or the students, begets boredom. Being bored is the opposite of being passionate; it diffuses the whole person. And boredom a kind of "shadow passion," a "negative spirituality," issues in violence as an outlet for its negative or unused energy. There is a lot of violence on campuses today—in dorms, in cafeterias, in lounges. And students, lots of them, are attracted to all kinds of spiritualities that are negative, or less than whole, where the violence of mind-control is visited upon the devotees by their "gurus," and then by the devotees on others in relentless proselytizing.

Spirituality is religion embodied, incarnate, religion informing all of life. The life of the university is teaching and learning. How we teach and learn, especially when these exercises take up hours of our lives, is preeminently a spiritual matter.

Passion needs discipline. The passion to know needs the channeling of "the disciplines." But no academic discipline can create the passion to know. Without that passion, we are left with techniques. We become educational technicians, teachers and students alike.

In a sacramental universe, to teach and study mathematics can be, and in fact is, as holy as to teach and study the Bible.

Transformation, conversion, salvation, wholeness is God's business. The business of those who minister, "who are aware of being people living in relation to salvation . . . is to provide the type of formation that is suited to transformation. That means modifying the secular structure for the purpose of salvation."[6] There, in broad outline, is the call and the purpose of ministry in that enormously important formative secular structure called the college or the university.

To end at the end, our spirituality is our ministry is our life. To serve in a particular world means taking that world seriously, means embodying our service in that world. Of course, campus ministers must serve all kinds of needs on campus. They must do individual counseling, work for humane living conditions, raise awareness of social issues such as world hunger and nuclear power.

But the inevitable conclusion for me from these reflections on ministry in higher education is that the life of that world, teaching and learning, must be ministered to, must be formed for transformation. And, because it is worship that calls to mind that transformation is what life is all about, worship in an academic community must remind us in every possible way—by the substance of its preaching, by the strength of its music, by the beauty of its surroundings, by the clarity of its language—that the life of the mind is holy.

NOTES

1. H. Richard Niebuhr, *Christ and Culture* (New York: Harper and Row, 1975), pp. 11–29.
2. Bernard Lonergan, *Method in Theology* (New York: Seabury Press, 1972), p. 105 and *passim.*
3. Rosemary Haughton, *The Transformation of Man* (Springfield, Ill., Templegate Pub., 1967).
4. Niebuhr, p. 17.
5. Niebuhr, p. 18.
6. Haughton, pp. 252–53.

EVANGELICAL SPIRITUALITY ON COLLEGE CAMPUSES*

Rebecca Manley Pippert

FALSE APPROACHES TO EVANGELICAL SPIRITUALITY

Otherworldly

I have a friend who is so spiritual she has never, that I can recall, admitted to having a bad day. Her tone is saccharine; her attitude is "Victory! No matter what, victory!"

Once she began, "Isn't this an absolutely marvelous day!" It was raining, so I began to think of all the reasons why it wasn't. Then she said, "Praise the Lord! My car was just totaled. All things work together for good . . . !"

"Yeah, it's a great day," I mumbled, "But . . . what did you say? Your car was what?"

"Totaled! Praise Jesus!" she responded.

Thinking I must have misunderstood, I said, "Wait a minute. Did you just say your car was totaled?"

"Yes, I did," she answered with a glow.

"But that's terrible!" I shrieked.

"Oh, not when you have Jesus. Let's just praise his name." And off she went on a celestial cloud.

Meanwhile, I pondered some earthly questions. Could her understanding of spirituality tolerate pain or face up to any real crisis? Did she not simply want to live in the world of the Spirit, and let us less spiritual types stay down here to struggle with the mundane and the negative?

Short on Reason

A freshman told me he had just finished his history final in five minutes. I replied that I was in awe of his intellectual prowess, but he assured me that it was no such thing.

"I spent those five minutes writing to my professor that it was a waste of time to study history when Jesus is coming soon. Then I asked him, 'Are you ready?'"

The student assumed that Jesus' return preempted every other activity except evangelism. The only book he wanted to read was the Bible, but he approached the Scriptures in the same cavalier way he approached history—taking verses out of context and misconstruing their meaning. That did not faze him, as long as he could warm himself emotionally.

Legalistic

I have some Christian friends who feel that one's eternal destiny would be doomed by lighting up a cigarette. I have other evangelical friends who are utterly committed to justice for the poor. They laugh and shake their heads over their legalistic brethren, but they would suspect the spirituality of a person who worshiped in a Brooks Brothers suit and sat down afterward to a cut of prime rib.

The point here is neither to undermine a much-needed identification with the poor, nor to equate true liberation with an after-dinner cigar. Rather, it is the confusion of both the older and newer legalism in identifying external disciplines with spirituality.

Ego-centered

It was equally alarming to hear, at an evangelical conference, students defining spirituality solely in terms of "ego-building" and "self-fulfillment." Jesus was reduced to being merely the answer to one's lack of security and self-esteem, rather than being the Lord of compassion for others.

Spirituality, divorced from pain and crisis may be a gnostic brand, but it cannot be an evangelical one. Nor can true spirituality be merely experience-oriented, severed from reason. And the spirituality which proudly wins points for what one does not do (although frequently the disease of the devoted) is an aberration of discipleship.

EVANGELICAL SPIRITUALITY

It Is Total

True spirituality controls the whole person. It is not all sentiment and no action; rather, it is something that comes from the very cen-

ter of a person's life. It is what shapes and motivates a person. It is
not what one *has;* it is what one *is.* We do not give the gospel; we are
the gospel. Jesus did not say, "Go out and try to drum up a little salt
in your life. " He announced, "You *are* salt" (Mt. 5:13). "Now start
acting like it."

Its Source Is Jesus Christ

In the evangelical Protestant tradition we believe that our spirituality proceeds from God the Father and the Son through the work
of the Holy Spirit in God's people. It is what God the Father has
said and done in Jesus Christ, together with our believing response
of gratitude and submission to the Holy Spirit, that constitutes our
spirituality. Indeed, the Spirit is the one who makes this response
possible.

It is the incarnation, the unique entrance of God among people in
the person and flesh of Jesus, who is fully God and fully man, that
gives us a correct understanding of spirituality.[1] Our view of the incarnation affirms that Jesus Christ is our spirituality. It is his life,
death, and resurrection that makes us acceptable to God. Spirituality begins not with emotional experience, nor the keeping of laws,
nor social activism, but with Christ.

The *divine* dimension of the incarnation calls us to be holy as God
is holy, creating in us a desire to seek God and imitate Him. And the
human side of the incarnation calls us to the world, with both its
hurts and ribaldry. As Robert Webber points out, when Christ's humanity is overemphasized, we develop a spirituality that concen-
trates almost exclusively on the Christian's relationship to the
world—as is the case with some social activists. When Christ's divinity is overemphasized we have a spirituality that is too otherworldly—as in the story of the woman with the totaled car.

We need spirituality that makes us more than passive pietists or
activistic Boy Scouts. The incarnation, Webber says, "breaks down
those false distinctions between the spiritual and the material, the
sacred and the profane, the supernatural and the natural."[2] To fail
to demonstrate spirituality through the holiness of our lives, or to
live without a passionate active concern for justice, truth, and humanity is to fail our tradition.

It Rings with Assurance

A key characteristic within the evangelical tradition is the conviction that our spirituality is coupled to a sense of an assurance of sal-

vation. Reference to evangelical language such as being "born again," "making a commitment to Christ," getting "saved," etc. is often misconstrued as pride or arrogance. But it is, at root, no more haughty than Luther's experience of liberation when he realized that he was "justified by faith." This assurance comes both from the knowledge that the Christ of history has procured salvation by objective historical events—the cross and resurrection—and from the power of the Spirit who enables me to call the God of the universe my Father (Rom. 8:15-16).

Evangelicals have had a wide variety of salvation experiences. Some cite a date of conversion; others feel their pilgrimage with God has been progressive, nurtured by a believing home life. Regardless of how they got there, all evangelicals would say that they experience personal contact with God through Jesus Christ.

It Is Marked by Vitality

Evangelical spirituality frequently has vitality and fervor. This atmosphere of vibrance and celebration, often characteristic of fellowship meetings—especially if recent converts participate—springs from an awareness of the reality of God, an awareness akin to what Israel experienced in its relationship to the "living God" (e.g., Ps. 84:2).

This was not a comfortable God so much as a transcendental Interferer. He was alive. And the best way to communicate His aliveness was to describe Him in the most graphic, specific language possible: they pictured Him speaking, listening, laughing, walking in the cool of the day, and promising to wipe away our tears. You can love Him, hate Him, argue with Him, reject Him. But above all—you can *know* Him.

THE SPIRIT AT WORK NOW

Where, we may ask, are current evidences of the Spirit's work? In many ways the Spirit is using the same tools he has always used: the Bible and prayer, fellowship and evangelism.

The Bible

There is very little difference among the campus evangelical ministries in their emphasis on Bible study, prayer, daily devotions, and Christian fellowship. The Navigators, a group that started with a ministry in the Navy and then extended it to the campus, have a wealth of Bible study materials.[3] So do Inter-Varsity[4] and Campus Crusade.[5]

The general approach to group Bible study would be inductive—a student-led exercise that focuses on observing the text carefully, then interpreting the meaning of the observation, and finally applying its meaning to life today. The students dig for information instead of being spoon fed.

During the past several years a method of Bible study, known as the "manuscript method," has been developed by the western Inter-Varsity staff, especially Paul Byer.[6] This method involves use of a manuscript of a book of the Bible without chapter or verse markings. The absence of these artificial markings—the original documents themselves had no such divisions—compels the students to work carefully enough to discover the inherent divisions in the text.

"If their minds are alive," Byer says, "questions will come to them out of the text itself, which forces them to go back into the text to find answers. These answers create more questions and this evolution occurs each time at a deeper level."

Inter-Varsity's previous format for Bible study had been to lift out various passages of Scripture for study without trying to connect them to the whole book. Byer had often used scattered incidents in the Gospel of Mark, but, in ways akin to redaction criticism, he wanted students to become curious as to what Mark's overall intention was, why Mark put the Gospel together the way he did.

What are the results of this study? First, it helps students to see a book as a whole. And they develop much greater appreciation for and sensitivity to the author's style and the way he develops his message. Since that message centers in the story of Jesus, his person becomes more alive to the students through a manuscript study of a Gospel.

Another result of Byer's method is that it reveals the power of a good story. Students feel they can sit down with their skeptic friends, read or tell them a gospel story, and talk about Jesus in an easy, clear way. It frees them to use Scripture in conversational evangelism. To a nonbeliever who does not have a theological framework, an isolated Bible verse may not make sense. But if we tell a story out of life—and life is already a shared framework—then the meaning of the story may be understood.

Community and Fellowship

The experience of community in a small group also helps produce changed lives. Students are urged to build intimacy within their small group as well as to get enmeshed in the life of their dorm or living unit. A balance between good scriptural study that leads to obedience to God and the healing and growth that often come from intimate sharing can be very powerful.

Music has always played a major part in evangelical fellowship. There are many hymns written today whose music is beautiful as well as lyrically profound. The songs of Ken Medema, Bill Gaither, André Crouch, and Jimmy Owens are all examples of this, along with the new charismatic songs and psalms set to music. Even with the rich combination of the new songs and the older ones in the Inter-Varsity hymnal, not all evangelical bad taste has been eliminated: one can't help but sense a few students itching to get back to the "I love Jesus" number sung to the Coca-Cola soundtrack.

A Fresh Look at the Gospels

Since the Reformation the evangelical tradition has been doctrine-oriented. Hence, some evangelicals have tended to regard the Epistles, with their rich doctrine, as the real "meat and potatoes" and the Gospels as light snacks for the spiritually young. But that seems to be changing as an increasing number of evangelicals reexamine the Gospels to see what Jesus valued and what he placed priority upon. This fresh look at these documents is compelling us to take several corrective steps.

We had sometimes let evangelism slip into the sales department, with too much dependence upon technique and strategy. If we had been examining and emulating the quality of life that Jesus calls us to, evangelism would have been more natural, flowing from our lives instead of from some memorized scheme.

Again, evangelicals often have focused on being "justified by faith" and have minimized "good works." Faith has frequently been misinterpreted as a simple decision, without wholehearted commitment to all its implications of worship, love, and service. Practice is proof of authentic discipleship. Behavior must spring from faith and doctrine, and the Gospels, with their insistence that we must "hear and obey" (paraphrase of Lk. 7:22), offer an antidote to barren doctrine that is unable to produce the fruits of behavior.

The evangelicals I work with are seeking to stir students from quietism by calling them to radical obedience to Jesus Christ. They are urging them to evaluate the depth of their commitment not by flawless articulation of doctrine, nor by pleasing their local staff worker—a contemporary temptation not present in the sixties—but by behavior that takes Jesus' words seriously.

Evangelism

Virtually all evangelicals can support a common definition of evangelism, like that expressed in the Lausanne Covenant (1974) and expounded by evangelical missioners like John R. W. Stott.[7]

Evangelism . . . is the proclamation of the historical, biblical Christ as Saviour and Lord, with a view to persuading people to come to him personally and so be reconciled to God. In issuing the gospel invitation we have no liberty to conceal the cost of discipleship. Jesus still calls all who would follow him to deny themselves, take up their cross, and identify themselves with his new community. The results of evangelism include obedience to Christ, incorporation into his church and responsible service in the world.

Though the Spirit also is moving in evangelism, it is here that we see some of the greatest differences among the sister movements—not in definition but in style. In Campus Crusade for Christ, a chief emphasis is witnessing to strangers. Crusaders frequently use religious surveys to open up conversations with a non-Christian. If the student is receptive, they will read the "four spiritual laws,"[8] their summation of the gospel. If they think the person is open spiritually, they ask the student to become a Christian.

Inter-Varsity encourages students both to communicate their faith and to care for persons with whom their lives naturally intersect. One hears the term "incarnational evangelism" in groups like Inter-Varsity and Young Life, a ministry to high school students. The emphasis is to proclaim the Word *and* to live it out—the whole gospel for the whole person.

Inter-Varsity's approach to evangelism usually takes place in several stages. The first is "pre-evangelism," establishing close relationships out of our shared humanity. I rarely meet a student in my movement whose aim is "mow them over for Jesus." Usually Inter-

Varsity students are so afraid of turning people off, or of being identified as "Bible bangers" who push tracts and nab strangers, that they remain silent. So the first level of training is to summon the students out of sequestered "holy huddles" and into authentic relationships with others.

Jesus' call to relationship also prohibits an "us and them" mentality and encourages a "come and see" approach. Consequently, the role of Christian community has taken on new importance. Instead of Christians isolating themselves from nonbelievers except for an occasional "evangelistic service," they are inviting their skeptic friends into their fellowships, making them feel at home, encouraging them just to "hang around" and see how they live.

A word of warning is in order: probably at no other time have people become so attracted to a "relational" approach. The 1960s brought a spirit of activism; the early seventies, introspection. But since the late seventies, students have seemed starved for relationships and community. They are open to both the beautiful and the ghastly.

Their attitude is all too often, "Love me—and I'll believe anything you want." This explains in part the seductive appeal of the cults and the terrible horrors of Jonestown. If there are only the "warm fuzzies" in our fellowship meetings but no clear proclamation of truth, then we could be building upon the students' emotional vulnerability. This is why we emphasize the proclamation of truth as much as the building of relationships.

The second stage, after establishing a relationship, is to arouse curiosity in the hearer, as the Apostle Paul did (Acts 17:2–3). There are many ways of stimulating interest, but the key is not to "dump" a message before the hearer is open.

The third stage is to relate the message itself. Alfred Krass,[9] in *Christian Century*, describes how Louis Alemen breaks down the verbal message into three parts: (1) telling his story (the drama of God's deeds with its central act in the life, death and resurrection of Christ); (2) telling my story (which isn't the gospel message but illustrates its power); and (3) seeking to show how his story relates to and is relevant to the story of the person to whom we are witnessing (i.e., your story). This integration of all three "stories" is a *sine qua non* of witnessing.

Many evangelicals have an increasing aversion to "cheap evangelism." They resist the notion that a "decision" is the whole transaction rather than a mere beginning. We call students to obedience to Christ, not merely to a decision. Navigators, for example, place great emphasis on building solid disciples. Among others, Rene Padilla and Samuel Escobar, Inter-Varsity leaders in Latin America, have helped us interpret the nature and implication of repentance in conversion. We must tell the seekers plainly both the joy and cost of following Christ. I have frequently heard a fellow staff worker, when encountering students who blithely say, "I can't think of any reasons not to become a Christian," reply to them frankly, "Well, I can, and let me name a few." As Jim Wallis writes:

To convert means far more than to experience the psychological, emotional aspects of change through inner experience. The biblical accent is clearly on a reversal of direction, a transfer of loyalties, a change in commitment leading to the creation of a new community. . . . We have forgotten that a relationship to Christ means a relationship to the purposes of Christ in history.[10]

Lastly, we must say a few words about the role of apologetics in evangelism. Our students are constantly encouraged to use their minds and to know why they believe. The problem is this: just when they seem to get their minds all in order and feel there are no lurking inconsistencies among their presuppositions, they go boldly forth and find that their non-Christian friends have all sorts of inconsistent and cherished beliefs floating around in their heads. For example, they frequently advocate sexual freedom in their conviction that there are no more moral absolutes. Yet they are rigid moralists over social injustices like child abuse, sexism, or the nuclear arms race.

The problem and challenge, therefore, is this: how do we speak of truth and absolutes in a world in which our concept of truth has been so drastically eroded that something is true merely if it turns you on or comes from sincere motives? Any discussion of absolutes seems absurd to a relativistic culture, yet without them the truths of God and the gospel can readily become trivialized.

Integration of Mind and Spirit

Linking head and heart has been a strong emphasis in Inter-Varsity, while Josh McDowell has given Campus Crusade a powerful voice in apologetics.[10] One of Inter-Varsity Press's best sellers was Os Guiness's *The Dust of Death,*[11] a 1973 book that explored the malaise settling on Western establishment culture as well as the so-called counterculture and then projected a "third way"—what Guiness called "constructive Christian radicalism."

Other writers with impact on students are John R. W. Stott, rector emeritus of All-Souls Church, London, and an honorary Chaplain to the Queen. His *Basic Christianity*[12] is a continuing best seller. Francis Schaeffer, an American who founded L'Abri Fellowship in Switzerland, has related rational evangelical orthodoxy to a presuppositional approach to theistic argumentation. His earlier books, *The God Who Is There* and *Escape from Reason,*[13] were especially influential among students.

The problem is to get students to see how their faith affects their world view and the way they use their gifts. Peter urged us to be prepared to give "a reason" for our hope (1 Pet. 3:15, KJV). Our job, then, is to arouse intellectual curiosity in the Christian faith in spite of our culture's drift toward adoration of experience alone.

As academic disciplines (natural sciences, philosophy, social sciences) have developed with an increasingly humanistic and not a theistic world view, believers often casually and uncritically have accepted their conclusions. "This has resulted in the creation of a cadre of Christians who live 'with two caps,'" Webber says. "The one cap is worn in church or in the doing of 'religious things.' The other in thinking or living in the world. Consequently, spirituality is no longer connected to 'thinking' and has become for some an experiential, emotional 'feeling in my heart.' "[14]

While I was an Inter-Varsity staffer at Reed College in Portland, Oregon, we had statewide conferences on topics such as "Morality in a Pluralistic Society." The resource persons tried to make students sensitive to the problems of integrating their faith with their academic majors and vocational goals.

For example, an evangelical reporter in the mass media told journalism students that the job of the journalist is not merely to report objectively both sides of a controversy, but to pursue *truth* and to publish it. A literature professor asked English majors, "How do Shakespeare's understanding of evil in Richard III or Camus's understanding of evil in the person of Clamonce in *The Fall* relate to a Christian understanding of evil?" A Christian architect saw the design of God's work in creation as a model for her own drawings. An urban planner acknowledged that he was striving to see what being a Christian meant in his work, which has such impact on the poor and the powerless.

"Dorm talks" dealing with the rational basis of Christianity are useful in probing the connection of mind and spirit. A staff member may speak briefly on topics such as, "Evidence for the Resurrection" or "The Reliability of the New Testament Documents." After the talk, the staffer urges those attending to ask questions. There is no pressure put on them to convert, only to consider.

Social and Ethical Concerns

While evangelicals always have placed a high value on personal morality (and this is, after all, a vital part of the ethical issue), there has not always been an equal passion for social justice. Yet the Spirit is doing new things here.

What is hard to account for is, as Martin Marty writes, "fundamentalism's departure from the older evangelical concern for social issues as it now relates to the whole social fabric."[15] Millard Erickson makes a similar point: "During its long history, orthodox, or conservative, Christianity has stressed the application of its message to social ills. . . . As the twentieth century moved on, however, fundamentalism neglected this emphasis. . . ."[16]

By and large, this evangelical social silence lasted from the 1930s until the 1960s. Happily, it has now been shattered. Although there is controversy within evangelicalism today over whether we view social concern as part of evangelism or whether it flows from discipleship, the consensus is that it must be present.

Martin Marty points to an awakening of this social concern among such younger evangelicals as Richard Pierard, Richard Quebedeaux, Richard J. Mouw, the editors of the *Reformed Journal*, the Southern Baptist Convention's Christian Life Commission, the *Sojourners*, authors of the Chicago Declaration of Social Concern (among whom were William Bentley, Sharon Gallagher, Nancy Hardesty, Wes Michaelson, David Moberg, John Perkins, Clark Pinnock, Wes Pippert, Ronald J. Sider, and John Howard Yoder), and others. Marty notes that they "have taken up this theme with a vengeance and totally part company with the fundamentalist pattern. . . . In the case of the prophetic criticism and occasional radicalism of the new evangelicals, it is often possible to see the mainline forces actually being eclipsed."[17]

How much has this new awakening touched the college campus? There is little question but that such magazines as *Radix, The Other Side,* and *Sojourners;* books by Ron Sider, John White, and Mark Hatfield; organizations such as Campus Crusade's Prison Ministry and World Vision International, which deals with hunger; leaders like Samuel Escobar and Tom Skinner; and even the increasing number of evangelical families who cook less lavishly—all have had an influence on students. The question is, how many?

Some Inter-Varsity staff members identify two groups within evangelicalism, one which accommodates itself to culture and one which criticizes culture. They observe that many evangelical students come to college with a comfortable mentality that has difficulty separating American cultural values from biblical faith. But an increasing number, a "vital critical group within," as Marty puts it,[18] are living out lives that reflect repentance instead of consumption. Furthermore, their models inspire others to consider local or even world problems. I have found that evangelical students from across the nation are articulating their concern about the nuclear threat, terrorism, famine, racism, sexism, and other urgent matters of the day—and they are putting their words into action.

Weekend Conferences and Urbana

Conferences and retreats have been greatly used by God's Spirit within evangelicalism. For example, one type of conference offers three levels of instruction on three different weekends: (1) the basis of what the gospel is and the spiritual disciplines of being a Christian; (2) the rudiments of Bible study; and (3) integration of one's faith with one's gifts or vocational interest. The participating students must do homework before coming; afterward, a staff member meets with them three times.

The largest conference of all is Inter-Varsity's triennial missionary convention held at the University of Illinois, Urbana. What is there about Urbana that deepens lives spiritually and redirects them? Students often say that they go to Urbana excited to hear "big gun" speakers. But when they return to their campuses, they find that it was the experience of being with thousands of others of like commitment that was most impressive. The "festival" dynamic at

Urbana is almost incomparable for most students. If it is exciting for students to experience *koinonia* at a statewide conference of, say, 150 students, imagine the impact of seventeen thousand. It is the closest thing to the Christian pilgrims in Jerusalem on Palm Sunday marching, singing, praising. The hymn singing at Urbana and the communion service on the closing evening are poignant and powerful. The speakers do influence the students, particularly as they insist that we American Christians abandon our success-oriented, materialistic mentality for real discipleship and consider the challenge to world mission.

CONCLUSION

Where does this leave us? What then are our hopes for the 1980s? Too often we haven't lived up to our heritage. So a starting point for the eighties would be simply to give the world what we have been given.

In a culture like ours, swayed so easily by the most recent fad or cause, where students often seem like burned-over ground because they have heard every trip, cause, cult, or trend imaginable, we need a fresh foundation. We need something true and trustworthy upon which to build our lives and the world.

Our fundamental point of trust is God. He says he is good, faithful, knowable—and we believe Him. We do not contend that we have God in our hip pocket, or that we have solved all transcendental mysteries. We have not searched out the unfathomable depths of His identity. Rather, He has given *us* identity and wholeness.

And what makes trusting and knowing God so exciting is that He is indeed the "living God." "Plato has told you a truth; but Plato is dead," writes G. K. Chesterton. "Shakespeare has startled you with an image, but Shakespeare will not startle you with one anymore. But imagine what it would be like to live with such men still living, to know that Plato might break out with an original lecture tomorrow, or that at any moment Shakespeare might shatter everything with a single song." The person who lives in contact with the Living God is a person "always expecting to meet Plato or Shakespeare tomorrow at breakfast."[19]

Our second point of trust is the Scriptures. Because we believe in their essential truth, we need to study them carefully. Nothing is so dangerous as misguided zeal over a misunderstood verse. The numerous cults—and their tragic adherents—illustrate the horrors that happen when leaders, even religious ones, depart from the authoritative patterns of the Bible.

Our third point of trust is our relationship to others. We need confidence in ourselves as well as the foundation of truth so that we can reveal who we are to others and relate to them authentically. We need the model of Jesus to show us how to be examples to our family, our neighbors, our colleagues. We need God's Spirit to give us perception and sensitivity to them.

In order to give this kind of care and love we ourselves need to be touched by God's love. Then, we can offer three things:

1. *A radical identification with the world.* By this I mean walking empathetically alongside fellow human beings. When we see the degree of brokenness in so many relationships, the need for profound identification becomes clear. Furthermore, in light of the divorce statistics, and the as yet unseen emotional scars of children with single or overworked parents, students may increasingly need parental models, as Willimon[20] has suggested.

We must remember what C. S. Lewis wrote:

There are no *ordinary* people. You have never talked to a mere mortal. . . . But it is immortals whom we joke with, work with, marry, snub, and exploit—immortal horrors or everlasting splendours. . . . Next to the Blessed Sacrament itself, your neighbor is the holiest object presented to your senses.[21]

2. *A radical difference from the world.* Jesus tells his disciples in Matthew 6:8, "Do not be like them." Some evangelicals are so heady with their attempts not to be legalistic that they ignore the call to be different. But Jesus makes it clear in the Sermon on the Mount that we are to be different, and he spells out how: by our character (we thirst for righteousness and are peacemakers); by our influence (we are light and salt in our communities); by our relationships; by our worship, and our purpose and goals. As Bloesch put it, "When the church becomes acculturized and secularized, it can no longer penetrate the world as a leaven; instead it contributes to the vacuity and dissolution of the surrounding culture."[22]

3. *A model of sacrifice.* We live in a culture where our dogs may eat better than people in other parts of the world, and where the evident goal of our culture (and, sadly, of many believers) is to attain the comfortable life, self-fulfillment, and "my rights." Christianity often sounds like a quick means to maturity and enrichment, to health and prosperity.

The greatness of Jesus is not only in the heights to which he was elevated, but also in the depths to which he came down as he established solidarity with the oppressed. "Moreover, the goal of the Christian life is seen not as personal integration or wholeness nor as the realization of human potential but rather as the sacrifice of the self to the cause of the kingdom and the glory of God."[23]

If we live repentant life styles, the world will listen when we speak. For our repentance (evidenced by our servanthood in relationships and our belief in Jesus Christ) reflects neither a lack of self-esteem nor a negation of life. It yields, rather, service and gratitude. *Gratitude,* because even with our sin we have been declared acceptable by God—and, consequently, our lives reveal standards not of the world, but of the will of the living God, the ground and goal of all human existence. *Service,* because the real test of our belief is whether we love others as He loved us.

And lastly, what will appeal to the eighties is what has forever arrested people through the ages—joy. "Joy which was the small publicity of the pagan is the gigantic secret of the Christian."[24]

NOTES

* The following works can fill in some of the historical background of the primary campus ministries discussed in this chapter:

    a. On English roots of Inter-Varsity Christian Fellowship: Oliver R. Barclay, *Whatever Happened to the Jesus Lane Lot?* (Leicester, Eng.: Inter-Varsity Press, 1977).

    b. Campus Crusade for Christ: Richard Quebedeaux, *I Found It!* (New York: Harper and Row, 1979).

    c. History of Navigators: Betty Lee Skinner, *Daws* (Grand Rapids, Mich.: Zondervan, 1974).

    d. On IVCF in North America: Stacey Woods, *The Growth of a Work of God* (Downers Grove, Ill.: Inter-Varsity Press, 1978).

1 Robert Webber, *Common Roots* (Grand Rapids, Mich.: Zondervan, 1978), p. 222.

2. Ibid., p. 232.

3. Navigator Bible studies and philosophy of movement: *Design for Discipleship* (Colorado Springs, Colo.: Navigator Press, 1973), a series of six books; *Studies for Christian Living* (Colorado Springs, Colo.: Navigator Press), a series of nine books; *The Life and Ministry of Jesus Christ* (Colorado Springs, Colo.: Navigator Press, 1977); and *The Lost Art of Discipleship*

Making (Colorado Springs, Colo.: Navigator Press and Grand Rapids, Mich.: Zondervan, 1978).

4. Inter-Varsity Press Bible Studies: *Discovering the Gospel of Mark; Discussions on the Life of Jesus Christ; Jesus the Life Changer; Fruit of the Spirit; Patterns for Living with God; Lifestyle of Love; Caring in Crisis;* and many others guides for Bible study, (Downers Grove, Ill.: Inter-Varsity Press).

5. Campus Crusade for Christ Bible studies: William Bright, "10 Basic Steps" and "5 Steps to Christian Growth" (Arrowhead Springs, Cal.: Campus Crusade for Christ).

6. Stan Slade, "The Manuscript Method of Inductive Bible Study: Essay in Hermeneutics," a paper presented at Fuller Theological Seminary, Pasadena, California.

7. John R. W. Stott, *Christian Mission in the Modern World* (Downers Grove, Ill.: Inter-Varsity Press, 1975).

8. William Bright, "4 Spiritual Laws" (Arrowhead Springs, Cal.: Campus Crusade for Christ).

9. Alfred Krass, "What the Mainline Denominations are Doing in Evangelism," in *Christian Century,* May 2, 1979, pp. 490-493.

10. Jim Wallis, *Sojourners,* May, 1978, p. 14.

11. Josh McDowell, *Evidence that Demands a Verdict* (Arrowhead Springs, Cal.: Campus Crusade for Christ, 1972).

12. Os Guiness, *The Dust of Death* (Downers Grove, Ill.: Inter-Varsity Press, 1973).

13. John R. W. Stott, *Basic Christianity* (Downers Grove, Ill., Inter-Varsity Press, 1971).

14. Francis Schaeffer, *The God Who Is There* and *Escape From Reason* (Downers Grove, Ill.: Inter-Varsity Press, 1968).

15. Robert Webber, *Common Roots,* p. 220.

16. Martin Marty, "Tensions Within Contemporary Evangelicalism," in *The Evangelicals,* ed. David F. Wells and John D. Woodbridge (Grand Rapid, Mich.: Baker Book House, 1975), p. 201.

17. Millard Erickson, quoted, by Martin Marty, "Tensions. . . ," p . 201.

18. Martin Marty, "Tensions. . . ," p. 202.

19. Ibid., p. 198.

20. G. K. Chesterton, *Orthodoxy* (Garden City, N.Y.: Doubleday Image Books, 1959), pp. 154-155.

21. William H. Willimon, "Remember Mama: Thoughts on Motherhood and Ministry," in *Christian Century,* May 9, 1979, p. 521.

22. C. S. Lewis, *The Weight of Glory* (Grand Rapids, Mich.: Eerdmans, 1949), pp. 14-15.

23. Donald G. Bloesch, *The Evangelical Renaissance* (Grand Rapids, Mich.: Eerdmans, 1973), p. 18.

24. Donald G. Bloesch, *Essentials of Evangelical Theology,* Vol. 2 (New York: Harper and Row, 1979), p. 59.

25. G. K. Chesterton, *Orthodoxy,* p. 160.

THE DISCOVERY AND NURTURE OF THE SPIRIT IN THE MAINLINE TRADITIONS OF THE CHURCH

Edwin E. Beers

There are some people who hope to grasp the spirit of the sonata by dismantling the piano.

—SIMONE WEIL

Prayer to God is the chief part, yea the main thing in religion. For the design of the whole truth respecting salvation, is to teach us that our life depends on God and that whatever belongs to eternal life must be hoped for and expected from him.

—JOHN CALVIN

"We can't deal with the radicalness of the gospel without the discipline of prayer, otherwise we are forced to trivialize it."
"But that prayer has to be communal."
"That means it has to occur in one's own community, where you work or live. You can't go running off all the time to other communities and escape the reality of your own."

—FROM A CONVERSATION WITH A FRIEND

Indeed! If God is really in this room, as we know God is, we can't be in too much trouble now, can we?

—THOMAS MERTON

To his shipboard companion, J. D. Salinger's Teddy remarks, "It's very hard to meditate and live a spiritual life in America. People think you're a freak if you do."[1] In the 1950s, when the story first appeared, Teddy's observation had the ring of truth. Ironically, this was also a period of record membership and attendance in the churches of the Protestant mainline tradition.

In our own time, which appears to be one of declining interest in the church as institution, someone who wants to meditate, who is on a spiritual quest, has some credibility. For years the word *spiritual* had little standing in religious circles, but it has recently reentered the realm of ordinary discourse, not only in the churches of the mainstream where the phrase "spiritual development" now describes a legitimate educational task,[2] but the word *spiritual* is also being used to describe a therapeutic focus in groups with a secular orientation as well.

Why is it that the word *spiritual* and the phenomenon the word describes have been restored to the cultural scene so abruptly as a cursory glance at the index of some mainline journals will indicate?[3]

I suggest that the increasing quest for *spirit* or for *spirituality* in the latter part of our decade represents a response to a malaise that is so much a part of our cultural fabric that it needs little description. The spiritual quest is also a response to the state of the churches, which are viewed by many, especially the young, as preoccupied with organizational technique and so focused on managerial notions of institutional health as to be only remotely sensitive to the Spirit as source and spring of the church's life.

A description of the relationship between spiritual quest and cultural malaise comes from a comment by a mainline minister (UCC) whose travels take him among young people of three continents. When asked by a reporter why there was such a fascination with prayer and with spirituality among young people, he replied, "There was a time when we had to tell young people that prayer was important; now perhaps we have to tell them that the intellectual dimensions of faith are important too. To be interested in prayer seems to be part of our time. There seems to be no solution, no way of affecting those who control our lives, so you use whatever lever you have. The popularity of mystical groups, the charismatic movement, are all reactions against despair."[4]

Similarly, criticism has been leveled against Protestant churches, that they are too imitative of corporation style. "We have taken on the corporate image, become business-like, industrious, and bureaucratic, but alienating many people in doing so."[5] It is as if peoples' intuition has been grasped by Paul Tillich's observation that "*the spiritual community* is the inner telos of the churches and as such is the source of everything that makes them churches." But the search for spiritual community in the churches most often reveals pseudo-community where people continue to relate to each other on the basis of function and prestige just as they relate to one another in organizations.

In spiritual community people are not judged by their functional capacity. Such community was disclosed in recent interviews with students related to Lutheran Campus Ministry (LCA-ALC), who gave the following response: "In the university our concerns are grades, jobs, pressure. Campus Ministry is a place where we are evaluated differently, not for our productivity as we are in school, but here we can be who we are. Here we have space." "These students," said one minister, "really respond to readings from Henri Nouwen and from Thomas Merton."[6]

A theologian has observed, "As the religions increasingly lose their cultural power and importance, believers will increasingly only be and remain such because they have *had* religious experiences."[7] Whether the quest for that experience is designated as search for Spirit or search for prayer, whether the disenchantment that motivates the quest rises from the social malaise or from the absence of humane community and the bureaucratic tendencies of the church, there has been a notable absence of those affirmative qualities, catalogued as the "fruit of the Spirit" (Gal. 5:22–23), in the lives of many people who regard themselves as part of the Church. But there is a hopeful turning, and whether that turn (*metanoia*) that is occurring in our time is *Eastward*[8] or *Inward*,[9] clearly there is a turn to rediscover the vitalities, impulses, and the animating powers which are understood to belong to the nature of Spirit which is disclosed in the biblical tradition itself.

BRIEF HISTORY: THE SPIRIT AS MOVEMENT AND MISSION

Spirituality might be described as a conscious awareness of the presence of God in human affairs. It is a way of picturing that participation and discerning that presence.

To live spiritually is to believe that life is animated and authorized by the Spirit of God (*ruach*). To live spiritually in the Christian community is to be aware of the Holy Spirit as the empowering force gathering, edifying, sending forth the community, and enabling the gospel to be lived faithfully.

Spirituality provides hope, vitality, and a compelling vision of the kingdom. Such vitality and hope were present in the spiritual awakenings in North America in the eighteenth and nineteenth centuries. Inspired by the preaching of Jonathan Edwards (1703-58) and George Whitefield (1714-70), Americans in the eighteenth century hoped that the presence of the kingdom on the colonial shores would then become the source of inspiration for other nations.

The awakenings of the nineteenth century contributed to the expansion of the churches and to the abolition movement. Historians estimate that prior to this second spiritual awakening only ten percent of the American population was part of the Christian church.

The same spiritual impulse inspired voluntary Christian groups of students on the campuses of the newly founded universities, which had themselves been founded by "pious and learned gentlemen." These groups often represented a small remnant of the entire student body. For example, at Williams College in the late 1790s only five of ninety-three students professed their faith publicly, and at Dartmouth in the class of 1799 there was only one professing student.[10]

In the following decade, however, a worldwide mission movement began at Williams College, followed later by the founding of the YM-YWCA and the Student Volunteer Movement. Later in the century, John R. Mott (1865-1955), a Methodist layman who had studied law at Cornell, directed the Student Volunteer Movement for more than thirty years. It is estimated that, between its founding in 1888 and 1945, more than twenty thousand students served overseas through the SVM.

It was during the first decade of the twentieth century that student foundations began to appear on the campuses of land-grant universities, a phenomenon that gave rise to denominational boards of Christian Higher Education. What marked the campus religious movement was the impulse toward unity and mission. In 1895 the World Student Christian Federation (WSCF), uniting Northern European and North American student movements, was founded in Sweden. The stated purpose of the movement was

to lead students to become disciples of Jesus Christ as only Saviour and as God; *to deepen the spiritual life of the students;* to enlist students in the work of extending the kingdom of Christ throughout the world; to collect information regarding the religious condition of students in all lands.[11]

In the WSCF constitution there is a clear commitment to mission, unity, and witness in the academic community, and to peace and justice and to growth in the Christian life. While the national student movements acknowledged their autonomy, they worked interdependently and were involved in relief programs after World War I and in rehabilitation following World War II.

In North America in 1944, a Christian Council emerged which, combined with other movements, became the National Student Christian Federation (NSCF), combining the strengths and purposes of many previous groups.

It is especially interesting to note that some of the major figures in the leadership of the World Council of Churches (WCC)* have also been leaders in the WSCF: such figures as D. T. Niles; Phillipe Maury, the first secretary general; Willem Visser 't Hooft; and the present secretary general of WCC, Philip Potter.

The movement throughout northern Europe and North America was characterized by a strong network. In North America it took the form of quadrennial conferences, especially in the 1940s and the 1950s. It was in the 1960s that the climate of the movement began to shift, gradually focusing on political issues, and less and less attentive to the Bible study and worship that previously had been part of the movement's tradition.

In 1965, the ministries of the mainline denominations gathered in Minneapolis, where Harvey Cox's *Secular City* was the textbook and the central focus was on urban plight, civil rights, and the escalation of the Southeast Asian war. In 1967, the University Christian Movement, an attempt to bring together mainline denominations and Catholic ministries in higher education, held a conference in Cleveland. The meeting was organized entirely around sociopolitical discussions and was based on ideological concerns, informed by the "desacralized" theology of the time. The movement voted itself out of existence, bringing to an end, for a time at least, any vital campus Christian networks as they related to the mainline traditions.

The spiritual impulses that had previously marked the presence of the liberal Protestant traditions of the church in higher education seemed to have reached a plateau. The Lutheran Campus Ministries retained a student movement. But, by and large, the mainline ministries, while engaging in some important work on social issues and values in the life of the university, seemed to have lost, with some exceptions, the animating force of the Spirit. Perhaps a comment by a campus minister points to the difficulty. She remarked, "It seems that the center of the Christian movement on the campus has shifted from the Spirit and has been replaced by Marxist rhetoric. Of course the Marxists are right. Structures need to be changed. No argument about that. But where's the community of comfort and joy? So often structures for ministry get too analytical, representing a loss of hope. They're too tied to the present powers. All the juice and joy is gone as people try to live their ministry in a negative intensity. You know, you still need to attend to the pastoral and the personal. This, in part, is what the charismatic movement keeps telling us."

A clue to the loss of Spirit may be found in words of Søren Kierkegaard, who lamented the loss of Spirit in his culture in the last century: "There is no lack of information in a Christian land. Something else is lacking, and that is something that one man cannot communicate directly to the other." For him the power of the gospel had deteriorated and Christian truth had become a series of generalizations, a reminder that the celebration of thinking alone can become another way of avoiding life.[12]

I would say that hope for renewal of the Christian movement in the university setting lies not in social analysis, as important as that process is for the understanding of contemporary life. But a Christian movement will become vital only if social concerns also restore attention to serious biblical study, prayer, celebration, and worship. I think the popularity of the youth movement emanating from the European-based community of Taizé can teach us. I have been astounded at the way in which students, lukewarm in response to some of the worship of local churches, will make any sacrifice to travel a great distance to a community such as Taizé in order to participate in the prayer, the liturgy, and the silence.

In calling for worship to return to the heart of the renewal of ministry, Jim Wallis reminds us that "there is sometimes among us what the Bible would call 'works righteousness' justifying ourselves on what we do and what we accomplish. But we have found the greatest strength when we have been in community where forgive-

ness, joy, and hope are daily marks of our lives. In celebration we
are strengthened . . . because we have first learned to say yes, we
are able to say no."[13]

Urban Holmes has written that a major agenda for contemporary
ministry is to enable people to rediscover their capacity for intuition
and wonder. "The fact that religious experience is considered so rare
among us does not mean that God is no longer present but that in
our western culture we have made so little of imagination, intuition
and wonder to discern within our culture the presence of God."[14]

The critical question regarding the loss of Spirit has been gathered into poetic words by Roger Schutz, prior of the Ecumenical
Community of Taizé.[15]

If festivity were to vanish from people's lives. . .

If we were to wake up, one fine morning, in a society well organized,
functional, and contented but devoid of all spontaneity. . .

If Christian prayer became an intellectual exercise, so secularized that
it lost all sense of mystery and poetry, leaving no room for the prayer of
gesture and posture, for intuition or emotion. . .

If the overburdened consciences of Christians made them decline the
happiness offered by Him who seven times over declared "Happy" on the
Mount of the Beatitudes. . .

If those living in the Northern hemisphere, worn out by activities, were
to lose the source of the spirit of festival, a festival still so alive in the
hearts of the people of the Southern continents. . .

If festival disappeared from the Body of Christ, the Church, in all the
world where could we find a place of communion for the whole of
mankind?

RESURGENCE OF SPIRIT: SOME HOPEFUL SIGNS

It was John XXIII who, in opening the Second Vatican Council,
prayed, "O Holy Spirit renew your wonders in our day as by a new
Pentecost." His successor, Paul VI, guiding the church through its
reforms, observed that the first need of the church is always "to live
Pentecost." The awakening of the Spirit that occurred through the
Second Vatican Council continues to effect in a profound way the
mainline Protestant traditions.

A campus minister, a leader in the United Methodist tradition
with a good sense of the winds and whims of ministry, observes that
renewal of worship and prayer in the liberal ministries seems to

occur where those traditions are not isolated from the liturgical churches. Where they remain in close touch with Lutheran, Catholic, and Episcopal campus ministries which have always insisted on a pastoral and sacramental center, a new vitality is likely to occur.

As early as 1943, a papal document (*Divino Afflante Spiritu*) enabled the convergence of biblical scholarship between Catholics and Protestants; and since the beginning of the century there has been a movement toward the renewal of liturgical life on an ecumenical basis. A survey of recent volumes of *Worship*[16] discloses the vitality of that renewal, though James White, United Methodist liturgical scholar, acknowledges that ignorance and indifference continue to hinder its progress. There has been a sufficient resurgence of interest, however, to produce revisions of hymnals and prayer books. For example, the new Lutheran Book of Worship includes daily offices of prayer with musical accompaniment; and The Hymnal of the United Church of Christ, recently published, has a much clearer focus on structured liturgy and the centrality of the sacraments. Enhanced by the work of the Consultation on Church Union (COCU), the renewal is helping to restore mainline people to their own history. At one time this included the discipline of daily prayer and before the nineteenth century included communion at every service on the Lord's day. It was not until the last half of the nineteenth century that infrequent communion became normative.[17]

As early as 1970, a consensus was reached by various confessions within the Protestant tradition, along with Roman Catholic and Russian Orthodox, regarding *communion.* Movements such as these explicit gestures toward the recovery of Christian unity deserve more attention in the mainline churches and are especially important in the academic community where the scandal of division is heightened and often places unnecessary barriers in the way of those who might otherwise be attracted to the community of faith.

Keith Watkins (Disciples of Christ) has described the irony of the fact that this gift of new life in the mainline churches is coming not from the Protestant establishment, but primarily from Catholic liturgical structures. He recalls Langdon Gilkey's observation[18] that Protestantism has become so identified with the culture of the West that its genuine religious ethos has been surrendered. He argues that the previous isolation of Catholics from the modern world has preserved the genuine gospel which can now be available to those who

have lost it. Gilkey claims that even though conservative Protestantism has kept the word, moderate and liberal Protestants who
have abandoned conservative Christianity and are not likely to return seem ready to look toward that older and more dominant
course—the Roman Catholic church, its liturgy and lectionary.[19] In
our own city, for example, there are already three groups of mainline
ministers and laity who meet regularly to study the lectionary texts.

Another example of the resurgence of spirituality is occurring in a
renewed interest in *Bible study.* On some campuses there is a new interest in the "Depth Bible Study" method developed by Professors
Sharon Ringe (UCC) and Walter Wink (UMC). While the method
takes critical scholarship seriously, it also helps students to become
aware of archetypal imagery and feelings lurking in the human
depths. The method links artistic expression, dance, music, and
sculpture as means for encountering the biblical message. Like liturgical renewal, this method of Bible study can reawaken the
power of imagery and symbols, so long neglected in much of Protestant worship. The method is also a reminder that the life of the
Spirit is an integrated life that embraces the affective and volitional,
as well as the rational, dimensions of life.

Another hopeful manifestation of Spirit that has influenced the
mainline resurgence has been the *Charismatic movement.* The initial
resistance that met the charismatic impulse seems to have softened,
and now mainline denominations have published study papers
which interpret the meaning of the movement and try to describe its
value to the entire church. While there seems to be increasing openness to people who refer to themselves as charismatic, others feel
threatened and confined by those who use that label.

An important contribution of the charismatic movement may be
in nudging those who do not share the explicit experience to begin
to ask themselves, what does my own faith mean when I'm up
against people whose attitudes and whose bases for interpreting life
are so different from my own?

As it affects the mainline churches and ministries, the charismatic
movement is both threat and promise. The threat is that the movement, already influenced by a cultural trend toward introspection,
can simply reenforce that luxury, simply offer an emotional release,
and turn in on itself, without impact on the social order.

The promise of the movement lies in the fact that it takes account

of the whole of a person's life, breathes new vitality to conquer the
sterility that has characterized so much of Western religion.

The experience of one campus couple is illuminating. Presently
members of the United Church of Christ, they recount their own
pilgrimage:

> We had been a part of the civil rights movement and the antiwar move-
> ment, but in the face of all this we concluded that our activism was
> empty. All my life I've learned the facts about the Christian faith, but I
> had no experience. All our actions didn't produce it.
>
> A few years ago we observed some people who seemed to be able to
> bring into balance the rational and the experiential. About that time we
> started a study group on the Holy Spirit, and we were drawn into a whole
> new world of wonder and excitement.
>
> The campus provided an ecumenical group for exploring this new
> world.
>
> Perhaps, we thought, the Holy Spirit *is* for people seeking balance in
> their lives. We discovered that there are people in the liberal Protestant
> tradition who live by trusting in prayer. We also noticed that in a strange
> way the Scriptures started coming to life, and to our astonishment the Eu-
> charist began to disclose a healing power we didn't previously under-
> stand. In short, our pilgrimage has a vivid experiential quality we hadn't
> known before.[20]

In 1847 the following entry appeared in Søren Kierkegaard's
Journal:

> There is no doubt that the present, and Protestantism always, needs
> the monastery again. . . . The monastery is an essential dialectic fact in
> Christianity and we need it there like a light house in order to gauge
> where we are even though I myself would not exactly go into one. But if
> there is to be true Christianity in every generation there must be individu-
> als with that need.[21]

I take it that Kierkegaard was calling for that critical perspective
which might summon Christians to listen intently (the root meaning
of obedience) in order to hear the gospel again. It was also a summons to acknowledge the indigence of the human spirit in the face
of a false triumphalism to which the faith had fallen victim. For
him, the monastery stood as a warning against the perpetual shal-
lowing of life. It beckoned humanity to reawaken to contemplative
wonder in order to see the world as it is, to be able to love it and to
trust the future, not to human control and manipulation, but to
God's faithfulness.

The reawakening of interest in monastic and communal disciplines is suggested by the success of courses offered at the College of Wooster[22] and at Oberlin[23] and by the increasing attention Protestants have paid to the writings of Thomas Merton and Henri Nouwen.

Merton's contribution to the current search for spirituality lies in part in the candor with which he shared every step of his pilgrimage and his willingness to disclose his own spiritual struggles. Merton also exposed the sheer violence that the human spirit suffers in Western culture ". . . surrendering to too many demands, committing ourselves to too many projects, wanting to help everyone in everything."[24] For Merton, this means to succumb to a violence that is destructive to spirit and that kills the root of our inner wisdom. He spoke of the imperative to protect the spirit from the ambushes of busyness and schedules. "Inside yourselves you shouldn't be running all the time."

He also lifted up the importance of spiritual guides, exposing a void in the development of Protestant spirituality, where attention to any kind of interior formation has been relegated largely to the realm of psychology.

Examples of serious search that integrates yearning for spiritual depth and commitment to peace and justice are occurring on the margins of the university, where an increasing number of committed people are forming *intentional communities.* The following comments by members of a community indicate that they are attentive to the wisdom offered by the example of Christian monasticism; and while they do not structure their lives according to the traditional models, they can share with monastic communities the longing for spirituality ". . . which can help us live our own vocations with greater interior peace, joy, and strength."[25] Formed and led largely by people from mainline traditions, residents of this community see themselves trying to reverse the assumptions for living in American culture.

We're trying to learn to place our sense of security, not in prestige or power, or material, or intellectual, or even spiritual wealth. We try to trust more and more in what Paul calls the "folly and weakness of Christ."

We try to support each other in decisions, whether they have to do with larger matters, such as our vocational choices or daily concerns, whether we are talking about what we eat, where we will set the thermostat, etc. We try to make these decisions in the light of the beatitudes and the gospel.

We're not trying to be anything special. We misunderstand each other and we're sometimes unfaithful to our vision; but we try not to let our unfaithfulness invalidate our vision, but to be aware of our unfaithfulness. We've been living in the tension between the vision the gospel gives and the reality we're aware of and see around us. Through prayer we keep returning to the struggle.

Are we a community of resistance? I think we are more a community of affirmation. Being a community of affirmation will probably lead us to resist certain things in the culture, for example, the whole phenomenon of mass culture. But in community we don't feel bound to live up to cultural expectations. We can resist material and intellectual accumulations by which most of us tend to insulate ourselves. If we are faithful, our resistance will lead us to resist patterns of destruction. If we should define ourselves by resisting evil, soon evil defines who we are and controls us. For us it's important that our identity comes from affirming life and the gospel.[26]

In spirit this community is closely linked to communities growing out of the European Protestant tradition such as Taizé and the Sisters of Grandchamp. The residents also feel a strong connection with Sojourners Fellowship and the communities of L'Arche founded by Jean Vanier.

Another hopeful phenomenon of renewal is the very serious and personal *search for spiritual depth* that continues among individuals. An observer whose listening posts are primarily in Europe and Asia tells of the number of students and other young people who ask fundamental and personal questions about prayer and do not care if the answers come from Protestants or Catholics. They often have little interest in any church but are interested in meeting spiritual men and women, no matter what church or even what religion they belong to.

A journalism student, who has made several trips to explore spiritually oriented communities, wrote following her visit to Findhorn in Scotland:

Personally, I still feel displaced in the church as it is right now. The evangelicals I've met seem to have a lot of passion for Christ, but their doctrines are too rigid for me. And the more modern Christians seem to have intellectualized the faith until it is secular, dry, and cold. Yet the more exposure I have to Eastern and to New Age Spirituality, the more confirmed I feel in Christianity. I feel we live in a very crucial age and that a tremendous spiritual change is going on. But I feel that in abandoning Christianity as so many members of my generation have, we lose our roots and have no context in which to understand these changes. My hope is that as a more spiritual way of life matures, there will be a revitalization of Christianity.

Perhaps the Spirit is descending upon mainline Protestantism, not in its fullness, nor at the center, but lingering, waiting to be discovered along the margins. It is as if the mainline church is in a provisional time, in which as 1 John admonishes, the Spirits are being "tested to see if they are of God."

On Pentecost Sunday a few years ago, I worshiped at the American Cathedral in Paris. What might have been a rich moment of worship struck me as insipid and bland. The hymns and readings, the prayers, authentic as they were, fell awkward and heavy upon my ears. No words to enliven the heart, they remained impotent and even drab. The contradictory experience was sharpened by the extreme formality and by the continuing reminder that worshipers were largely Americans even though Pentecost is one of the most world-unifying, horizon-expanding, international moments of the entire church year.

Immediately following that experience, which seemed devoid of any sense of celebration or of the presence of the Spirit, I left by train for the Burgundy region for a visit to Taizé and arrived in time to join in the office of evening prayer.

What struck me with great force was the climate, the mood of worship. Though the worshipers numbered in the thousands, everything was preceded by intense silence. There the Word was read, not from a distant lectern, but in the very center of the gathered people. The international, world-unifying nature of the liturgy was apparent. Readings and prayers were offered in at least four languages. Despite language barriers, there was spontaneous participation in the response and the alleluias, though about fifteen different countries were represented.

At Taizé people gathered in every sort of costume—shorts, dhotis, sandals, and barefoot. Kneeling or seated on the floor, the whole body found space to pray. In this motley gathering in silence and simplicity, one could sense the interior movement of the Spirit, an empowerment, a vitality, everything that the Pentecost text which had been read in the Paris cathedral had been admonishing me to understand.

What was it about Taizé that had made the Spirit's presence such a reality? For one thing, a community such as Taizé takes seriously the organic nature of the church. It is not an organization. The concern of the brothers is that spiritual community takes time and steady focus. They remain centered in their concern for persons. The worship is personal, intimate, and directly related to the realities of the community and its visitors. As the prior says, "We have no method, no system. We have one passion: helping young people discover how to live creatively with the gifts they possess."[27]

Secondly, the vitality of the Spirit in a community such as Taizé lies in its continuing solidarity with the poor, with the people of the Third World. People from the Third World are a continuing presence at Taizé; and fraternities of brothers live among the poor in Asia, Africa, Latin America, and New York City.

Taizé, then, is an example of a servant community, vulnerable to and wholly dependent upon the action of the Spirit—and never for a moment able to separate liturgy and prayer from its understanding of mission.

Finally, Taizé, with other communities like it, seems not to be obsessed with judging outcomes or results of its ministry. The community knows the reality of failure, but does not despair. Its understanding of mission coincides with the counsel Thomas Merton gave to James Forest, of the International Fellowship of Reconciliation:

> Don't depend on the hope of results . . . you may have to face the fact that your work will be apparently worthless and even achieve no result at all, if not results opposite to what you expect . . . . In the end it is the reality of personal relationships that saves everything.
>
> The real hope then is not in something we think we can do but in God who is making something good out of it in some way we cannot see . . .[28]

Such a model for hope, naive as it may appear to some, is certainly not the only way for ministry to become open to fresh vitalities of the Spirit. But for many it can become the beginning of renewal, the triumph of hope, and the victory of grace.

NOTES

* Abbreviations used in this chapter: UCC = United Church of Christ; UMC = United Methodist Church; LCA = Lutheran Church in America; ALC = American Lutheran Church.

1. J. D. Salinger, "Teddy," in *Nine Stories* (New York: New American Library, 1954), p. 138.

2. For an example of increasing interest in "spiritual development" in the mainline churches, see *Spiritual Development and Christian Community: Report of a Seminar* (New York: Office for Church Life and Leadership, United Church of Christ, 1978).

3. "Index: Volume XCV, July-December," *The Christian Century* 43 (1978): 1275. Compare with previous issues.

4. William R. Wineke, "Concern of Today's Youth About Prayer Is A Reaction Against Despair, Monk Says," in *Wisconsin State Journal,* January 18, 1975, sec. 3, p. 1, cols. 3–6.

5. Arthur Moore, "Church Image Worries Pastor," in *Milwaukee Journal,* December 16, 1978, p. 4, cols. 1–4.

6. Reported by the Reverend Alan Heggen of Lutheran Campus Ministry, Madison, Wisconsin.

7. William M. Thompson, "A Spiritual Journey Within the Psychoanalytic Tradition," in *The Ecumenist* 4 (1977): p. 49.

8. Harvey Cox, *Turning East* (New York: Simon & Schuster Touchstone, 1977).

9. Jacob Needleman, *The New Religions* (New York: E. P. Dutton, 1977).

10. Robert H. Eads, "A Brief History of Student Christian Movements," in *The Campus Ministry,* ed. George L. Earnshaw (Valley Forge, Penn.: Judson Press, 1964), p. 66.

11. Ibid., p. 74.

12. Fred B. Craddock, *Overhearing the Gospel* (Nashville: Abingdon, 1978), discusses at length both the indirectness and the concreteness of the gospel's address.

13. Jim Wallis, "Christians' Strongest Weapon Against Spiritual Evil," in *Sojourners,* August 1978, p. 19.

14. Urban T. Holmes, *Ministry and Imagination* (New York: Seabury, 1966), p. 88.

15. Rex Brico, *Taizé, Brother Roger and His Community* (New York: Collins, 1978), p. 153.

16. *Worship,* "A Review Concerned with Liturgical Renewal," published bimonthly by the Monks of St. John's Abbey, Collegeville, Minn.

17. Doug Adams, "Free Church Worship and Sunday Work," in *New Conversations,* 3 (1978/79): p. 14.

18. Keith Watkins, "Protestants Rediscover the Word?" *Worship* 53 (March 1979): p. 125.

19. Ibid., p. 125.

20. An experience related by Mr. Howard Kanetzke, who with his wife, Lucetta, is a member of the Community of Hope (U.C.C.).
21. Søren Kierkegaard, *The Journals of Kierkegaard* (New York: Harper Torchbook, 1958), p. 130.
22. Richard H. Bell, "Poetry and the Spirit in Community: An Experience," in *Religion in Life* 62 (1973): pp. 478–495. A presentation of student experience in Christian Communities drawn largely from the journals of the participants who with Dr. Bell and his family visited monastic communities in France and Great Britain in the summer of 1972.
23. George F. Simons, "A Monastic Experiment by College Students," in *Monastic Studies* 11 (1975): pp. 205–213. A month-long monastic experience for students as part of Oberlin College's 1972 winter term. Interpretation of the experience has been expanded into book form.
24. Thomas Merton, *Conjectures of a Guilty Bystander* (Garden City, N.Y.: Doubleday, 1965), p. 73.
25. From a discussion with residents of *La Samaritaine,* a contemplative community sponsored by First Congregational Church (United Church of Christ) who are attempting a life of prayer, simplicity, justice, and peace. Location is the University of Wisconsin campus, Madison.
26. Ibid.
27. Brico, *Taizé*.
28. James Forest, "Thomas Merton: Prophet in the Belly of a Paradox," in *Sojourners,* December 1978, p. 18.

III

Contemplation and Action in Higher Education

CONTEMPLATION AND ACTION IN HIGHER EDUCATION
An Interpretation

Parker J. Palmer

At the heart of the word *contemplation* stands the root of the word *temple*. In Latin, temple or *templum* means "an open place for observation marked out by the augur with his staff." The augur, I understand, was a Roman religious official whose duty was to discern the meaning of certain omens, and on this basis to predict future events and advise on the course of public business.

Allow me to play with these images for a moment and suggest that the campus minister is the unofficial augur of the university whose task, in part, is to mark out an "open place for observation" in the midst of academic life, a clearing in which members of the university can see past the thickets of disciplinary fragmentation, the biases of class and culture which hedge in the campus, into the needs of the world community, the yearnings of the human heart, the divine requirement for love and justice. (Indeed, since campus ministers often work in teams these days, it is literally true that this clearing is to be "marked out by the augur with his—or her—staff!")

The core meaning of contemplation is simply to see clearly. And when we see clearly, the apparent contradiction between contemplation and action is resolved. Contemplative insight reveals that all of life is organically related, notwithstanding our cultural assumptions of individualism and autonomy. Contemplative insight reveals that we "act" upon each other whether we want to or not simply by virtue of our organic state of being. So the problem of contemplation and action can be put in very simple terms: Ordinarily, we see what our culture allows us to see. To contemplate is to see what is really there. Ordinarily, we do what we want to do. To act contemplatively is to act in awareness of what reality requires.

Reality is not the easiest word with which to begin an essay! But reality is what all the religious traditions are about, and in this introduction to Part III and the chapters that follow, writers from several of those traditions respond to the question, "What is real?" Though these traditions differ in emphasis, they share these convictions: to contemplate is to see the reality of God's presence in the world. To act contemplatively is to act in response to that presence. Part of the ministry on campus is to call academic people to such a vision and such a way of life in which contemplation and action are one.

CONTEMPLATION IN THE ACADEMY

To call the university to contemplation is not (as some might think) to divert its mission, but to remind it of its own tradition. The precursor of the university was the monastery, and in its earliest years the university had a monastic vocation: to transmit knowledge of the sacredness of life, to channel the spiritual formation of individuals and whole cultures.

If contemplation involves seeing clearly, seeing beneath the surface and beyond the appearance of things into their inward realities, it can be argued that the university *has* stayed faithful to its tradition. Not only does the academy practice a kind of contemplation, but it is one of the last institutions in society where that practice is sustained and rewarded. Every discipline in the university's curriculum (at least in the liberal arts) has as its aim "to see beneath the surface." Physics reveals the invisible structure of the visible world; literary studies uncover the hidden patterns and powers of language; psychology deals with the underlying regularities of seemingly random behavior.

My own undergraduate work was in sociology, and I still recall the sense of X-ray vision which came as I developed and began to use "the sociological imagination."[1] That phrase belongs to C. Wright Mills, and by it he meant the ability to see the intersection of history and biography in the context of social structures. For me, it meant "seeing through" the taken-for-granted world of the white, suburban, upper middle class. It meant an awareness that behaviors, attitudes, and opinions I had assumed as normative were, in fact, reflections of certain economic interests. It meant coming to terms with the possibility that social class was a more powerful determinant of one's life commitments than religious belief; indeed, that religious belief itself was largely a function of social class. For me, the sociological imagination was an early and compelling experience with contemplation of the inward reality of things, and it bred in me a critical and sometimes creative tension with my taken-for-granted world.

In fact, many of the tensions between university and society can be traced to the academy's faithful practice of this sort of contemplation. Any social system functions more smoothly when its members take it at face value. So the social pressures against "seeing into things" are often considerable, and the punishment for those who see too well are sometimes severe. At its best the university has served as contemplative critic of the seamless assumptions of popular culture, continually unraveling the fabric of fallacies which society weaves to cloak itself against self-knowledge. Although the university, like any human institution, easily falls prey to its own self-serving assumptions, it has probably done so no more often (and perhaps less often) than the church.

In fact, there is a certain irony about the campus ministry calling the university back to contemplation, since the church may well have fallen farther from this part of its tradition than the academic community itself! The American religious vision has been blinded by popular culture often enough to humble us believers, and even the current tide of churchly interest in meditation often seems more escapist than radical. If contemplation meant *only* "seeing beneath the surface of things," then the university should be calling the church back to its contemplative tradition, not vice versa.

But seeing beneath the surface is not the whole of contemplation. It is merely a first step in freeing one's vision from the illusions of culture. The next step is to move beyond critical analysis into the vision of wholeness toward which authentic contemplation leads. The true contemplative goes beyond the dissection and debunking so characteristic of academic culture into a living relation with that power beyond brokenness which wants to reconcile and heal and bring things back together. And here, I believe, the religious community possesses an insight into contemplative practice which the university has largely lost.

The university practices a partial contemplation, "seeing through things" with all the skepticism and cynicism which the idiom suggests: "You could see right through him." Contemplation in the university tends to terminate in a kind of debunking which allows the enlightened academic to announce to a benighted world that things are not *really* what they seem. Academic contemplation tends to be reductionistic, bringing all experience to a level where it is "explained away," reducing things to a kind of nothingness (rather than cultivating the wonder and amazement which come from realizing that things come out of nothing). The contemplation practiced in the university tends to fragment and disperse our world instead of bringing it to wholeness, with each discipline performing surgery on a different part of the body until nothing but a mutilated corpse remains.

Such was my experience with "the sociological imagination." The thrill of seeing beneath the surface of my social world was the thrill of seeing forbidden things, and with it came a host of destructive feelings. I felt anger, for example, at those who had kept these truths from my view; and as I realized that they had never seen these truths to begin with, and thus could not have shown them to me, my anger gave way to feelings of superiority and disdain. Indeed, I became alienated from a whole community of people, white and middle class like me, but unlike me (I thought) trapped in a world of illusion. It became impossible for me to participate in my own community without a sharp edge of skepticism and cynicism undercutting everything I said and did. The contemplation taught in the university had deprived me of a world rather than opening up a new one.

It need not have been that way. There is much in our world that needs dismantling, but only as a first step toward building new structures of greater truth and beauty. It is important, for example, to see how thoroughly our class interests condition, and even determine, our religious beliefs. But having seen that, we should be in a position to believe more freely, to transcend the bonds of economic interest; this should be part of the "liberation" available through the "liberal" arts. Yet seldom does the academic community find the power and vision to move beyond demolition into new creation.

There is, I think, a fundamental difference of assumptions behind contemplation in the spiritual tradition and contemplation in the university. The intellectual eye looks around the world and sees smug, self-serving, largely bourgeois notions about the nature of things and looks for a scalpel to dissect them with. The spiritual eye looks upon that same world and sees, beneath those desperate and wishful notions, brokenness and fragmentation and alienation, and proceeds to seek a source of healing and wholeness.

Clearly, both assumptions are valid. Clearly, the scalpel must often be applied before healing can occur. But the two approaches must be placed in right order, and that requires some effort to discern the nature and needs of the patient. In an earlier era the American consensus was so strong that the university's capacity to "see through things" was needed to maintain openings in a closed system of thought. But today there are more openings than there is system. There is no common culture worthy of the name, and the greatest need is not for surgery, but for sewing up. The most creative thought in our time may begin in analysis but it will always drive toward synthesis, toward contributing to that common vision without which "the people perish." A great many illusions have been stripped away in our time and the inward disease lies exposed to view. The great task now is to contemplate still more deeply, to find our way into a wellspring of healing and health for the individual and the body politic.

What religious traditions know, and the university needs to learn, is that to contemplate ultimately is to learn to love. It is to see so deeply into another that one identifies with the other. It is to see beyond the facade of unity and beyond the inner brokenness into that loving source which sets all life in motion and yearns to restore us to our original wholeness.

I think again of "the sociological imagination." It is one thing (and an important thing) to see the "suburban captivity" of minds and hearts constrained without knowing it by economic interests and class structures. It is another thing (also important) to see that I myself am part of that scene, and that in hating it I hate myself. And it is yet another thing (most important of all) to see that there is a power of love which desires the liberation of all people from all such constraints; a power which can work through me for my own liberation and the liberation of others.

The fruit of true contemplation is not to set one above and against others by virtue of possessing secret knowledge. Instead, it is to give an inward understanding of the needs and hopes of a captive people, and of one's own captive heart, so that one becomes a loving servant to self, to community, to truth, to justice, to freedom—becomes, in a word, a servant of God.

THE UNITY OF CONTEMPLATION AND ACTION

If contemplation is problematic for the university, even more so "action." One of the most persistent myths of academic life reserves the university as a realm for thinking, not doing. The academic community understands itself to be involved in observing, analyzing, commenting, judging—but not acting on its findings. Academic freedom, as one wag put it, means the freedom to be academic. And this myth of the academy is supported by outsiders who are fond of scoffing at the "ivory tower," or of putting down professors who cannot know the world of action because they have "never met a payroll."

Of course, both the outside and the inside view distort the facts. Obviously the university "acts" in the sense of exerting a profound influence on the surrounding society. By its very presence as a gateway to employment, wealth, and status, it shapes the behavior of millions who wish to achieve the rewards it waves before them—and millions of others who either failed to do so or never had the chance. The intellectual life of the university is constantly flowing into action through the careers pursued by its graduates; through the impact of its research on business, industry, government; through its power as arbiter of ideas in our higher culture.

Often, when campus ministers think about the problem of action in academic life, the question becomes, "How can we make the university a staging ground for social action?" But that question is narrow and misleading, for the university is already a staging ground for action of all sorts. It is delusory to think that the problem has been solved once we have managed to bootleg some sort of "social action" program onto the university campus. The real question seems to me twofold: "How can we help the university overcome the illusion that it does not act?" and "How can we help the university become more reflective and directive of the influence which it exerts on the surrounding society?"

These questions presuppose a relation between contemplation and action, but as we begin to explore that relation we must recognize that the university's own analytic mindset, its dualistic way of subdividing reality, has forced us to frame the questions as if contemplation and action were separate entities, unrelated in nature, which we must somehow bring together. The problem is false. We should not be asking how to relate contemplation to action, but how to overcome the habit of seeing them as separate. And we can begin to do that by recognizing that our habitual dualism does not reflect the nature of things so much as it serves certain of our self-interests.

For example, when we separate contemplation from action we can justify our frequent (and typically American) instinct to act for action's sake. Many of us—formed as we are by a society which has sought salvation through doing—find it painfully difficult not to act when confronted with a problem. We are programmed to believe that every problem demands action, personal action, immediate action, any action—for the sake of our own catharsis if nothing else. Problems create a tension within us, and that tension is released through action whether or not the action is a suitable response to the problem.

The violence which is endemic in America is perhaps the best example of this syndrome. Violence never solves a problem, it merely compounds the old one or creates a new one; but violence does serve as a temporary release of emotions, not only for individuals who feel powerless but also for frustrated nations. Contemplation sees through such action; in contemplation we gain insight into the motives and outcomes of what we do; and through contemplation we come to love the other in a way that makes violence impossible. If we were better schooled in the unity of contemplation and action, we would be denied the catharsis of action as an end in itself, we would be given the deeper and truer catharsis of understanding, and we might be given the grace to live out the sometime truth in the ironic counsel, "Don't just do something—stand there!"

By the same token, if we understood the unity of contemplation and action, we would no longer have the luxury of a self-contained contemplation which fails to find appropriate outcomes in action. Contemplation has a bad name among activists these days because it is so often practiced as an exercise in escape, avoidance, abdication of our responsibilities to a suffering world. Clearly, such escapism is not authentic contemplation any more than violence is authentic action. Both perversions begin in the artificial separation we have made between contemplation and action, a separation which enables us to do what we wish in either sphere, without the claims and demands of the one guiding the life of the other.

If we can rid ourselves of the habit of dualism, we can see that the unity of contemplation and action runs deeper still, deeper than the fact that contemplation can clarify our action, that action can bear the fruit of our contemplation. For there are times when action *is* a kind of contemplation, when action opens up the hidden structure of reality in ways that detached observation never can. When a person takes a stand of conscience—refusing, for example, to pay war taxes—he or she quickly learns things about the boundaries of permissibility in our society which are not visible from an unengaged stance. When John Howard Griffin dyed his skin and went about as a black man, he learned things about America's systemic racism which no detached white observer will ever fully see.

And there are times when contemplation *is* a form of action, when the very presence of a self steeped in contemplative truth ripples the surrounding waters in ways which influence events. Witness "The Fighting Cock" which Taoist master Chuang Tzu wrote about; here is our model of nonviolent power!

> *Chi Hsing Tzu was a trainer of fighting cocks*
> *For King Hsuan.*
> *He was training a fine bird.*
> *The king kept asking if the bird were*
> *Ready for combat.*
> *"Not yet," said the trainer.*
> *"He is full of fire.*
> *He is ready to pick a fight*
> *With every other bird. He is vain and confident*
> *Of his own strength."*
> *After ten days, he answered again:*
> *"Not yet. He flares up*
> *When he hears another bird crow."*
> *After ten more days:*
> *"Not yet. He still gets*
> *That angry look*
> *And ruffles his feathers."*
> *Again ten days:*
> *The trainer said, "Now he is nearly ready.*
> *When another bird crows, his eye*
> *Does not even flicker.*
> *He stands immobile*
> *Like a cock of wood.*
> *He is a mature fighter.*
> *Other birds*
> *Will take one look at him*
> *And run."*[2]

Perhaps we can see the ultimate unity of contemplation and action by seeing that both of them are, finally, religious problems, religious responses. Our dualism has misled us again by suggesting that the relation of contemplation to action is like the relation of the sacred to the secular, that contemplation is somehow a way of bringing religious dimension to the worldly business of action. But action is as much a religious phenomenon as contemplation itself, for action comes, however unconsciously, out of deep human hopes and needs, longings which can rightly be called religious in nature. I mean the longing to overcome differences and be united with others; the longing for one's life to make a difference; the longing to transcend the dailiness of life, the trivial and the mundane; the longing, in fact, for a kind of immortality through the acts one leaves behind. The perversions to which our action is vulnerable stem from these soul-deep needs, needs which must be illumined and clarified and purified by the light of contemplation. Action is a religious problem, and authentic contemplation is a prayerful way of responding to that fact.

The quality of the university's action, its impact on society, is directly related to the quality of its contemplation. At its worst, the university's way of dividing reality into pieces and parts has led to manipulative forms of action which assume that the parts can be moved at will into whatever configuration pleases the mover. To the extent that the university's contemplation has portrayed the heart of reality as essentially amoral, to that extent has it fostered amoral forms of action. In a world where all truth is relative, action becomes unglued from common values and is guided largely by self-interest and the limits of what is possible.

In true contemplation, contemplation which sees not only beneath the surface but beyond the brokenness as well, we tap a well of love from which flows action that wants the best for the other, action that wants to unite rather than divide, action that wants to serve the whole rather than manipulate the parts. This is a contemplation which places us in organic relation to all that is, so that our action becomes as responsive to the needs of the whole as a healthy internal organ is responsive to the needs of the body. When we see all things in the light of love, there is no question of where contemplation ceases and action begins. As Thomas Merton once wrote:

Love has its seat not only in the mind or in the heart; it is more than mere thought and desire. Love is action, and it is only in the action of love that we attain to the contemplative intuition of loving wisdom. This contemplative intuition is an act of the highest degree and kind; it is the purest kind of love. And this love does away with the apparent contradiction between action and contemplation.[3]

CONTEMPLATION AND ACTION IN FOUR FAITH TRADITIONS

In the chapters that follow, the reader will find four statements on contemplation and action written by persons who share a concern for the ministry on campus, but who come to it from different faith traditions: liberal Protestant, evangelical Protestant, Catholic, and Jewish. In writing this essay, I have resisted the constant temptation to speak of the substance of my own religious beliefs because I want, instead, to focus on the rich interplay of convictions which these four writers open to us. Of course none of them can "represent" the whole of his or her tradition, for each of these traditions is so splendidly complex that its "typical version" would be merely a mediocre fiction. But each writer witnesses to something essential and unique in the tradition, as well as something essential and unique in his or her own refraction of it. In trying to capture the essence of what each has to say, I shall focus on these essential and unique elements. In doing so, I hope I can show how these papers reveal both a diversity of approaches to the problem of contemplation and action and the promise inherent in trying to listen and learn from each other across traditional lines.

Beverly Asbury, writing from a liberal Protestant point of view, begins by acknowledging the impact of the world on the "evangelical, pietistic, fundamentalistic" faith of his childhood: "I would never recover the certainty which had marked my earlier life." This sense of loss (however necessary) is typical, I think, of liberal Protestant autobiography, and leads to Asbury's understanding of what contemplative insight means on campus: the capacity to see by the light of faith while perceiving without blinking that the facts of modern life offer little warrant for faith. Thus, the title of his essay, "Despite All Appearances to the Contrary."

For Asbury (and, I think, for much of liberal Protestantism), linking contemplation to action means seeing the ambiguity and contradictions of life and developing the capacity to live with them.

Asbury quotes H. Richard Niebuhr approvingly: we must maintain "loyalty to the idea of God when the actuality is a mystery." He calls us to acknowledge the savage God whose reign of death dominates so much of the experience and imagination of the modern age, while at the same time affirming faithfulness to a God who bade us "choose life."

And what is the foundation of such faith? It is "the conviction that God has acted and disclosed his/her being in certain particular, distinctive moments in human history. . . . Abraham, the Exodus, the deliverence from captivity . . . . Jesus who was crucified, dead, buried, and raised to new life . . . ." We have memory, and we have hope—despite all appearances to the contrary. But we earn the right to be heard in the modern world not merely by our faith, but by our refusal to avert our gaze from the world's terrors. To contemplate is to learn a way of seeing which gives death its due, yet penetrates beyond death to a true source of life.

From this vantage point, Asbury is able to see clearly and critically a fatal lapse in the contemporary university. Speaking of Freudians, Marxists, and other materialists who wish to discredit religious faith, he says:

It is worth noting the irony that many who make such assumptions still seem more fearful of the God of our faith traditions than they are of the savage God. . . . With religion in so sad a state, one would have thought that the secular and humanistic reductionists in our universities would have moved with consciousness and clarity . . . to the task of constructing new systems of viewing and reordering reality. Alas, few even seem to make the attempt . . .

When Asbury turns directly to the problem of action, he scarcely resembles the stereotype of the liberal Protestant (a stereotype which is now badly dated). Not only does he see ambiguity between faith and worldly facts, but also between the intents and the results of action. Not only does he quote Niebuhr, but also Jacques Ellul:

Ultimately, politics obsesses us and gives us hallucinations, fixing our eyes on false problems, false means, and false solutions; we must therefore leave politics behind, not in order to abandon all interest in the *res publica* . . . but . . . to achieve it by a different route, to come to grips with it again in a different way, on a more real level, in a decisive context.

As Asbury admits, "I have not found it easy to follow Ellul's advice." But, clearly, he represents a new generation of liberal Protestants who find action as ambiguous as the world itself. The campus ministry, as Asbury sees it, must work to establish a "pole of tension" with the illusions of academic culture, politics, the world. Sometimes this pole of tension is established by acting, sometimes by withdrawing from action. But, either way, the underlying discipline for those who would minister is a contemplation which allows us to see God's truth "despite all appearances to the contrary."

Ronald Sider writes from the perspective of an evangelical Protestant Christian, and he is very explicit about the context in which Christian contemplation must occur: Scripture, the "radical judgment of biblical revelation." In particular, Sider argues that there are three "central biblical foundations" which ground our contemplation and give basis for our action: the prophets' assertion that to know God is to do justice; the biblical doctrine that God is on the side of the poor; and the bodily resurrection of Jesus of Nazareth as the cornerstone for our hope that justice will prevail.

Although Sider acknowledges that worldly vision does not see the truth of Scripture, he is not troubled by that fact. Commenting on the inability of many moderns to believe the "prescientific" claim of Jesus' resurrection, Sider says:

I am convinced that that skeptical conclusion rests on intellectual confusion. It is sheer nonsense to suppose that more and more precise scientific data about the way nature regularly works can tell us whether there is a God who transcends natural processes, who might intervene in nature if he chooses.

And he proceeds to develop the biblical evidence which establishes the historicity of the resurrection.

For Sider, the resurrection is more than a historical event, kept alive in memory against the negative evidence of the present moment; it is a present reality, more real, more vivid, more compelling than anything science can authenticate. For Sider, the end of contemplation has already been achieved: the vision of God, incarnate in Jesus Christ, manifest in our world as a presence of both love and judgment.

And the judgment is clear: it falls upon those who, having seen the vision, fail to act on behalf of justice for the poor. Like many evangelicals, Sider calls liberal Christians to "acknowledge and rectify their heretical neglect of evangelism and central biblical doctrines like the deity and resurrection of Jesus Christ." But Sider also calls his own community of evangelical Christians to "confess and correct their heretical neglect of the biblical summons to do justice." Indeed, he makes a fascinating case that evangelicals, in their disregard of the biblical call to justice, have "fallen into theological liberalism":

Notice what the methodological essence of theological liberalism is—it is allowing our thinking and living to be shaped by surrounding society's views and values rather than by biblical revelation. Liberal theologians thought that belief in the deity of Jesus Christ and his bodily resurrection was incompatible with a modern scientific world view. So they followed surrounding "scientific" society rather than scripture.

Evangelicals rightly called attention to this heresy—and then tragically made exactly the same move in another area. We have allowed the values of our affluent, materialistic society to shape our thinking and acting toward the poor. . . . We have allowed our theology to be shaped by the economic preferences of our materialistic contemporaries rather than by Scripture. And that is to fall into theological liberalism. We have not been nearly as orthodox as we have claimed.

To Sider, there is only one "solid foundation for campus ministry in the 1980s" and that is "a thoroughly biblical—and therefore thoroughly radical—faith." In a brief but compelling sketch of two colleges (Wheaton and Oberlin), Sider reminds us that both of them began in the mid-nineteenth century with a "holistic combination of evangelism, community and social passion," while today both colleges lack passionate concern for the oppressed and both are far removed (though along quite different routes) from the authentic evangelical wellsprings of their early years. The direction for campus ministry, Sider argues, is back toward those deep sources of Christian conviction and action for justice.

Arnold Wolf writes from his years of experience as a rabbi and as director of a major Hillel foundation. His article is as revealing in its form as in its content, for he presents his case by telling stories of Jewish lives as they are being lived on campus today. His very form suggests that "contemplation" and "action" are not analytic categories in Jewish tradition, but are to be understood as integral and interwoven strands of life experience, and to be told about not with abstractions, but through stories.

Wolf's stories tell of persons who combine "a desire to assimilate to WASP culture with the need to protect and intelligently defend the Jewish people. . . ." And for these Jewish students, faculty, and administrators, assimilation has become the major tactic of protection and defense. As one of Wolf's students put it, "The Holocaust made Amerian Jews acutely aware of the need for power—political and economic power." The route to power is clear: it is through WASP-dominated institutions like the prep school, the elite university, on into the law firm or the brokerage or the multinational business. For these academics, as Wolf suggests, "the true answer to the Holocaust is found, finally, at the Harvard Business School and Exxon."

From this point of view, "action" is clearly not a specialized activity aimed at protesting or changing social ills. Indeed, such action is discouraged among the persons Wolf writes about because it diverts one's energies from the quest for power and endangers one's access to the corridors of power. By their view, as Wolf writes, we must stop worrying about other people's skins for the sake of saving our own necks. Instead, action here becomes whatever one does in the strategic pursuit of power, especially the kind of power represented by career. As Wolf's student comments, "Working on my 'Note' for the *Law Review* is more important to me than demonstrating over apartheid in South Africa."

And by this view, what is "contemplation"? In Jewish tradition, as Wolf notes, the cognate for contemplation is "disinterested study of the Torah. To study and restudy God's Word . . . is what human beings must do when they aspire to insight and obedience." But today, Wolf argues, Torah has become secularized for many young Jews. Now, study in the university is "the royal road to power . . . we learn not what God wants but Caesar, and in learning well, we become Caesar's successor."

Having portrayed a rising generation of Jewish academics, Wolf goes on to speak for himself, and, against the formula of salvation by assimilation, Wolf poses the grave danger of the loss of Jewish identity: "I do not believe that those who choose to assimilate in order to serve the Jewish people will remember how to do that,

much less remember how to serve the ancestral God.... Some ...
may call this success, but to me it is the death of the spirit and the
end of anything worth being called Judaism any more."

In the midst of these facts and this prospect, the task of the rabbi
on campus is, first, "contemplative": to possess a "relentless willingness to see the world I live in, judging but not judgmental, perceptive but not least of the beam in my own eye." And, second, given
what he or she sees on the campus and in the larger culture, the
rabbi "should ... not only present alternatives to the monolithic-
pluralistic university, but be one.... The chaplain must represent
assumptions that are unprovable and commitments that only a
whole life can validate." So the second requirement is action, action
that comes in and out of an entire life pattern. Contemplation and
action, discerning and living the difference, this is the task of the
Jewish teacher in the secular academy.

Mary Luke Tobin writes from her experience as a Roman Catholic sister whose vocation has included both long hours of contemplative prayer and long hours of meeting and marching to protest
the cruelties and injustices of our time. For her, contemplation
"is essentially a listening in silence, an expectancy. Contemplative prayer begins with a return to the heart, finding our deepest
center ... "

For Tobin, the central function of contemplation is to reveal the
image of God in our own heart and in the heart of every other person. The end of contemplation is the realization that each life is infinitely valuable, centered in sacredness, a "glorious manifestation of
God." And this contemplative insight, gained in silent waiting, is to
be buttressed by the steady reading of Scripture. In Scripture, Tobin
writes, "I ... saw that Jesus set the importance of the human person
and the sacred value of each one above all else. What else can we
infer from his subordination of the law and the Sabbath to the needs
of the human person? ... I began to understand Jesus as defender
and liberator of all those who had been dominated." And "to think
of Yahweh as other than One who is for the suffering, poor, and oppressed is, to me, unfaithful."

Tobin believes that the link between contemplation and action
will begin to be forged as we let contemplative insight and the words
of Scripture "question us," as we are confronted with the "sobering
contradictions" which exist between the sacredness of the human

self and the brutalities of the world. "Only when we become aware of the difference between the possibilities to which the gospel calls us and the unjust world of which we are a part can our faith really impel us forward toward action. Recognition of this contradiction will not allow us to ignore what is happening in our world."

So, out of the contradiction between contemplative insight and the conditions of human life, there arises the seamless consistency of contemplation and action for justice. There is no doubt in Tobin's mind that contemplation and action belong together and feed each other, that "the deepening insights and clarity of contemplation occur in relationship to the ever-widening initiatives of action. . . . Contemplation becomes more all-embracing, reaching ever new depths, even as action grows more determined and courageous."

For Tobin, the university community can relate to both contemplative and active life: "If the university is a place where there exists some space and time for thought, prayer, and the discerning process, those of us engaged in campus ministry must labor to protect jealously this milieu." She goes on to cite a few cases where successful social action campaigns have been mounted by university groups, but also speaks critically of the upsurge of "spirituality" among campus groups in recent years: "Unfortunately—and I would like to believe I'm wrong—their prayers are seldom related to the actions needed to take issue with the harsh reality of our world."

Throughout Tobin's essay, the image of "the rock" appears and reappears. It is her image for the reality we discern through contemplation, as well as her image for the place where we may stand as we take action which puts us at risk. It is an image which comes in part from Tobin's own Christian tradition, a symbol for God and Christ in many biblical texts. But Tobin uses it in a way which avoids theological exclusiveness, a way which opens into relationship with other cultures and religious traditions. This is a central theme of contemplation and action for her, this unity beyond doctrinal divisions which we find when we say yes to life. Writing of her experience on a mission to Saigon toward the end of the Vietnamese War, Tobin says:

Looking about me at my fellow marchers, I somehow knew that it was possible, fitting, and right to rank oneself with all those Christians, Buddhists, and others seeking the liberation of persons, especially the powerless. I saw, as I had not seen before, that we are all one people, and that the realized union of all persons in the one God had to come. And I knew this would be possible only if one had a rock to stand on. . . . The house that stands, Jesus says, is one which so firmly clings to the solid rock of God that it withstands the rains and storms. . . . What is this rock if not the place where the contemplative spirit seeks a union of solidarity with the work of justice?

On "Mutual Irradiation"

As I think about these four pieces—Catholic, Jewish, liberal and evangelical Protestant—I am struck by both their similarities and their differences, and not all of them at the predictable points! Indeed, I am impressed by how far removed these traditions are from our stereotypes of them; impressed by the ways in which, for better or for worse, they have already borrowed from each other. And for all these reasons, I am struck by the rich opportunities that exist here for "mutual irradiation" between the four faith traditions, and for the enrichment of campus ministry which might follow. On too many campuses these ministries work in isolation, and even in competition with each other. Perhaps here, in the shelter of a book, we can encourage a quiet conversation which would benefit not only each tradition, but the whole of ministry as well.

To begin with similarities, I find the four writers surprisingly close on their conception of the university; and I am surprised, too, at how closely they adhere to the university's historic tradition. One might expect that such activists as these would want the university to transform itself into an agency of social change. But while asking the university to become more fully engaged with the human diminishments of our time, each of these writers respects the university's role as a setting for a kind of contemplation. Each of them asks the university to begin by honoring that part of its historic mandate more fully than it does now: to help people learn to see more deeply beyond appearances into the inwardness of things. (It is interesting that Ronald Sider, writing from an evangelical position often caricatured as apolitical, comes closest to advocating direct action in academe by recommending the model of mid-nineteenth century Oberlin College, whose evangelical commitments and attendant abolitionist beliefs caused the college to become a stop on the "underground railroad.")

But even as these four writers call the university to a kind of contemplation, they share the conviction that the university is so monolithic in its epistemology, so thoroughly empirical and rationalistic, that "seeing beyond the surface" may be infrequent if not impossible. So they ask (rather modestly, I think) that the university make space within its precincts for alternative visions, alternative ways of viewing the world. And believing that the university is unlikely to do this of its own accord, all four writers see the main task of campus ministry as one of offering alternative ways of seeing, of establishing the contradictions.

This, I think, is the most powerful convergence among these four viewpoints: the common vision of campus ministry as standing over against the conventional assumptions and perceptions of academic culture. Asbury speaks of posing a "pole of tension." Sider sees biblical revelation in radical judgment of both campus and campus ministry itself. Wolf asserts a historic Jewish faithfulness and life style against the quest for secular security. And Tobin calls us to let prayer and scripture continually question our lives. Sometimes campus ministry establishes the contradiction by a particular program of action; sometimes by articulating the faith in preaching and in prose; sometimes by personal witness to a peculiar way of life; sometimes by strategic withdrawal from conventional institutions. Whatever the mode, the consensus is clear: all four of these writers want campus ministry to challenge the university's monopoly on ways of viewing and responding to what is real.

If campus ministry is to establish alternative modes of contemplation on campus, what are the foundations of contemplation for these writers? This question, of course, takes us to the core of faith, so now the picture becomes more complex as each writer develops the special genius of his or her tradition. But, despite these divergences, the four share a common foundation—namely, the texts which transmit the historical memory of the faith, the accounts of God's mighty acts on our behalf; texts from which our own living memory can be kindled and inspired. Though not all texts are shared, and though each writer appropriates them in a different way, there is enough common text—and enough mutual appreciation of the role of memory in faith—to make conversation among these viewpoints possible and fruitful.

But, then, the differences emerge. For Asbury, contemplation is grounded in memory and upheld by hope but includes a kind of existential honesty about the world before one's eyes; thus, contemplation is a continual tension as one tries to bring two divergent views into a three-dimensional whole. For Sider, contemplation reveals the contemporary reality of memory's witness, and leads to a proclamation of living truth (especially of the resurrection) which worldly vision will never apprehend. For Wolf, contemplation means the disinterested study and restudy of God's Word wherever it is found ("Pentateuch, Bible, all of the religious traditions ultimately") in the context of an historical community committed to discovering what the Lord requires. And for Tobin, though Scripture is central, contemplation also involves a silent receptiveness in which we can discern the rock on which we stand, the sacredness which underlies all humanity.

To me, the most fascinating differences between these writers emerge when they come to the subject of action; here is where I find the greatest diversity of approach and the least predictability! For Asbury, coming from a liberal Protestantism which has often been portrayed as action-happy, the whole problem of acting is surrounded with Ellulian cautions and hesitations and even negations. For Sider, coming from an evangelical tradition often portrayed as quietistic, the failure of evangelicals to work through politics for justice is nothing less than heresy. For Wolf, action means the whole network of one's commitment of time and energy and gifts; it is as if this rabbi has written with a Protestant notion of "vocation" in mind. And for Tobin, coming from a tradition in which "Catholic action" has had broad and diffuse meaning, action means specialized efforts for change aimed at well-defined problems—notably, for her, the nuclear threat to humankind's survival.

It is always tempting to say that, despite apparent differences, all religions finally mean the same thing; and perhaps someday they will. But the differences are real, and if we brush them aside too easily we will miss a chance to expand the scope of our own understanding. It is worth noting, for example, that Beverly Asbury devotes only a paragraph or so to the rehearsal of God's saving actions in history and spends pages analyzing the problem of "seeing" in academic context, while Ronald Sider spends pages explicating the scriptural foundations of faith and shows little interest in the epistemological complexities of academic culture. Arnold Wolf takes great care to understand the particular mentality of the secularized Jewish academic (arguing that such people must reclaim their religious particularity), while Mary Luke Tobin tries to reach beyond Catholic creed through the symbol of "the rock" to embrace a community of people who discern the sacredness of life regardless of their religious affiliation.

I hesitate to say that these special emphases, these commissions and omissions, represent the potential and limitations of the current moment in liberal Protestantism, evangelical Christianity, Judaism, and Catholicism. But I do believe there is some truth in that claim. I shall *not* say how splendid it would be if we could form a super-religion which combined the strengths of the four traditions, for in some sense these strengths cancel each other out; every strength is shadowed by a weakness. But I will assert that these four approaches to the problem of contemplation and action on campus indicate the imperative for campus ministries of all sorts to be in serious conversation with each other. When that occurs, we will sometimes illuminate each other, sometimes infuriate each other, sometimes correct and humble each other. But all the time we will be learning the better to love each other so that we can better love God and the world. And that, finally, is what contemplation and action are all about.

NOTES

1. C. Wright Mills, *The Sociological Imagination* (New York: Oxford University Press, 1959).
2. Thomas Merton, *The Way of Chuang Tzu*. Copyright © 1965 by the Abbey of Gethsemane. Reprinted by permission of New Directions, New York, p. 109.
3. Thomas Merton, "Introduction," in Ernesto Cardenal, *To Live is to Love* (New York: Doubleday Image Books, 1972), p. 12.

JUDAISM TRIUMPHANT (MORE OR LESS)

Arnold Jacob Wolf

The generation that is in charge of the American educational establishment now includes many Jews. To be sure, most of them are not very "Jewish," and some of them, in fact, are deeply ashamed of their origins or conflicted about their responsibilities. A significant number of others, though, see these origins and responsibilities as fully congruent with where their heart is (and they may be right).

That generation, my generation, had its hands full in getting advanced degrees from the best schools, finishing the dissertation or the professional internships, trying to stay married and raise a family—all this in the wake of the Holocaust which killed a third of our brothers and sisters and wounded every Jew of our generation. We helped create Israel, we helped build a thousand new synagogues and schools, we worked out our own Jewish life alone and in communities of fellow seekers. We succeeded. We failed. But, I believe, it is the next generation, our children's, that will face the issue of commitment and/or success more squarely and more fully than we. We look like them, but our heads are often those of our parents' and theirs before them. We never fully assimilated; most of us never meant to in the first place. We are, after thirty years at the university or at the hospital or in court, not very different from what we once were.

But what is "Jewish"? If it means religious commitment, then those who are not ashamed or conflicted about this appellation are private, noncommittal on this issue. Unlike many high administrators of Christian background, they are neither conspicuously believers nor skeptics. One has the feeling that faith is not the locus of their undoubted Jewish concerns, at least not in any theological sense, not in a "Christian" sense. They are comfortable in being Jewish and, if there is a problem, it is that they are, perhaps, too comfortable in being Jewish. There is no apparent conflict between their origins and their ambitions, between their principles and their accomplishments. They have absorbed at least the ethical imperatives of their background and carried them forward successfully in their personal and crucial vocation. I do not know how much they think about God, but I know they are deeply and unswervingly Jewish, in some sense.

If Judaism, or at least Jewishness, is no problem, then what is the problem? Perhaps just that! We Jews have been accustomed to seeing our role as interstitial, marginal, alienated. But here are, apparently, integrated human beings. Does that look like smugness or like premature adequation of our religious heritage to the American university setting? Do we miss tension, struggle, a Judaism which judges and, in part, rejects modernism? Or have the people of whom I speak gone through these conflicts and come out the other side? In any case, Judaism seems alive and well not only at home, but in offices where it has never been welcome before.

A brilliant recent graduate of Yale College and the Stanford Law School wrote out an autobiographical fragment in response to Irving Howe's *World of Our Fathers.* It reveals his history and, above all, his goals. He comes from a deeply committed Zionist family in the Midwest and has had a far better than average Jewish education. He is also a fine person—able, genial, and handsome. He is also incredibly open about what he wants and why. He says what many of his cohorts cannot even permit themselves to think. He is a product of post-Holocaust, post-Israel Jewish history. He is a product of Yale, Stanford, ruling-class America. He is unique; he is an indicator of things to come.

I have shortened his autobiography and rendered it more anonymous, but I have neither added to nor subtracted from its basic thrust. I believe it is too important to be fictionalized. "Third Generation," however, is my title, and X will not be identified. But his views are clear and, as I shall argue after reproducing his document, devastatingly indicative of the direction Jews may be headed in as our century comes to a close.

Third Generation
by X

All four of my grandparents were born in the western fringes of the Soviet Union. I know little about their precise origins, other than that gleaned from infrequently told family tales. The more interesting of my two sets of grandparents are on my mother's side. Her mother came from Lithuania, one of the richest and most cultured points of origin in eastern Europe. X was their American name and, after arriving at Ellis Island, they left for Colorado because of rumors about a silver boom. They flourished for a short period of time as merchants in the rough and tumble mining town. My grandmother's brother was mayor of Silver Plume, Colorado, after the boom was over and and it had become a ghost town. My grandmother was a scholar of German language and literature, the first woman admitted to the University of Colorado, and a close friend of the author of *Little Women.* She moved eastward to Chicago to work at Hull House as a social worker (having given up a potential career as a writer), became an ethical culturist, and ended up in Cleveland where she met her husband. He was a *fusgeyer* or, as Howe explains, an immigrant who literally walked across eastern and central Europe to Hamburg in order to escape the tyranny of the Russian army, which had conscripted him at the age of twelve. He became a successful real estate businessman and a partly active attorney. As dynamic as he was, his premature death before my birth makes my memory of him most incomplete. My grandmother's brothers also had interesting careers—one moved to Seattle and did retail business at I. Magnin, another wrote speeches for Huey Long until he committed suicide at the age of twenty-eight, another convalesced at a Turkish bath resort on the Sea of Galilee, and still another taught at Columbia University.

My father's parents were more typical immigrants—penniless, uneducated, and clannish. They met in Rhode Island, moved to X, and started a furniture store. Our name is most certainly an abridged version of some Russian name. Grandpa was the son of a long family of rabbis. But that is no big deal since rabbis were as plentiful in the shtetl as lawyers in America. His wife was a shrewd woman who took the meager profits from the furniture store and invested them in General Motors and other blue chip companies, providing the wherewithal for my father's education at an institute of technology.

The higher status of my mother's parents is reflected in my mother's more cosmopolitan experiences. She was on the same ship as Haile Selassie when she was eight years old. The emperor was ejected from Ethiopia by the Italians in 1936. Both were on their way to Palestine, a safe harbor in those days while the depression was wreaking chaos at home. My father can be best described as a no-nonsense person who comes from a hard-nosed, parochial, and striving immigrant family. "Striving," of course, is a matter of degree since every American Jew, in my opinion, is striving toward something.

The values that my parents have are fairly coherent—a firm belief in political liberalism, the separation of church and state, secularism, modernism, industrialization, growth with inflation, the Democratic party, Israel, and most of all education. My parents set out to achieve an apparently contradictory task: I was to be inculcated with Jewish values by parochial, immigrant teachers at Hebrew school, and I was to receive a first-class education. The contradictions of my educational background are my parents' greatest gift, enabling me to transcend the parochialism of my Jewish forebears without surrendering one iota of my Jewish identity. Of course, my foray into the Wasp world of a laboratory school caused occasional consternation within the family. Before my bar-mitzvah in Israel, they discovered me dating Holly, daughter of an alcoholic, anti-Semitic, wealthy Irish demogogue. The same day that the Soviets offended international law by invading Czechoslovakia, I transgressed criminal law by joyriding on a "borrowed" motorized minibike.

I followed my older brother's path to valedictorian at school. Yet my brother and I are two different animals. The laboratory school he went to was just beginning to open its doors to non-Wasp minorities, whereas the top ten students in my class of sixty-nine were all Jewish. My brother was, like Howe's immigrant, entering new and foreign ground and confiding in a close group of friends. My arrival at school was much more gregarious. I knew who the good teachers were, and I was eager to attain success on prep-school terms—in sports and in social life—as well as in academics. My little brother, who graduates from laboratory school this spring, senses that his eldest brother was brilliant, but I was important.

History repeats itself at Yale, where I followed my brother right into the same major. But again, differences are apparent. Whereas he devoted his extracurricular energies to forming and leading the Israel Committee, I was more attracted to East Coast educated preppies like Jeff from Darien, who is about to leave the Stanford Business School for a career in Citibank's elite multinational finance division; Bill, grandson of a premier World War I flying ace and son of a now-bankrupt former Yale football captain (Bill is currently editor in chief of a semitrashy paper with a circulation of nearly 250,000); and James, traveling boutique clothes salesman and scion of a great New England family of educators.

When I say that I retained my Jewish identity, I mean that I had a core of experiences that my Wasp friends lacked. I came from a family that placed an immense value on achievement. Everywhere I looked in my family, I saw increasing success, upward mobility, sources of future prestige. One of my parents' curious traits was a refusal to discuss unpleasant things. My mother's brother was shielded from me because he was categorized a "manic-depressant." My father's sister was taboo because she was a "schizophrenic." Both were brilliant students who somehow could not adapt to the post-World War II "conform and get ahead" mentality of American second-generation Jews.

My "core of experiences" includes four trips to Israel—modern Israel—land of young, vital soldiers who could vanquish enemies twenty times their size. Second-generation American Jews educated in the pre-World War II era mimicked the Wasp because we never again want to be outside the governmental power that failed to divert Allied planes in order to bomb the death tracks to Auschwitz. I mimic the Wasp not from a position of inferiority, but, rather, from a position of internal (and, in many ways, external) superiority.

Someday I will argue that the Holocaust was the best thing that ever happened to American Jewry. Since the Holocaust, we witness a dramatic social and economic ascendance of American Jews, first in small businesses, then in the professions and academe, and now in large corporations and government. The Holocaust made American Jews acutely aware of the need for power—political and economic power.

One source of power, though a bit anachronistic, is a sovereign state designed primarily for the perpetuation of the Jewish people. A second source of power is through our accomplishments in law and public service. Whereas second-generation American Jews sought economic security, my generation seeks political security, real power. Hence, the overweening presence of Jews in law schools, particularly in prestigious ones that provide the credentials for future government posts. Hence, the overweening presence of Jews in the media, an arena where the American public can be manipulated and shaped according to the ideology of the media industry. Hence, the presence of Jews in banks, large corporations, the State Department, and the Pentagon, all of which make transactions that could mean life or death for the state of Israel.

Second-generation Jews also wanted prestige and power, but could not attain it without first securing the economic means required for upward mobility. As Professor Lindblom of Yale points out, "Wealth and income, along with many values that tend to cluster with wealth and income, such as education, status, and access to organizations, all constitute resources that can be used in order to gain influence over other people." The shrewd decision of my parents' generation to cast all their eggs in the education basket is largely responsible for the disproportionate political influence of their offspring.

The very notion of "getting ahead" that is the hallmark of the Jewish immigrant and his offspring runs counter to the egalitarian values of the New Left. Working on my "Note" for the *Law Review* is more important to me than demonstrating over apartheid in South Africa. As Hillel, an ancient talmudic scholar reportedly said, "If I am not for me, who else will be?"

Meritocracy is the key to the ascendance of American Jewry, especially since World War II. The need for qualified elites to manage the post-industrial society has led to greater emphasis on SAT scores and grades as a device for screening out the mentally able from the average and the crippled. As gruesome as the notion that someone is not good enough to enter a certain school is, such is the cost of running our complex society.

And, so the argument continues, if we Americans forsake our commitment to finding the best and the brightest, we will lose our leadership in the world. Logic runs against egalitarianism. Only the fear that the social system will crack if we become overtly elitist explains the persistent re-

fusal of the vast majority of American Jews to align themselves with the
Republican party, benefactor of big business and country club.

The ascension of third-generation American Jews to the pinnacle of
political and economic power carries with it a contradiction. In order to
become an executive of a large organization, the Jew must adopt the gen-
teel mannerisms and social graces of the Wasp. One young Jewish partner of an investment bank warned me that the world of the corporate and
government elite demands a style different from that of the entrepre-
neurial builder. "They watch you for a long time," he added. The Jewish
style is rebellious, impatient, questioning, unwilling to conform, brash
and showy. The collision course can be run successfully only if the Jew
can make it to the top on his own terms. The image of the corporate or
political executive must and will change as non-Wasps begin to fill the
role. This change is necessary because, if the Jew adopts totally the Wasp
persona, he will surrender the genius that enabled him to make the initial
rise. He will become, instead, Jay Gatsby—rich, eccentric, and self-
destructive.

The trend away from liberalism will continue as American Jews become more firmly entrenched in established circles. The insularity of the
Jewish community in large metropolitan centers will erode further, yet
consciousness of Jewish identity will persist. A new stereotype, the Jewish
preppie, will replace that of the uncouth genius from Bronx High School.

This document is remarkable for many reasons. It is frank, strong,
clear, and unashamed. It says what a good many Jewish students, at
least in the better universities and graduate schools, are secretly
thinking. It combines a fine sensitivity to Jewish issues and concerns
with a strong desire for personal career success, and imaginatively
buttresses the one with the other. Unique about this statement, in
my view, is that traditional Jewish values interpenetrate the ambition of a gifted young man. He speaks of what he personally wants
as a religious obligation; he speaks of Jewish obligations as his personal drives. Above all, he combines a desire to assimilate into
WASP culture with the need to protect and intelligently to defend
the Jewish people from whom he springs and whose life he
cherishes.

We are told in Hansen's law that the third generation remembers
what the second generation tried hard to forget. Thus, assimilating
Jewish parents, themselves children of immigrants, may have children who return unexpectedly to *kashrut* and Zionism. But, as we
see here, things are often more complicated. The third generation
can be, indeed, proudly and fearlessly Jewish, but the themes to

which they return have been utterly transformed by their experiences in the American milieu. They return not to what was, but to their image of what was, to their own version of the millennial Jewish situation which has been greatly transformed, if not wholly reversed. The third generation *does* remember, but in the way it has been taught to remember by the culture of the American university.

For Jewish tradition the highest virtue (*k'neged kulam*) is disinterested study of the Torah. To study and restudy God's Word (Pentateuch, Bible, all of the religious tradition, ultimately) is what human beings must do when they aspire to insight and obedience. Study is the study of sacred texts in a sacred community, with the goal of serving a Holy Master. But in the third generation we find a wholly different version of Jewish education; study is goal-directed; it is, in fact, the royal road to power in our meritocracy. Study is learning what the ruling class needs in order to serve that class, share in its power, and finally replace it. Careerism is the name of this game: we learn not what God wants but Caesar, and in learning well, we become Caesar's successor. There are no sacred texts, but there are magical ones (law books, business school protocols) which open all doors, including the sealed gate to our redemption. Redemption, of course, no longer means oneness with God and with a messianic world, but oneness with those who rule on earth already.

Israel is also a value, but in complete transvaluation. What was once perceived as a Holy Land, full of need and full of the power to bestow grace, the land of the prophets and sages, the land where God's commandment requires us to live, the land where Jewish self-definition is most plausible and most rewarding—that land has become a very different kind of paradigm for our writer. Israel now means power, particularly naked military power. X achieves status in his prep school by identifying with Moshe Dayan and the Israel defense forces. Israel is still a task, but it is now the task of protecting the Jewish community in its own land by attaining power in other lands (particularly in the United States) where Israel's future will be decided. We must assimilate in order to become expert in violence, in order to protect valid Jewish interests in Israel and around the world. Zionism is no longer a motive for separatism, but precisely the opposite: it mandates becoming like the nations in order to make it possible for some fellow Jews to live as a nation.

The Holocaust is also transformed under the reconsideration of third-generation perspectives. In most Jewish thinking it looms very large: as theodicy, as martyrdom, as tragedy, at once terrifying and problematic. But here the Holocaust serves exclusively as a warning: if Jews are powerless they will be killed, hence they must never be powerless again. The street fighters of the Jewish Defense League are right to emphasize that we are surrounded by enemies and that our chief obligation is to destroy them before they destroy us. But they have no real idea of how to do that: by marching, by throwing Molotov cocktails into Soviet embassies, by mobilizing the *ressentiment* and righteous indignation of the lower middle class. These methods are doomed. They are what the impotent do in their rage at being impotent. The point is to become powerful, and the way is by becoming more assimilated than the assimilationists, more American than old American families. Poor Jews, separatist Jews, cannot protect the Jewish people. Only we, university educated, well connected and successful beyond any previous generation of Jews, can do that. We will honor the Warsaw ghetto fighters and the victims of Auschwitz best by refusing to become victims ourselves, and that means by refusing categorically to be interstitial any longer in the American polity. The true answer to the Holocaust is found, finally, at the Harvard Business School and Exxon.

Jews were often left-liberals in the past because they were poor and because they continued to identify romantically with the poor even when they moved up the economic-social ladder, says our young critic. But we have no time for these romantic illusions any longer. They are dangerous and regressive. It is time we identified openly with the upper-class party and the upper-class club and the upper-class ambition that fit our present situations. Judaism really teaches "if I am not for myself, who will be?" It requires of us that we forsake any pseudo-ideals that obscure rational self-interest.

But we may doubt that our young careerist speaks the whole truth. Not only because Hillel the Elder added, "but if I am only for myself what am I?" but, rather, because the whole meaning of his key phrase is quite different from X's. As Professor Urbach has pointed out, the meaning is properly: if I do not perform the holy *mitzvot* myself, who can do my job for me, and if I do perform them only for a reward, what reward have I, and if I do not begin now, when shall I? Left-liberalism among Jews is conditioned not only by a transient sociology, but by a pervasive, millennial interpretation of

Jewish piety and prophetism in the everyday obligation of politics. Of this our writer knows nothing and cares nothing. If our sole obligation is to move up in the Gentile world, old-fashioned Jewish ethics must, he insists, be transcended. For the sake of the Jews, we may be required to stop being so Jewish. For the sake of saving our necks, we must stop worrying about other people's skins. Egalitarianism is a handicap in a meritocracy; so it is time we stop pretending we care very much about others and start moving to the top where we belong—not only, of course, for our own sakes, but for the sake of an embattled Western world and a vulnerable Jewish folk.

X contends that, while it may be true that the military-industrial complex has long been a hotbed of anti-Semitism, its elite must know by now that they need Jewish leadership. They cannot continue to exclude Jewish brains from top positions unless, like the Soviets, they are willing to pay a tremendous price, ultimately an unacceptable price. The third generation (often, I'd correct him, the fourth) of American Jews is ready at last to enter the sacred precincts of American capitalism and to begin to take over key roles. We are needed; no one can any longer keep us out. Especially because the "we" that is going to move in is a much more acceptable "we"; Choate and Yale and Stanford Law School have done their task for hundreds of us. We are now *salonfahig,* acceptable everywhere. What our former masters may not know is that, though we look very different, we are as proudly (if not as "religiously") Jewish as any previous generation. We are not only a fifth column in the corporate world, but also heirs of the Rothschilds and Warburgs. We are where we belong, at last.

Thus, says X, we can surrender a Jewish style which was only transitional, in any case. It is no loss to give up lox and Yiddish. Woody Allen has already demonstrated that such a Jewishness was sexually debilitating and personally counterproductive. So have more profound critics more profoundly, writers like Hannah Arendt and Jean Paul Sartre. We are finally ready to slough off immigrant habits and feelings in order to take our place in American social life. We shall not need to become Reform Jews (that measure was, in any case, too little and too late); theology is neither a stumbling block nor an advantage, it is merely irrelevant. But we *shall* need to dress differently and talk differently and experience differently. That's all, and that's enough.

But, we may ask, are Jewish modalities really so completely separate from Judaism? Is our "style" nothing but east European *shtetl* memories, or is what we are determined by Jewish fate, if not also by Jewish faith? Can we dismiss as mere nineteenth-century baggage what seems to embody an essential way of "being in the world"? We can, of course, easily give up lox and old-fashioned clothes. But how about our sexuality and parenting and philanthrophy and even our learning? Is it obvious that we have nothing to lose by changing these crucial modalities of service and survival? Is the way we pray utterly irrelevant to how we live, our Bible and Talmud to what we have become? I do not believe that those who choose to assimilate in order to serve the Jewish people will remember how to do that, much less remember how to serve the ancestral God. If we buy into American (or Soviet or Israeli) society without reservation, we shall, inevitably, have sold out something once precious to us and to God.

The Jewish hero was once upon a time the scholar-saint. Then, later, it was the scientist and student of Western culture, the soldier and the *kibbutznik*. Is it now to be the aging preppie, the successful meritocrat, the Marrano manager in General Motors who cleverly masks his Jewishness with a Jewish mask? In the Enlightenment period, we were advised by Jewish thinkers to be Jews at home but human beings abroad. Now the roles are to be reversed: outside we shall flaunt our Jewish colors, our loyalties to fellow Jews, our fearlessness to be what we want. But at home, inwardly, we shall have transformed ourselves into something other. There will be no Jews to protect, not in a Jewish state, even one that is strong enough to survive but not to embody the millennial dream, not in a diaspora that has won every game but the last and most important. Some, like our X, may call this success, but to me it is the death of the spirit and the end of everything worth being called Judaism any more.

What is it like to be a rabbi to an American campus on the brink of the eighties? Both difficult and fascinating. Difficult, because young Jews are in rapid movement, often ambivalent about their heritage, often nakedly opportunistic in their ambitions. Fascinating, because there is much conern with Jewish identity and Jewish values even, or especially, among those who are most ruthless in their upward mobility. There are a great many Jews at Yale (or Columbia or Haverford or Oberlin or Stanford), far more than most alumni of those schools realize or, perhaps, approve. There is a great variety of Jewish activity on all these campuses: Sabbath worship in three or four styles; *havurot* (communal house "churches"); Zionist public action; fund raising for Israel and for Jewish education; courses for credit and for pleasure in philosophy, Bible, Jewish problems and Jewish history, music and Midrash, self- and people-hood. But there is not much action for world peace, or for feeding the hungry, or for civil rights, just now. Jewish hearts are still in the right place more often than Jewish legs are marching in protest or in parade.

A rabbi is a teacher. He must learn and teach above all else. I have learned much from my teachers and more from colleagues and most from my students, including a great deal I'd rather not know. When I offer a seminar in twentieth-century Judaism, five times as many students sign up than Yale will let me include. But when we celebrate minor holidays, the numbers sharply decline. Many will come to a Seder meal or build a *sukkah* or get dressed up for a *Purim* carnival night, but won't study medieval texts or ways to improve Arab-Jewish relations. They are utterly postmodern, and I am not yet fully modern myself. They are too ambitious for my taste, and I am too slow moving for them. They are too conservative politically and too modern in theology and practice for me; I confuse them, though also I sometimes surprise or even delight.

They do not seem very happy with their successes. If Yale psychologist Seymour Sarason is right, they are not going to be very happy doctors or lawyers, either. The Yale faculty seems to drink too much, divorce too often; its members look like unfulfilled, if resolute, joggers and tennis players. But a suburban synagogue presents a very similar picture. What is unexpected (at least by me) is how happy these unhappy Jews think they are. The medical student does not usually think much of the profession, but still rather enjoys medical school. The law student masochistically delights in his own persecution, though he will not admit to anyone that, when he graduates, he will, in fact, practice law. Beside them, I feel myself at once very "together" and yet profoundly unfinished, as well.

A chaplain should, I believe, not only present alternatives to the monolithic-pluralistic university, but be one. The school necessarily stands for critical thinking (about everything but critical thinking itself). The chaplain must represent assumptions that are unprovable and commitments that only a whole life can validate. A rabbi, working with both Orthodox and orthodoxly alienated Jews, must be as hard as a rock and as flexible as a reed. The usual biblical figure for fruitfulness is a tree with deep roots and gently fluttering leaves. My roots are not deep enough, I fear, and some of my leaves are already desiccating in the chill. But while I want my people to be happy, I have a different goal for myself: to be worthy of their trust.

Trustworthiness means a relentless willingness to see the world I live in, judging but not judgmental, perceptive but not least of the beam in my own eye. Trust (*emunah*) means letting God save the world and convert the Jews to Judaism, while my task is to show Him where the Jews are and to help Him bring the Messiah by not getting in His way. The sixties were all prophecy and black consciousness and the Six-Day War. The seventies were nonattachment, the Yom Kippur War, dropping out and making out and making it. The eighties will be very different again, I am sure, but no easier. But I am not free and you are not free to abstain from the future task just because neither of us is commanded to bring it to completion. Let us begin—again.

TO BUILD WITH LIVING STONES

Mary Luke Tobin

I

In the garden of Ten Ruji, near Kyoto in Japan, is a lake of moving green water in which are placed several large stones arranged in a Zen pattern. They invite the visitor to pause and reflect. Since I have a picture of that lake, taken on the spring day on which I saw it, I am able to recall the scene vividly.

Last summer I spent several fascinating hours with some other stones. I explored a number of petroglyphs, made by early American Indians at Ring Lake, Wyoming. Pictures carved with a sharp instrument on the faces of huge boulders in the area of a lake in the Tetons depict strange images of spirits or animals. Often these images are shown wearing exotic clothing, elaborately decorated, representing the gods or spirits of an early tribe. These relics, symbols, left by unknown wanderers dating from the twelfth and thirteenth centuries, are preserved for us because they were carved on the almost unchanging face of the ancient rocks. Perhaps, at the very time of their ritualistic carving, the knights of England were wresting their demands for participation in government from the king. Rocks, by their enduring solidity, help us to make connections, to hold in mind two widely separated events. There is so much to learn about stones.

I recall my amazement when, as a child, I first learned that stones are living things and go through their transformations like other living things, though very slowly. Despite the appearance of immobility, rocks do change. They are not without life, but it is a life subtly emanating from their substance.

My reflections on rocks have become a framework for the topic we are discussing here: the spiritual quest in which action and contemplation come together. The peaceful, meditative image suggested by contemplation and the vigorous moving figure suggested by action may seem to have little in common. But they do share the

same source, I believe, and I hope that my reflections may throw
some light on this conviction. For my own experience has led me to
the conclusion that the deepening insights and clarity of contemplation occur in relationship to the everwidening initiatives of action.

II

When I was deciding, as a young woman, on my choice of the
kind of religious life that I wanted to live, I thought seriously of entering a contemplative community, one where the first order of the
day, according to the Catholic tradition, would be the practice of
prayer. Would this not lead me more quickly into a more direct experience of the presence of God? I pondered the choice seriously,
but I finally opted for an "active" order where prayer alternated
with teaching. The ideal of the life of Jesus in which work and
prayer were interwoven was the attraction which swayed my eventual decision.

My life in the order, then, developed with teaching and prayer
forming the fabric of every day. I was engaged steadily in a search
for an ever-richer life of contemplation; action, on the other hand,
took the route of the day-to-day work of teaching. I was not involved in the societal struggles of the forties, and World War II
touched me but little. How could I have been so unaware of a whole
civilization in terrible crisis? Why was I not agonizing over the crucifixion of six million Jews and questioning my complicity in their
suffering? Why was I so unmoved and so indifferent, indeed, like a
rock without life? Were the roots of contemplation not deep
enough? Where was true compassion?

The very "stones had to cry out" before I could see what was so
obviously a profound connection between action for human liberation and a life of reflective prayer. The progressive happenings of
the intervening years were to make me more conscious of the center
from which all action and contemplation flow.

III

One of the fortunate experiences of my life was meeting Thomas
Merton, the Christian poet-mystic who wrote luminously on contemplation during the fifties and sixties. Contemplation, he suggests,

is essentially a listening in silence, an expectancy. Contemplative prayer begins with a return to the heart, finding our deepest center, awakening the profound depth of our being in the presence of God, who is the source of our being and our life.

"Contemplation is the highest expression of a person's intellectual and spiritual life. It is that life itself, fully awake, fully active, fully aware that it is alive. It is spiritual wonder. It is spontaneous awe at the sacredness of life, of being. It is gratitude for life, for awareness, and for being. It is a vivid realization of the fact that life and being in us proceed from an invisible, transcendent, and infinitely abundant Source. Contemplation is, above all, awareness of the reality of that Source.... Contemplation is a sudden gift of awareness, an awakening to the Real within all that is real."[1]

Reality, of course, is a word difficult to define; and yet, it is a useful word because it is broad enough to hold within itself several levels of meaning. I use *reality* here to encompass not only the happenings of our everyday life, but also the interaction of events in a complex world. For the believer, reality also includes, at the deepest level of human existence, a union between God and each human person.

"God is in our 'center,' " to continue Merton's thought, "and that 'center' is all that is left when we die. Real freedom is to be able to come and go to that 'center.' When we die, everything else is destroyed except that which is important, the true, inner self, the 'center.' The only thing which is important is this inner reality, for God preserves it and is identified with it. Nobody can touch or hurt this 'center.' We must be free to be in contact with this 'center.' ... We have to train ourselves to choose what will let this 'center' operate. If you choose to handle everything that comes up so that you are in contact with this 'center,' you will have freedom.... The reality which is the will of God can keep us in contact with this 'center' at every moment. We must respond to it."[2]

But Merton also had some words to say about the unity of action and contemplation. His own development records his coming to an acute awareness of the human reality in which he saw not only "God alone," but also all men and women as glorious manifestations of God. Once this "vision" possessed him, he spared no effort or words in speaking out against social evil, especially the oppressions of racism and war.

"There is no contradiction between action and contemplation," Merton said, "when Christian activity is raised to the level of love. On that level, action and contemplation are fused into one entity by the love of God and our brothers and sisters. But for action to reach this level, prayer must be deep, powerful, and pure.[3] . . . God is the very ground of what we know, and our knowledge itself is his manifestation: not that he is cause of all that is real, but that reality itself is his epiphany. God is never shown by the Bible, for example, merely as a *supplement* of human power and intelligence, but as the very ground and reality of that power. This is our greatest human dignity, our most essential power, the secret of our humanity."[4]

Another great teacher of our time who wrote about prayer and action was Abraham Heschel—Jewish writer, mystic, and teacher. He said of prayer, "The primary purpose of prayer is to praise, to sing, to chant. Because the essence of prayer is a song, and one cannot live without a song."[5] And yet, he, too, was well aware of the relationship between prayer and action. Once, asked about the prophets concerning whom he had written at length, he replied, "The prophet is one who is able to hold God and the human person in one thought, at one time, at all times. This is so great and so marvelous. It means that whatever I do to a person, I do to God. When I hurt a human being, I injure God. God has made human beings to his own image and likeness. Now, God is invisible. But to find God among us it is necessary to look only as far as the next human person. There is, I believe, a partnership of God and human beings. God needs our help. I would define a human being as a divine need. God is in need of men and women."[6]

I heard Abraham Heschel meditate on peace before a group of antiwar protesters at the Capitol rotunda in Washington. This talk revealed to me the integrity of prayer and action for justice in his own life. I recall that he expressed himself in words similar to these: "The Vietnam War is the greatest religious issue of our times. For what does God demand of us primarily? Justice and compassion. What does he condemn above all? Murder; killing innocent people. How can I pray when I have on my conscience the awareness that I am co-responsible for the deaths of innocent people in Vietnam? In a free society, some are guilty; all are responsible." His identification of the war as a religious issue tells us something deeply significant about this committed man whose faith and action formed one bond.

IV

Both Merton and Heschel, in exalting the dignity of the human person, have taught us a key lesson about contemplation related to action. They have taught us that we are touched by empowering love when we are responsive to the mystery and beauty of each person. By this contemplation we are impelled to resist by action, by word or deed, whatever degrades or destroys the image of God.

What I find in my own experience is an expansion of my sense of the unity and presence of God in a commitment to social justice. I can think back now to those influences in my life which assisted this process. My outlook was gradually broadened from a narrower perspective of personal faith to wider horizons which include not only a larger community of fellow Christians, but also a greater solidarity with the whole human community.

At first I did not identify with God's call the need to open my eyes to the injustice and alienation of our times. It would be misleading to pretend that I am not still struggling for the implementation of this consciousness in my own life. But I would like to enumerate several experiences/events which have helped me to develop it. Not only individual persons, but also communities, insights, happenings, and the interweaving of scriptural reflection in my life have constituted stepping stones along the way.

The life of a religious sister has built into it quite ample blocks of time for personal as well as communal prayer. I have mentioned Thomas Merton as an important figure in helping me understand the integration of prayer and action. His writings in the fifties delighted me with their penetrating and illuminating disclosures of the ways of prayer. He was able to point out paths and obstacles, and to do so in the discerning language of the poet. I was surprised then, and a little shocked, when he began to write less about personal prayer experience and more about the harsh realities of racism and war. He was clearly sensitive to the nuclear danger as early as 1961.

On one occasion in the early sixties, he brought Daniel Berrigan to a gathering at Loretto, Kentucky, where I looked forward to hearing Berrigan speak about his own poetry. The imagery of his words and figures had always delighted me; thus I was eager for him to share his poetic insights into prayer. Again, I was disappointed that, during the hours he talked to us, he spoke not of his poetry, but only of the poverty and suffering of people in the South. He seemed interested only in recruiting young college people to give up their summers for volunteer work for the poor in the South.

These disturbing developments obliged me to look further than the familiar, and I was forced to bring my faith into confrontation with the cruelties of racism and war. I began to have to deal with the fact of social evil in my neighborhood and my country. To involve myself as a responsible Christian and a citizen with a voice, to integrate these new insights into my own life of prayer became imperative.

Nor was I alone in this: my own community, the Sisters of Loretto, was moving into a larger vision. New currents of theology were appearing in the church, and it was exciting for me to learn about them from the persons within our community who were studying at universities both at home and abroad.

Central to these insights, it seemed to me, was a fresh emphasis on and perception of the value of the human person. There was a new stress on and recognition of human talents and potentialities, in particular the dimension of openness to the transcendent, to the infinite. What a great thing is a human person, and how valuable is each one's life! "Worth without price," to quote Paul Ricoeur. Further, the interplay of our changing times with our newly awakened sensitivity to the person was itself a theological venture.

Although Scripture had always been an abundant resource for personal prayer, it took on a new richness for me. It seemed to me, as I reflected on a number of passages in the Gospels, that there was ample evidence for seeing the relationship of the words and actions of Jesus to the social evils I had been learning about. I now saw that Jesus set the importance of the human person and the sacred value of each one above all else. What else can we infer from his subordinating the law and the Sabbath to the needs of the human person? It now seemed pivotal to my own development that I began to understand Jesus as defender and liberator of all those who had been dominated.

During the late sixties, the community of the Sisters of Loretto began to move corporately toward realizing the connection between the gospel and the societal evils of the world in which we found ourselves. Some of our members had marched at Selma and, here again, I was learning to incorporate the consciousness of the evil of racism in a more pertinent way into my own faith perspectives. In 1967, my community, for the first time, took a stand on a controversial public issue, agreeing to work in opposition to the Vietnam War. At the same time, the community made a policy decision supportive of the conscientious position of individual members: "The courage of a Sister of Loretto to act on her Christian conviction deserves the support of her sisters. A common application of the Gospel to any public issue may never be reached by us, but respect for another's integrity and conscience is a value that we affirm and pledge ourselves to preserve."[7] Such firm and unequivocal stands supported the members of the community who felt a greater urgency to act against the war on racism, as well as those who were reluctant to move into more radical action.

It is probably impossible to assess the influence and support of a vital community in forming one's ideals and affirming one's positions. I certainly cannot overestimate this element in my growing awareness of social evil. While I do not suggest that a religious community is the only place where such affirmation is possible, it seems true that, in a community where prayer and reflection on Scripture are daily priorities, one stands a better chance of being reminded of the "justice Yahweh asks."

V

In the early sixties, I had been able to participate in the great renewal drama of the Roman Catholic church at Vatican II in Rome, where I was an observer, or rather an "auditor," having been invited there, with a few other women, to "represent women" in some small token participation. With some kindred souls among the other women at Vatican II, I became part of a small, even though silent, "cheering section," so to speak, for the voices of those bishops and their advisors opposing atomic warfare and speaking up for other social justice issues. As differences developed and struggle ensued in the speeches of the bishops at the Council, I realized with excitement and hope that I was present at an event of great significance in the history of the Catholic church.

At the Council, the new reality of ecumenical engagement and the warmth of friendships made with Protestants present there was a joyful ingredient in my growing social consciousness. Meeting Robert McAfee Brown among the Council observers was to have many repercussions in the years ahead. Being a companion with him and others like him at so many antiwar events and demonstrations in the next eight years was a strengthening support in a much wider scene than that of the strictly religious area of ecumenism. In this mutual commitment to action for justice together, many of us have experienced a new understanding of ecumenism and its values.

By working with women here and at the Council, my perceptions of the injustice of sexism were intensified. My heightened awareness of the issue of the subordinate status of women in church and society had thus already been awakened. Therefore, at the Council I was heartened by the voices of some bishops stating the need to take seriously women and the issues they were raising about themselves. A statement in the Council document, *The Church in the Modern World,* admits the problem of discrimination: "Every type of discrimination . . . whether based on sex, race, . . . is to be overcome and eradicated as contrary to God's intent."[8] Unfortunately, I must add that the promise given by these speeches and texts has yet to be fulfilled. Though it was remarkable that fifteen women were invited as observers to Vatican II, there is no denying our token status.

After Vatican II, I continued to be deeply interested in the problems women face in church and society. But for the decade of the sixties and early seventies, all of us social activists were so occupied with "stopping the war" that the feminist issue was seldom raised. It took the crying out of the "living stones" of active feminists outside the church to awaken us women in the Christian community and to question us. The events of the Women's Ordination Conferences in 1975 and 1978 served as consciousness-raising points for Catholics. The profound mistrust of women which is widespread in the church, and well documented, can only be perceived and then confronted, I believe, in the full context of the liberation of all oppressed peoples. Jesus, as liberator of all the oppressed, again sets the parameters for change.

My growing social awareness was also deepened at this time by an experience with a group of leaders from women's religious communities. Marie Augusta Neal, then teaching at the Harvard Divinity School, was assisting the group to formulate methods of renewal in the light of the developments of Vatican II. For the first time, I heard the expression *structural evil,* and had to learn to explore its meaning in the creating and preserving of an unjust status quo in the social and economic structures of our society. I began to see far-reaching implications for justice in the social documents of the church, and to question my own and the religious communities' indifference in the face of a critical world situation.

Nevertheless, I have been grateful for the messages coming from church sources directed not only to the value of the human person, and of human rights, but also to the urgency of working for justice and against war. In 1971, the Catholic bishops declared in their international synod that "social justice is a constituent element of the Gospel."[9] Further, illustrations from the words of the present Pope, John Paul II, continue this theme. In his first encyclical, March 15, 1979, he said, "Peace comes down to respect for inviolable human rights ... while war springs from the violation of these rights and brings with it still graver violations of them.... We all know well that the areas of misery and hunger on our globe could have been made fertile in a short time if the gigantic investments for armaments at the service of war and destruction had been changed into investments for food at the service of life."[10]

The implications of these strong words have not in large part been translated into action, however. It is my conviction that those who stand within believing communities must continually struggle and speak out so that the investments for armaments may be turned around and converted into investments for peace and better human living.

In the summer of 1970, I went to Vietnam, where I saw at first hand the effects of war in a small Asian country. How could one reconcile the strong and clear implications of the social teachings of the Gospel with the continuation of an obviously futile war?

I had joined a little group of "fact finders" from the American Friends Service Committee and the Fellowship of Reconciliation who had traveled together to Vietnam. We went to ally ourselves with students, press, and other antiwar protesters who were seeking an end to United States involvement. We found ourselves in a land of charming and beautiful people who quickly endeared themselves to us. As we listened to the stories and testimony they presented to us, I had new motivation for protesting a wrongheaded and costly war. And as I marched with the students to present a petition to the U.S. embassy in Saigon, I felt a surge of elation at the opportunity to put words, actions, and prayer together. Looking about me at my fellow marchers, I somehow knew that it was possible, fitting, and right to rank oneself with all those Christians, Buddhists, and others seeking the liberation of persons, especially the powerless. I saw, as I had not seen before, that we are all one people, and that the realized union of all persons in the one God had to come. And I knew this would be possible only if one had a rock to stand on.

VI

My reflections on the Gospel, as I participated more directly in action for peace and justice, consistently affirmed this. In the New Testament, there is indeed a rock image of special significance in Saint Matthew's Gospel: "So then, anyone who hears these words of mine and obeys them is like a wise person who built a house on rock. The rain poured down, the rivers flooded over, and the wind blew hard against that house. But it did not fall, because it was built on rock. But anyone who hears these words of mine and does not obey them is like a foolish one who built a house on sand. The rain poured down, the rivers flooded over, the wind blew hard against that house, and it fell. And what a terrible fall that was!" (Mt. 7:24–27)

The house that stands, Jesus says, is one which so firmly clings to the solid rock of God that it withstands the rains and storms. "Yahweh is the rock of my salvation" (Ps. 18:2). What is this rock if not the place where the contemplative spirit seeks a union of solidarity with the work of justice?

Like a rock to stand on, then, our faith, continually nourished in prayer, keeps before us the sacredness of human life, that sacredness which compels us to defend life in words and deeds. Faith ever reminds us of the mysterious unity between the human person and the Creative Spirit.

As we deepen our reflection on the life and words of Jesus, especially as we ponder the Scriptures, we are drawn forward into a land of questions. Heschel tells us that it is the Bible which questions *us*, not we who question the Bible. And Merton remarks that, in the Bible, one's questions are answered not by clear and definitive answers, but by more pertinent and more crucial questions. In the progress toward understanding, then, one does not go from answer to answer, but from question to question.

As an example, we could consider the questions and contradictions that arise even in our daily prayer. Perhaps we begin with words of adoration and thanksgiving. Are we not blessed beyond measure with the means to live a healthy life, developing the marvelous potential of our gifts? We see both children and adults, like buds opening to the sun, growing into the persons they have the means of becoming. "That you may have life, and have it more abundantly" (Jn. 10:10). So, granting the diminishments present in all our lives, there is room for rejoicing and for thanksgiving. But no sooner have we expressed our gratitude, than our consciousness of world events reveals to us an inescapable truth: our good fortune is the lot of only a small fraction of the people of the earth. For we know that, each day when we rise, the gap between the rich and poor is greater than it was when we went to sleep. We are already being questioned by a sobering contradiction.

Faith tells us that God is manifested in reality. This God is present in the very world where sin, alienation, sorrow, oppression, and suffering are the daily food of powerless and helpless people. Reflection on the Gospel emphasizes the contrast between the new creation set before us by the words of Jesus and the harsh reality of our world.

For, in that new creation, the blind will see, the deaf will hear, the dead will be raised to life, and the poor will hear the Good News. Indeed! Here are the crucial questions, for here is the contradiction. Only when we become aware of the difference between the possibilities to which the Gospel calls us and the unjust world of which we are a part, can our faith really impel us forward toward action.

Recognition of this contradiction will not allow us to ignore what is happening in our world. This world, to quote John Paul II, is one in which "the increasing wealth of the rich has been achieved through the growing impoverishment of the poor."[11] This is a world in which there is not only the distressing gap between the rich and the poor; it is also a world in which rich nations, anxiously protecting their wealth, try to establish "national security" by methods which undermine world security. For this is a world in which superpowers are madly stockpiling towers of nuclear weapons in an act more foolish than the building of the Tower of Babel. And the stones which build the towers are lethal.

Of course, we are understandably frightened at this spectacle and do not want to look at it. It is hard to face what these towers portend; it takes courage to allow this grim vision to enter our quiet hours of contemplation. And yet, is this not what the epiphany of God, revealed in every living, suffering being, means? Is this not what it means to be invited by Scripture to "choose life instead of death" (Dt. 30:19)?

The anti-war movement compelled students to respond because it disclosed a callous disregard for human lives—not only the lives of the people of a small Asian nation, but also their own. The greater potential for human destruction inherent in the nuclear peril makes our meditation on the Scriptures' affirmation of life even more imperative. In the Book of Wisdom, for example, we read, "Death is not God's doing. He takes no pleasure in the extinction of the living. To be: for this he created all" (Wis. 1:13–14).

In the light of biblical reflection on God's valuing of life, how ironic it is that official military code names for various steps in the progressive deployment of nuclear weapons refer to religious symbols honored by Christian tradition. Thus, the world's first nuclear explosion, which took place at Alamogordo, New Mexico, on July 16, 1945, was called "Trinity." On August 6, the traditional day when the liturgy recalls the transfiguration of Christ, another explosion destroyed the city of Hiroshima, killing or wounding most of its people. A third "mother bomb" was exploded at Nagasaki on August 9. Our fourth bomb, completed shortly afterward, started the nuclear weapons stockpile. We know the successions after that.

In recent years, it is this spreading, unseen nuclear arsenal of which we have been largely unaware which increasingly alarms me. Today the United States nuclear cache contains at least thirty-five thousand nuclear warheads. The world total is about twice as great. Continued development and stockpiling of new weapons by the superpowers is the most threatening form of nuclear proliferation, for it implies the capability of destroying civilization.

The free choice of global suicide, made in desperation by world leaders and ratified by the consent and cooperation of their citizens, would be a moral evil whose magnitude defies comprehension. Whether such a choice is made with the highest motives and the most urgent purpose in no way lessens its horror. Neither is its horror lessened if it is made on the gamble that some might escape. The destruction of civilian centers by nuclear annihilation is genocide. How can it be reasonable or right to leave this decision to a largely anonymous power elite that, thanks to our passivity, is driving us all toward ruin? Worse than ruin is this denial of the free choice which is the birthright of persons: their awesome power of saying yes or no. We have to make ourselves heard.

VII

I am reminded that Merton once drew a comparison between wise madness and foolish madness, if we can accept for a moment the paradox of these terms. To the foolish madness of super-powers each building its own Tower of Babel, we must oppose a wise madness which is willing to dissent from the overwhelming current of opinion favoring the construction of such towers, deadly stone by deadly stone. It is hard to see how we can accomplish much by our outcry. Our protest, indeed, will be regarded as mad. But, as Christians and as believing people, we have the resources of faith to give us courage in our resistance. We know that we have a foothold, a firm rock on which to stand, the rock of faith and prayer.

In 1962, Merton wrote some words about standing firmly on such a rock. In that year, he wrote a short essay, addressed to the community of the Sisters of Loretto in Kentucky, neighbors to the Trappist monks at Gethsemani. The occasion was the hundred and fiftieth anniversary of the community's founding. His words are applicable to every Christian or Christian community today: "There is a secret in our Kentucky valley which is a quiet mixture of wisdom and madness. A triumph of hope over despair. . . . When I say there is madness in the old walls of these houses, I mean a wise madness that, in spite of the public approval we have received, persists in the ironic suspicion that *all is not well with the world,* and we cannot be altogether a part of it. . . . We are, of course, engagés in the world of our time. Yet we still have to save ourselves from it, for unless we have a foothold that is not of this world, we will go down with it, and drag no one to safety."[12]

It is striking to discover that, in 1968, in Bangkok, Thailand, in the last formal talk of his life, Merton returned to this image: "If you want to pull a drowning person out of the water, you have to have some support yourself. If you are standing on a rock, you can do it."[13] All the years of contemplation between those two statements must only have confirmed his conviction.

The same is true of all of us. We experience an ever more revealing depth in the words of favorite Scripture passages as the years go on. When I reflect on familiar texts such as "You are my God; in you I trust" (Ps. 91:2), the expression carries a freight of meaning deepening through the years. To think of Yahweh as other than One who is for the suffering, poor, and oppressed is, to me, unfaithful.

I believe that, when seriously undertaken, contemplation and action grow mutually more supportive as they continue to be integrated. Which is to say, contemplation becomes more all-embracing, reaching ever new depths, even as action grows more determined and courageous.

Having built our tower of lethal stones, it was not long until their power was tested. The first victim, as we have seen, was Hiroshima. When I visited there in 1974, the series of pictures and memorials so poignantly presented made a deep impression on me. Among the pathetic relics of that tragic event is a rock—a very special rock. Onto its surface the shadow of a victim's hand is burned. Someone—in August 1945—left us this symbol of dreadful reality. In my view, reflecting on a symbol which points to a deeper meaning is a key element of contemplation leading to action, of contemplation in the midst of action. Often it is the poet or artist who opens the symbol to us. Let us listen, then, to Denise Levertov's poem about the shadow on the rock:

> *. . . the shadow,*
> *the human shadowgraph sinking itself*
> *indelibly upon stone at Hiroshima*
> *as a man, woman or child was consumed*
> *in unearthly fire—*
>   *that shadow*
> *already had been for three days*
> *imprinted upon our lives.*
> *Three decades now we have lived*
> *with its fingers outstretched in horror clinging*
> *to our future, our children's future,*
> *into history or the void.*
> *The shadow's voice*

> *cries out to us to cry out.*
> *Its nails dig*
> > *into our souls*
> > > *to wake them:*
>
> '*Something,*' *it ceaselessly*
> *repeats, its silence*
> *a whisper, its whisper*
> *a shriek,*
> > *while 'the radiant gist'*
> *is lost, and the moral labyrinths of*
> *humankind convulse as if made*
> *of snakes clustered and intertwined and stirring*
> *from long sleep—*
> '... something can yet
> be salvaged upon the earth:
> try, try to survive,
> try to redeem
> the human vision
> from cesspits where human hands
> have thrown it, as I was thrown
> from life into shadow....'[14]

To the profound appeal addressed to us by this poem, what response can we make? And yet, can we avoid response? If contemplation has made us open to the epiphany of God in our world, we will be urged inevitably to respond. "The shadow's voice cries out to us to cry out." What response can we make to those who have been "thrown (by our violence) from life into shadow"?

VIII

Elie Weisel has wisely said that the opposite of love is not hate, but indifference. Perhaps a greater problem than indifference is the paralysis of one's energies caused by a conviction that, when the obstacles are so great and the odds so overpowering, nothing can be done. Discouragement then enervates us and prevents us from moving into action. Young people on college campuses or elsewhere are perhaps more subject to discouragement than others because, of course, they are short on experience and often disheartened by the obstacles envisioned by those who are older. For this reason, they need some success stories, at least some small proof that the risks involved will be worth taking. Like the rest of us, young people need some modest supports for hope as they move into action: some successes, some friends, and some joy.

We should perhaps not be too quick to assign the reasons for student indifference simply to lack of interest or to apathy. The growing diminution of job opportunities, the need to prepare oneself for the forced competition of the marketplace, put unrelenting pressure on the college student. But if the university is a place where there exists some space and time for thought, prayer, and the discerning process, those of us engaged in campus ministry must labor to protect jealously this milieu.

There *are* some success stories in the field of social justice. The national INFACT (Infant Formula Action Coalition), created to combat infant formula abuses, for example, was founded by students at the University of Minnesota. And this group, working against certain multinational corporations' exploitation of Third World people, has built a strong support group across the country.

Several student groups have persuaded university officials to introduce shareholder resolutions to corporations, asking them to disclose facts about investments in South Africa. In Colorado, the Rocky Flats Action Group is a coalition of persons concerned about the local hazard and global threat posed by a plant which makes nuclear bomb triggers; the coalition includes students, professors, environmentalists, and a cross section of persons from the religious/academic community.

The corporate strength of the military-industrial complex is so great that those who work against its power and the increased militarization of the world have to be heartened by minimal successes. They have to learn to be content and even encouraged by the small percentage of company shares which may be voted to support their protest. Because a critical minority has turned the tide on some congressional votes, for example, other victories can be seen as possible.

Recently I represented my religious community in presenting a stockholders' resolution to Rockwell International, operators of Rocky Flats, asking the corporation to cooperate with a citizens' committee reviewing plant operations. On the same day, in Denver, there was a solidarity demonstration to coincide with the stockholders' meeting; and it was good to learn that students were involved with the justice and peace people who organized it. "Aurarians

Against Nukes," an organization from the city's Auraria campus, which comprises three metropolitan colleges/universities, were represented among the group.

Besides seeing examples of success, young people (but also, of course, the rest of us) need to be encouraged that others are working toward the same goals. They need to see that it is an efficient strategy to ally themselves with others—with small or large groups or communities who have been similarly motivated. Some of these are denominational and ecumenical groups; but also there are growing networks across the country built up, for example, by groups such as Mobilization for Survival in the disarmament struggle. These afford no small support. And it is my conviction that prayer and contemplation ought to be and can be a true part of such groups.

IX

In New York City in 1978, I met regularly with the Manhattan Task Force for Disarmament, organized and promoted by dedicated students. At the time of a disarmament demonstration in front of the United Nations, I was present at a special liturgy led by Daniel Berrigan in a crowded apartment living room on New York City's Lower East Side. The group was made up mainly of students and seminarians. As the cup was reverently passed among the students, some of whom would be arrested in a few hours for their nonviolent resistance, I became acutely conscious of the profound connection between heightened prayerful reflection and imminent costly action.

Challenging actions like these demand not only comrades and a sense of success, but also joy. When I asked a campus minister at the University of Colorado recently what interest in justice issues he found across the campus, he told me, "Very few are so interested, though the few are among some of the most committed. I could get only a handful to join me at an anti-nuclear demonstration last fall. However, if we brought a guru from a new religious movement to the campus, we'd fill the hall!" Pictures of young people exultantly singing, eyes closed and arms lifted, are everywhere to be seen in the press. Those of us engaged in campus ministry could help channel such spiritual energy into actions that take issue with the harsh reality of our world.

The stones have to cry out for these young people also. How can consciousness of our corporate and individual responsibility for the oppressed unfold in each person? Could not our joyful celebration of God be related to the satisfaction of taking at least some small steps toward the creating of a more human world? For we do need joy.

In the sober efforts for social justice, when we relate our contemplation to action, can joy be expected? Daniel Berrigan, who has long been an example of action motivated by contemplation, says something about Christian joy: "I believe we were created for ecstasy. And redeemed for it at considerable cost. Certain vagrant, unrepeatable moments of life tell us this, if we will but listen. Such moments, however, are clues to the whole native structure and texture of things: not merely are such glorious fits and starts meant to keep us going, a fairly unattractive idea; but ecstasy fuels and infuses us from the start, our proper distillation and energy of soul."[15]

The poets speak to our hearts. Return to the heart is where contemplation starts, moving back and forth to our center, where our reflection says yes to the action we must take. It is in this spirit that we will know how to respond when the moment comes.

I have written principally of one great threat in our times—the nuclear threat—because I believe it to be the greatest danger in our world. It should be encouraging that the nuclear peril and other urgent problems of our day (women's issues, racism, etc.) have been addressed by some courageous groups, including students. I hope that we as campus ministers, together with at least some students, can take some action, speak some word, be at some place where we can make ourselves heard. Perhaps we cannot do much, but there can be little doubt about the rightness of our action when it comes forth from that center where it has been energized by prayer.

Scripture itself speaks to us: "Come to the Lord, the living stone rejected by us as worthless, but chosen by God as valuable. Come as living stones, and let yourselves be used in building the spiritual temple, where you will offer . . . acceptable sacrifices to God through Jesus Christ" (1 Pet. 2:4–5).

Come as living stones—alive, alert, aware, contemplative, and active. In the quiet and silence of our contemplative moments, never separating the reality of our deepest unity from that of our troubled world, we can perhaps gain some fresh insight into the questions and answers that will keep us alive, alert, aware, ready for whatever action we have thus discerned, so that we may indeed become living stones, acceptable to build a living temple.

NOTES

1. Thomas Merton, *New Seeds of Contemplation* (New York: New Directions, 1972), pp. 1–3.
2. Merton, unpublished manuscript.
3. Merton, *Contemplative Prayer* (Garden City: Doubleday Image Books, 1971), p. 115.
4. Merton, *Opening the Bible* (London: Unwin Books, 1972), pp. 54–55.
5. Abraham Heschel, typescript of "A Conversation with Dr. Abraham Joshua Heschel," National Broadcasting Company, Inc., 1973, p. 4. (This material is copyrighted.)
6. Ibid., *passim.*
7. Proceedings of general assembly, Sisters of Loretto, 1967.
8. Walter M. Abbott, S.J., ed., *The Documents of Vatican II* (New York: America Press, 1966), pp. 227–28.
9. Text of statement from bishops' synod appears in Joseph Gremillion, *The Gospel of Peace and Justice: Catholic Teaching since Pope John* (Maryknoll, N. Y.: Orbis Books, 1976).
10. Pope John Paul II, *Redemptor Hominis* (text available in *Origins,* National Catholic News Service, Washington, D.C., March 22, 1979).
11. Ibid.
12. Merton, *Loretto and Gethsemani* (booklet privately printed), p. 5.
13. Merton, *The Asian Journal* (New York: New Directions, 1975), p. 341.
14. Denise Levertov, *Life in the Forest.* Copyright © 1977 by Denise Levertov. Reprinted by permission of New Directions.
15. Daniel Berrigan, "Priests, Women, Women Priests, and Other Unlikely Recombinants," in *Witness,* July 1979, p. 12.

RESURRECTION AND LIBERATION
An Evangelical Approach to Social Justice

Ronald J. Sider

Billy Graham's alma mater, Wheaton College in Illinois, is one of the nation's best evangelical colleges. In recent decades, it has been conservative in every way—theologically, economically, and politically. But it did not start that way. Its first president, the thoroughly evangelical Jonathan Blanchard, was one of the leading political radicals of the nineteenth century.

Oberlin College is one of the nation's best secular colleges. For many decades, it has been liberal in every way. But it did not start that way either. The leading spirit in its early years was Charles Finney, the most prominent evangelist of the mid-nineteenth century. Finney's Oberlin was a thoroughly evangelical college. It was also vastly more radical socio-politically than the Oberlin of the 1970s.

I believe that the Oberlin of the 1840s and 1850s offers a better model for discerning and doing justice in the 1980s than either Wheaton or Oberlin in the 1970s. Founded in 1835[1] after the Board of Trustees expelled radical abolitionist students from Lane Theological Seminary in Cincinnati, Oberlin College became the major refuge for radical students forced out of campuses all over the country for their anti-slavery views. Almost three hundred students flocked to Oberlin the first year. More came the next. Evangelist Charles Finney, the Billy Graham of the middle decades of the century, was a radical abolitionist who consented to become professor of theology only when he was promised that black students would be admitted.

Oberlin instantly became a hotbed of radical abolitionism. Almost immediately after Oberlin began, students formed the Oberlin Anti-Slavery Society. To the intense resentment of the conservative countryside, Oberlin was a major stop on the underground railroad. When state and federal fugitive slave laws required the return of captured slaves to the South, evangelist Finney and Oberlin's chairman of the Board of Trustees urged and defended civil disobedience. In the dramatic Oberlin-Wellington Rescue Case, which one historian has ranked with the publication of *Uncle Tom's Cabin* in the promotion of abolitionist sentiment, Oberlin's professor of Christian ethics and Oberlin's Sunday school superintendent did just that. Imprisoned for civil disobedience, they taught their ethics class and Sunday school students from a Cleveland jail.

Nor was abolition Oberlin's only concern. Oberlin was the first coeducational college in the world, graduating many of the early feminists. The peace movement was strong. Oberlin promoted educational reforms that encouraged "progressive education that governed by moral principles instead of the rod and the rule."[2]

Social reform, however, was not the exclusive preoccupation of Finney's Oberlin. There were frequent times of revival and college life was intensely religious. Both students and faculty spent their vacations conducting revival meetings. (One sin of which they regularly called sinners to repent was that of slavery.) Within two years, there were six different missionary societies on campus. In their missionary work with American Indians, they also opposed relocation schemes by the government and other violations of treaties! As the dominant influence in the early years, Finney insisted that Oberlin "make the conversion of sinners and the sanctification of Christians the paramount work and subordinate to this all the educational operations."[3] That was the foundation of the school known across the nation for its radical commitment to social justice.

If contemporary Oberlin has lost its evangelical religious foundation (and for that matter a good deal of its radical socio-political critique of the status quo), contemporary Wheaton has lost much of its founder's social passion. While at Oberlin, Wheaton's first president, Jonathan Blanchard, said that "every true member of Christ is a universal reformer whose business it is, so far as possible, to reform all the evils which press on human concerns."[4] Intensely active in the struggle against slavery, Blanchard became the American vice president of the World's Anti-Slavery Convention in London in 1843. Wheaton College's motto, "For Christ and His Kingdom," remains as a haunting memory of Blanchard's activist theology. Blanchard insisted that the kingdom of God preached by Jesus was "a perfect state of society," which although not of this world is certainly *in* it. He warned both against those who "locate Christ's kingdom in the future to the neglect of the present" and those who "construct a local heaven upon earth, . . . thus shutting out the influences and motives of eternity."[5] In the power of Christ, Christians can begin now to live in Christ's new kingdom even though it will come in its fullness only at the eschaton.

The past one hundred years have drastically transformed both Wheaton and Oberlin. In fact, one could write a fascinating, illuminating history of Protestant life and thought in the past century by tracing the slow, steady divergence of these two schools whose religious roots are so similar. One would need to describe "The Great Reversal," in which evangelicals largely lost their social passion in the late nineteenth and early twentieth century.[6] One would need to explore the way that theological liberalism and secularism permeated Oberlin. But that story cannot be told here.

Instead, I want to suggest very briefly where the Oberlin and Wheaton communities stand at the end of the 1970s. Oberlin's social passion, briefly resuscitated in the activist sixties, is now essentially dead. Oberlin's students, like the students of most prestigious (formerly Christian and now secular) colleges and universities, are primarily preoccupied with obtaining a secure niche in the status quo via good grades, which will open the doors of excellent graduate and professional schools. The student Christian organizations long connected with schools like Oberlin have lost their theological foundations and collapsed. In the 1940s, there were several hundred intercollegiate YMCAs; in 1979, there were about twenty-five. Increasingly preoccupied with radical politics, the University Christian Movement disintegrated at the end of the sixties after a brief, tumultuous history.

By contrast, Wheaton and the evangelical community which it symbolizes (scores of evangelical organizations have their national headquarters in the Wheaton area) throb with life. Evangelical campus organizations such as Inter-Varsity Christian Fellowship, Campus Crusade, Young Life, and Youth for Christ, which sprang up in the forties and fifties, are now the dominant Christian student organizations. Inter-Varsity now brings over seventeen thousand students to its triennial missionary convention held at the same place (Urbana, Illinois) where the YMCA, YWCA, and the Student Volunteer Movement used to assemble thousands for their national intercollegiate conferences.

But all is not well. Evangelicals failed to join in any significant way in the search for justice in the 1960s. Confirming Marx's charge that religion can be the opiate of the people, some actually promoted their evangelical student movement, which was largely devoid of significant concern for social justice, as a conservative safeguard against the student activism of the sixties. In spite of some significant exceptions, including a Jonathan Blanchard Society at Wheaton, the majority of students at evangelical colleges are as eager as their secular counterparts to obtain secure niches in the economic status quo.

To be sure, significant countertrends are emerging. John Alexander began *The Other Side,* the first evangelical social justice journal, while teaching philosophy at Wheaton College. When one visits Wheaton today, one quickly senses a new mood of expectant openness to questions of social justice. Probably a third of the campus is involved in some form of Christian service ministry with the elderly, poor, or hungry. *Sojourners* magazine, a widely influential biblical magazine devoted to issues of radical discipleship, community, and justice, began in the early seventies at Trinity Evangelical Divinity School in the Wheaton area. The Chicago Declaration of Evangelical Social Concern (1973)[7] and the statement on social responsibility in the Lausanne Covenant (1974)[8] also indicate that most evangelical leadership has begun to reassert the importance of concern for social justice in a dramatic new way in recent years.[9] But the pilgrimage toward a viable contemporary version of the kind of holistic combination of evangelism, community, and social passion exhibited at evangelical Oberlin in the mid-nineteenth century has only just begun.

I believe that the only solid foundation for campus ministry in the 1980s is a thoroughly biblical—and therefore thoroughly radical—faith. That means that evangelical Christians must confess and correct their heretical neglect of the biblical summons to do justice. That means that liberal Christians must acknowledge and rectify their heretical neglect of evangelism and central biblical doctrines like the deity and resurrection of Jesus Christ. Only if both groups can submit their thinking and programs to the judgment of biblical revelation—and Scripture will indeed judge both with equal severity—is there any hope for faithful Christian campus ministry in the 1980s.

BIBLICAL FOUNDATIONS

What are some of the central biblical foundations for a passionate commitment to the search for justice? I want to develop three theses:

1. In their summons to do justice, the prophets assert that knowing God is inseparable from, although not identical with, doing justice.
2. God is on the side of the poor is one of the central biblical doctrines.
3. The bodily resurrection of Jesus of Nazareth is the indispensable foundation of the Christian hope that justice will ultimately prevail.

That the prophets were centrally concerned with social justice need hardly be argued. "Let justice roll down like waters" (Am. 5:24) is their universal demand (Is. 32:1, 42:1–7). They plead for justice in the courts and in the economic system (Am. 5:10–15; Is. 5:8–15). They insist that God destroys nations, even his chosen people, if they tolerate social injustice (Am. 6:4,7; Is. 1:21–26; Jer. 5:26–29). They see that sin is social as well as personal and condemn participation in unjust social situations just as fiercely as commitment of personal sin.[10]

In fact, commitment to the search for justice is so critical that the prophets insist that one cannot know Yahweh if one does not seek justice. That is not to say, with Latin American liberation theologian José Miranda, that knowing God is nothing more than seeking justice for the poor and oppressed. Miranda says bluntly, "To know Yahweh is to achieve justice for the poor."[11] "The God who does not allow himself to be objectified, because only in the immediate command of conscience is he God, clearly specifies that he is knowable *exclusively* in the cry of the poor and the weak who seek justice."[12] Tragically, it is precisely Miranda's kind of one-sided, reductionist approach that offers comfortable North Americans a plausible excuse for ignoring the radical biblical word that seeking justice for the poor is inseparable from—even though it is not identical with—knowing Yahweh.

Jeremiah announced God's harsh message that King Jehoiakim did not know Yahweh and would be destroyed because of his injustice:

Woe to him who builds his house by unrighteousness,
and his upper rooms by injustice;
who makes his neighbor serve him for nothing,
and does not give him his wages; . . .
Did not your father eat and drink
and do justice and righteousness?
Then it was well with him.
He judged the cause of the poor and needy;
then it was well.
Is not this to know me?
Says the Lord. (Jer. 22:13–16)

Knowing God necessarily involves seeking justice for the poor and needy (cf. also Hos. 2:19–20; Is. 11:1–9). It is simply not possible truly to know the God of the Bible if one refuses to participate in the search for justice.

My second thesis is that the teaching that God is on the side of the poor is a central biblical doctrine. To say that God is on the side of the poor is *not* to say that material poverty is a biblical ideal; or that the poor and oppressed are, because they are poor and oppressed, to be included in the church; or that God cares more about the salvation of the poor than the salvation of the rich. But it does mean several specific things:[13]

1. At the central points of revelation history, God also acted to liberate the poor and oppressed.
2. God acts in history to exalt the poor and oppressed and to cast down the rich and oppressive.
3. God's people, if they are truly God's people, are also on the side of the poor and oppressed.

First, the three central points of revelation history: the exodus, the destruction of Israel and Judah, and the Incarnation. At the central moments when God displayed his mighty acts in history to reveal his nature and will, God also intervened to liberate the poor and oppressed.

God displayed his power at the exodus not just to keep his promises to Abraham and call forth a chosen people, but also to free oppressed slaves! When God called Moses at the burning bush, he informed Moses that his intention was to end suffering and injustice: "I have seen the affliction of my people who are in Egypt, and have heard their cry because of their taskmasters; I know their sufferings, and I have come down to deliver them out of the hand of the Egyp-

tians" (Ex. 3:7–8; cf. also Dt. 26:5ff.). We distort the biblical interpretation of the momentous event of the exodus unless we see that,
at this pivotal point, the Lord of the universe was at work correcting
oppression and liberating the poor.

The prophets' explanation for the destruction of Israel and then
Judah underlines the same point. The explosive message of the
prophets is that God destroyed Israel not just because of idolatry
(although certainly because of that), but also because of economic
exploitation and mistreatment of the poor (e.g., Am. 5:10–15, 6:1–7,
7:11; Jer. 5:26–29).

When God acted to reveal himself most completely in the incarnation, he continued to demonstrate his special concern for the poor
and oppressed. Saint Luke used the account of Jesus in the synagogue at Nazareth to give a programmatic definition to Jesus' mission. Jesus read from the prophet Isaiah:

> *The Spirit of the Lord is upon me,*
> *because he has anointed me to preach good news to the poor.*
> *He has sent me to proclaim release to the captives*
> *and recovery of sight to the blind,*
> *to set at liberty those who are oppressed,*
> *to proclaim the acceptable year of the Lord. (Lk. 4:18–19)*

After reading these words, he informed the audience that this Scripture was now fulfilled in himself. The mission of the Incarnate One
was to preach good news to the poor and free the oppressed.

Many people spiritualize these words either by simplistically assuming that he was talking about healing blinded hearts in captivity
to sin or by appealing to the later Old Testament and intertestamental idea of "the poor of Yahweh" (the *'anawim*). It is true that
the latter Psalms and the intertestamental literature use the terms for
the poor (especially *'anawim*) to refer to pious, humble, devout Israelites who place all their trust in Yahweh.[14] But that does not mean
that this usage had no connection with socioeconomic poverty. Indeed, it was precisely the fact that the economically poor and oppressed were the faithful remnant that trusted in Yahweh that led to
the new usage where the words for the poor also designated the
pious faithful.[15]

Jesus lived what he taught. He spent more of his time with the
poor in the cultural and economic backwater of Galilee than with

the rich and powerful in Jerusalem. He healed the sick. He spent time with oppressed women. And he warned his disciples in the strongest language that those who do not feed the hungry and clothe the naked will experience eternal damnation (Mt. 25:31–46). At the supreme moment of history when God Himself took on human flesh, we see the God of Israel still at work liberating the poor and oppressed and summoning his people to do the same.

The second aspect of the biblical teaching that God is on the side of the poor and oppressed is that God works in history to cast down the rich and exalt the poor (e.g., Lk. 1:46–53; Jas. 5:1). Why? Precisely because, according to Scripture, the rich often become wealthy by oppressing the poor or because they fail to feed the hungry.

James warned the rich of impending misery because they had cheated their workers (Jas. 5:3–5). Long before the days of James, Jeremiah knew that the rich were often rich because of oppression.

> *Wicked men are found among my people;*
>   *they lurk like fowlers lying in wait.*
> *They set a trap;*
>   *they catch men.*
> *Like a basket full of birds,*
>   *their houses are full of treachery;*
> *therefore they have become great and rich,*
>   *They have grown fat and sleek.*
> *They have known no bounds in deeds of wickedness;*
>   *they judge not with justice*
> *the cause of the fatherless to make it prosper,*
>   *and they do not defend the rights of the needy.*
> *Shall I not punish them for these things:*
>   *says the Lord.*
>
> (Jer. 5:26–29)

Isaiah (3:14ff.), Hosea (12:7–8), Micah (6:9–12), Ezekiel (22:23–29) and Amos (8:4–8) all repeat the same point. Because the rich oppress the poor and weak, the Lord of history is at work pulling down their houses and kingdoms.

Sometimes Scripture does not charge the rich with direct oppression of the poor. It simply accuses them of failure to share with the needy (e.g., Ezek. 16:49–50). But the result is the same.

The third aspect of the biblical teaching that God is on the side of the poor and oppressed is that the people of God, if they are really the people of God, are also on the side of the poor and oppressed. Those who neglect the poor and the oppressed are not really God's people at all—no matter how frequent their religious rituals or how orthodox their creeds and confessions. The prophets sometimes made this point by insisting, as we have already seen, that knowledge of God and seeking justice for the oppressed are inseparable. At other times they condemned the religious rituals of the oppressors who tried to worship God and still continue to oppress the poor. Worship in the context of mistreatment of the poor and disadvantaged is an outrage against God (Is. 58:3–7, 1:10–17; Am. 5:21–24).

Nor has God changed. Jesus repeated the same prophetic warning against those who try to mix pious practices and mistreatment of the poor (Mk. 12:38–40). The prophetic word against religious hypocrites raises an extremely difficult question. Are the people of God truly God's people if they oppress the poor? Is the church really the church if it does not work to free the oppressed?

God declared through the prophet Isaiah that the people of Israel were really Sodom and Gomorrah rather than the people of God (Is. 1:10). God simply could not tolerate their idolatry and their exploitation of the poor and disadvantaged any longer. Jesus was even more blunt and sharp. To those who do not feed the hungry, clothe the naked, and visit the prisoners, he will speak a terrifying word at the final judgment: "Depart from me, you cursed, into the eternal fire prepared for the devil and his angels" (Mt. 25:41). Jesus intends his disciples to imitate his own special concern for the poor and needy. Those who disobey will experience eternal damnation.

Lest we forget the warning, 1 John repeats it: "But if any one has the world's goods and sees his brother in need, yet closes his heart against him, how does God's love abide in him? Little children, let us not love in word or speech but in deed and truth" (3:17–18; cf. also, Jas. 2:14–17). Regardless of what we do or say at eleven A.M. Sunday morning, those who neglect the poor and oppressed are not the people of God.

But still the question persists. Are professing believers no longer Christians because of continuing sin? Obviously not. The Christian knows that sinful selfishness continues to plague even the most saintly. We are justified by faith, not our good works.

That response is extremely important and very true. But it is also inadequate. All the texts from both testaments which we have just surveyed surely mean more than that the people of God are disobedient (but still justified all the same) when they neglect the poor. These verses pointedly assert that some people so disobey God that they are not his people at all in spite of their pious profession. Neglect of the poor is one of the oft-repeated biblical signs of such disobedience. Certainly none of us would claim that we fulfill Matthew 25 perfectly. And we cling to the hope of forgiveness. But there comes a point—and, thank God, He alone knows where—when neglect of the poor is no longer forgiven. It is punished.

In light of the central biblical teaching that God is on the side of the poor, how faithful is the Christian church? Frankly, I am not sure that large numbers of Christians of *any* theological orientation have imitated God's special concern for the poor. Certainly, evangelicals must confess that we have been very unbiblical at this point. The evangelical community is largely on the side of the rich oppressors rather than the oppressed poor. Imagine what would happen if all evangelical campus organizations, colleges and seminaries, would dare to undertake a comprehensive two-year examination of their total program and activity to answer this question: is there the same balance and emphasis on justice for the poor and oppressed in our programs as there is in Scripture? I am willing to predict that, if we did that with an unconditional readiness to change whatever did not correspond with the scriptural revelation of God's special concern for the poor and oppressed, we would unleash a new movement of biblical social concern that would change the course of modern history.

But our problem is not primarily one of ethics. It is not that we have failed to live what our teachers have taught. Our theology itself has been unbiblical and therefore heretical. James Cone is right when he says:

Theologians of the Christian Church have not interpreted Christian ethics as an act for the liberation of the oppressed because their views of divine revelation were defined by philosophy and other cultural values rather than by the biblical theme of God as the liberator of the oppressed. . . . We cannot say that Luther, Calvin, Wesley and other prominent representatives of the church's traditions were limited by their time, as if their ethical judgements on oppression did not affect the essential truth of their theologies. They were wrong ethically because they were wrong *theologically*. They were wrong theologically because they failed to listen to the Bible.[16]

By largely ignoring the central biblical teaching that God is on the side of the poor, evangelical theology has been profoundly unorthodox. The Bible has just as much to say about this doctrine as it does about Jesus' resurrection. And yet we evangelicals insist on the resurrection as a criterion of orthodoxy and largely ignore the equally prominent biblical teaching that God is on the side of the poor and the oppressed.

Now please do not misunderstand me at this point. As the next section will demonstrate, I am not saying that the resurrection is unimportant. The bodily resurrection of Jesus of Nazareth is absolutely central to Christian faith and anyone who denies it has abandoned a central tenet of Christian faith. But if centrality in Scripture is any criterion of doctrinal importance, then the biblical teaching that God is on the side of the poor also ought to be an extremely important doctrine for Christians.

I am afraid that evangelicals have also fallen into theological liberalism. Of course we usually think of theological liberalism in terms of classical nineteenth-century liberals who denied the deity, the atonement, and the bodily resurrection of Jesus. And that is correct. People who abandon those central biblical doctrines have fallen into heresy. But notice what the methodological essence of theological liberalism is—it is allowing our thinking and living to be shaped by the surrounding society's views and values rather than by biblical revelation. Liberal theologians thought that belief in the deity of Jesus Christ and his bodily resurrection was incompatible with a modern scientific world view.[17] So they followed the surrounding "scientific" society rather than Scripture.

Evangelicals rightly called attention to this heresy—and then tragically made exactly the same move in another area. We have allowed the values of our affluent, materialistic society to shape our thinking and acting toward the poor. It is much easier in evangelical circles today to insist on an orthodox Christology than to insist on the biblical teaching that God is on the side of the poor. We have allowed our theology to be shaped by the economic preferences of our materialistic contemporaries rather than by Scripture. And that is to fall into theological liberalism. We have not been nearly as orthodox as we have claimed.

Past failure, however, is no reason for despair. I think we mean it when we sing, "I'd rather have Jesus than houses or lands." I think we mean it when we write and affirm doctrinal statements that boldly declare that we will not only believe, but also live whatever Scripture teaches. But if we do mean it, then we must teach and live, in a world full of injustice and starvation, the important biblical doctrine that God and his faithful people are on the side of the poor and oppressed. Unless we drastically reshape both our theology and our entire institutional church life so that the fact that God is on the side of the poor and oppressed becomes as central to evangelical theology and evangelical institutional programs as it is in Scripture, we will demonstrate to the world that our verbal commitment to *sola scriptura* is a dishonest ideological support for an unjust materialistic status quo.

My third thesis is that the bodily resurrection of the carpenter from Nazareth is the indispensable cornerstone of the Christian hope for ultimate justice and *shalom.* To understand the grounds for this assertion, we must recall Jesus' historical context. In the intertestamental period, apocalyptic thought—which divided world history into the Old Age (the present) of evil and injustice and a coming New Age of *shalom* and justice—became widespread among Jews. Most Jews longed for the days of the coming Messiah who would throw off the yoke of the oppressive Romans and bring justice and wholeness to the poor, sick, and oppressed.[18] In a dramatic, supernatural convulsion, the Old Age would end and the Messiah would inaugurate the New Age by destroying the wicked, resurrecting the dead, and pouring out God's Spirit on all who were part of the New Age.

It was into this charged religious atmosphere that Jesus came announcing the welcome news that the expected messianic kingdom was beginning in his person and work. He ministered to the poor, sick, and oppressed in keeping with Jewish messianic expectation. But he disappointed popular hopes when he failed to lead the crusade against Roman imperialism and, instead, summoned his followers to love their enemies, even Roman oppressors. Even worse, he offended the scribes and Pharisees by freely forgiving sinners, even claiming personal divine authority to forgive sins (Mk. 2:6–12). Jewish leaders accused him of blasphemy and the Roman establishment crucified him, as they did all messianic pretenders, as a political threat to Roman imperialism. Jesus had failed.

Almost immediately, however, his disciples began informing anyone who would listen that Jesus was alive. They said that God had raised him from the dead to demonstrate that Jesus had indeed been the long-expected Messiah. They believed that the Jewish view of history had been fundamentally altered. Even though the Old Age continued with the coming of the Messiah, the New Age had decisively broken into the old aeon. Jesus' resurrection and the gift of the Holy Spirit at Pentecost were decisive evidence that the New Age had begun, and that all people should therefore now begin to live in the new messianic kingdom of Jesus' disciples. By raising Jesus from the dead, God had won the decisive victory over the Old Age's evil and injustice. Certainly that victory was not complete, for the Old Age continued. But the resurrection was decisive evidence that the total victory would surely come when the Resurrected One returned to usher in ultimate *shalom.*

What is to be said of this astonishing early Christian vision? Is it one that critical collegians can share at the end of the twentieth century? To answer that, we need to review more carefully the central elements of the thesis just sketched.

What was the message of the carpenter from Nazareth?[19] Saint Luke answered that question with his programmatic account of the dramatic encounter in the synagogue at Nazareth at the beginning of Jesus' public ministry (Lk. 4:16–30). In recent years there has been lively debate over whether Jesus' reading from Isaiah 61:1 contained a conscious reference to the year of Jubilee.[20] (According to Leviticus 25, every fiftieth year was to be a year of Jubilee when slaves were freed and all land was returned to the original owners or their descendants without compensation.) A recent dissertation completed at the University of Basel by Robert Sloan has broken important new ground.[21] Sloan uses a Qumran text which comes from roughly the same time as Jesus, that links the Jubilee passage of Leviticus 25 and the sabbatical release of debts of Deuteronomy 15 with Isaiah 61:1. Furthermore, the Qumran text gives the Isaiah passage a specific Jubilee interpretation. Equally important, all three texts are placed in an eschatological perspective. Thus the Qumran text expects the economic and social reordering described in Leviticus 25, Deuteronomy 15, and Isaiah 61 to occur when the Messiah ushers in the New Age. In fact, Sloan has discovered that, in Jewish literature, the Jubilee text is almost always placed in an eschatological context.[22]

Luke 4:16ff. would seem to demand a similar interpretation. This means that, at the heart of Jesus' message, was the announcement that the messianic age of eschatological expectation was beginning in his life and ministry. ("Today this scripture has been fulfilled in your hearing."—v. 21) Right at the heart of Jesus' conception of the new messianic age was the special concern for the poor, the release of captives and liberation of the oppressed called for in the Jubilee. The New Age which he saw himself inaugurating had specific, radical economic and social content.

New Testament scholars have increasingly recognized that Jesus' announcement of the eschatological kingdom had both present and future elements. Scholars such as W. G. Kummel and George Ladd have demonstrated the inadequacy of both consistent eschatology (Schweitzer, etc.), which discarded or distorted the texts which speak of the kingdom being present in Jesus' life and work, and realized eschatology (Dodd, etc.), which largely ignored the texts which speak of the kingdom as still future.[23] Jesus taught that the messianic age had already broken into the present in himself (e.g., Lk. 11:20), but he expected its completion to occur in the future.

That the eschatological Jubilee was central to Jesus' thought and work is also suggested by other passages. When John the Baptist sent two disciples to ask if Jesus was the expected one, Jesus responded with words that alluded to Isaiah 61:1: "Go and tell John what you have seen and heard: The blind receive their sight, the lame walk, lepers are cleansed, and the deaf hear, the dead are raised up, the poor have good news preached to them" (Lk. 7:22). In the sermon in Luke 6:20ff., Jesus pronounced a blessing on the poor and hungry and promised that, in the New Age, they would be satisfied. Conversely, the rich and full would experience a woeful reversal (vv. 24–25). Drawing on Deuteronomy 15, he commanded his followers to live by the standards of the dawning messianic age and make loans, expecting nothing in return (v. 35).

Jesus' cleansing of the temple fits perfectly into this inauguration of the messianic Jubilee. Outraged that the wealthy priestly aristocracy was collecting huge sums from their monopolistic sale of animals for sacrifice, Jesus called their economic practices robbery: "My house shall be a house of prayer, but you have made it a den of robbers" (Lk. 19:46). And he drove them out. This was not armed revolution. But it was a dramatic act of civil disobedience designed to protest the misuse of the Temple to enrich the leading priestly families.[24] It is hardly surprising that the Sadducees and priestly aristocracy considered a person who announced and acted out such a radical call for socioeconomic change to be highly dangerous. Hence, they moved promptly to destroy him (Lk. 19:47). Within a few days, they had him arrested and turned over to the Roman governor as a dangerous revolutionary. One reason Jesus got crucified then was that he began to live out the kind of radical socioeconomic reordering expected when the Messiah would inaugurate the Jubilee.

But it would be a gross distortion to suggest that Jesus was crucified *merely* because he offended the wealthy establishment with radical socioeconomic proposals. He called people to live out the vision of the Jubilee precisely because the messianic age had begun in his own person and work. I am not unaware, of course, that considerable modern scholarship has denied that Jesus made any messianic claims. But I agree with Martin Hengel that the "thesis of a totally unmessianic Jesus has led a major portion of German New Testament studies along a false trail."[25] He took the term "Son of Man" from the eschatological expectation of a heavenly messianic figure and used it as his favorite self-designation. He clearly and explicitly set aside Mosaic teaching and placed himself above Moses with his bold, "You have heard that it was said, but I say to you" (Mt. 5:21-48). Thus he called into question the Torah that "to the Jew was identical with the law of the world, indeed with the cosmic order of the universe [and] that guaranteed Israel's election and right to dominion."[26]

Indeed, he went even further. He claimed the authority to forgive sins, which, as the Jewish bystanders immediately recognized, was a prerogative of God alone (Mk. 2:6-7). And at his trial, when they asked him if he was the Messiah, the Son of God, he said, "I am; and you will see the Son of Man sitting at the right hand of Power and coming in the clouds of heaven" (Mk. 14:62).[27] It is hardly surprising that monotheistic Jews charged him with blasphemy.

The Roman rulers, however, reserved for themselves the authority to mete out capital punishment. Hence, the Jewish authorities could not execute Jesus even though the Torah prescribed death for blasphemy. But since messianic pretenders were a clear political danger to Roman imperialism, Pilate was willing to crucify

Jesus on the *political* charge that he claimed to be the king of the Jews.

What an astounding person this Nazarene carpenter had been! He had gone about the country tenderly ministering to the poor, sick, and oppressed. He had announced that the messianic age had broken into the present. Therefore, he had said, the people of God should begin living out the eschatological Jubilee and transform the whole economic order. He had claimed to be the long-expected Messiah and had said he would usher in his kingdom with love (even for enemies) rather than the sword. Indeed, he had gone even further, setting his own personal authority above that of Moses, claiming divine authority to forgive sins and acknowledging that he was the Son of God. What an utterly astounding person. What fantastically exciting good news—if it was really true. What offensive megalomania and breathtaking blasphemy if it was false.

And then he died on a cross. He suffered the most despicable death possible. Paul's quotation from the Torah, "Cursed be everyone who hangs on a tree" (Dt. 21:23; Gal. 3:13), expressed the Jewish viewpoint. As for the brutally efficient Romans, they knew how to put down political threats. They regularly crucified political criminals, especially the constant stream of rebellious Jewish messianic pretenders. And it worked, too. Crucifixion had a decisive way of squelching messianic megalomaniacs. Jesus was finished. Perhaps the disciples and some of the poor masses had begun to fathom a little of Jesus' fantastic vision and claims. But the Roman and Jewish establishment did not believe such nonsense for a moment. And they killed him to prove they were right. German theologian Jürgen Moltmann is surely correct in insisting that the cross decisively destroyed the credibility of Jesus' message and claims.

He who proclaimed that the kingdom was near died abandoned by God. He who anticipated the future of God in miracles and in casting out demons, died helpless on the cross. He who revealed the righteousness of God with an authority greater than Moses, died according to the provision of the law as a blasphemer. He who spread the love of God in his fellowship with the poor and the sinners met his end between two criminals on the cross. . . . For the disciples who had followed Jesus to Jerusalem, his shameful death was not the consummation of his obedience to God nor a demonstration of martyrdom for his truth, but the rejection of his claim. It did not confirm their hopes in him, but permanently destroyed them.[28]

And then he rose from the dead!

But can an honest, modern intellectual believe that claim? Many people think not. They think that the use of modern science has made belief in alleged miracles like Jesus' resurrection an outdated superstition which only naive prescientific folk could accept.[29] Considerable New Testament scholarship supports this skepticism.[30] I am convinced, however, that this skeptical conclusion rests on intellectual confusion. It is sheer nonsense to suppose that more and more precise scientific data about the way nature regularly works can tell us whether or not there is a God who transcends natural processes, who might intervene in nature if he so chose.[31] Similar confusion reigns in much writing on the relationship between historical methodology and alleged miracles.[32] The most objective approach for the historian is not to assume either that miracles cannot happen or that they can. Instead, each instance of alleged miracle must be evaluated carefully on the basis of the evidence available in that particular case.

The evidence for Jesus' resurrection is surprisingly strong.[33] Of the many points that are often made, I will briefly mention four: (1) the change in the discouraged disciples; (2) the empty tomb; (3) the fact that the first witnesses were women; and (4) the very early evidence in 1 Corinthians 15.

What gave rise to the "resurrection faith" and the disciples' willingness to risk their lives to spread it? Professor Reginald H. Fuller, formerly of New York's Union Theological Seminary, has underlined the fact that this total transformation demands explanation: "Even the most skeptical historian has to postulate an 'X', as M. Dibelius called it, to account for the complete change in the behavior of the disciples, who at Jesus' arrest had fled and scattered to their own homes, but who in a few weeks were found boldly preaching their message to the very people who had sought to crush the movement launched by Jesus."[34] If one rejects the New Testament explanation that Jesus arose and appeared to his disciples, one is left with the extremely difficult task of proposing other grounds adequate to explain the dramatic transformation of very discouraged people. The late Professor Robert Grant of the University of Chicago has said, "The origin of Christianity is almost incomprehensible unless such an event took place."[35]

There have been a number of attempts to explain the empty tomb.

The old one of the theft is no longer accepted. It has been suggested that Joseph of Arimathea, or the Romans, or the Jewish leaders, removed the body before the women arrived; but, if so, the Jewish leaders would obviously have conducted guided tours to the real burial place as soon as the disciples claimed Jesus had arisen.

In his discussion of Jesus' resurrection, the prominent German theologian Wolfhart Pannenberg quotes Paul Althaus to underline this point:

> Paul Althaus has rightly seen this point: "In Jerusalem, the place of Jesus' execution and grave, it was proclaimed not long after his death that he had been raised. The situation *demands* that within the circle of the first community one had a reliable testimony for the fact that the grave had been found empty." The resurrection kerygma "could not have been maintained in Jerusalem for a single day, for a single hour, if the emptiness of the tomb had not been established as a fact for all concerned."[36]

Both the Christians and their Jewish opponents agreed that the tomb was empty.

The fact that women were the first people to visit the tomb and allegedly see the Risen Jesus speaks in favor of the authenticity of the accounts. Professor Moule[37] of Cambridge has recently pointed out that women were notoriously invalid witnesses according to Jewish principles of evidence. Hence, if the early Christians had made up the accounts of the first visit to the tomb and the first meeting with the Risen Jesus, they would certainly have claimed that men were the first witnesses. The best explanation for the priority of the women is that it actually happened that way.

The oldest evidence for the resurrection is in 1 Corinthians 15:3–7. Many scholars have pointed out that the words used in verse 3 (*delivered* and *received*) are the technical terms used to refer to the careful handing down of oral tradition.[38] Paul apparently taught this to all the churches. Furthermore, Paul says he received it, presumably, soon after he became a Christian just a few years after Jesus' death. That means that this witness to Jesus' resurrection received a fixed form very soon after the actual events.

As a historian, I find the evidence surprisingly strong. The most unbiased historical conclusion is that Jesus was probably alive on the third day.

It was the resurrection which dramatically transformed the life and thought of the discouraged disciples. Everywhere in the New Testament it is clear that it was the resurrection which convinced the discouraged disciples that Jesus' claims and his announcement of the messianic kingdom were still valid. Jewish eschatological expectation looked for a general resurrection at the beginning of the New Age. As the early Christians reflected on Jesus' resurrection, they realized that one instance of this eschatological resurrection had actually occurred in the Old Age. Thus they referred to Jesus' resurrection as the first fruits (1 Cor. 15:20–23) of that final general resurrection. Jesus' resurrection, then, was decisive evidence that the New Age had truly invaded the Old. Jesus of Nazareth was now called Jesus Christ (Jesus the Messiah) because his resurrection was powerful evidence that his messianic claims were valid.

Indeed, even more lofty titles seemed appropriate after his resurrection. Throughout Acts and the Epistles, it is clear that the resurrection was the decisive demonstration that convinced the disciples that Jesus was truly the Son of God (Rom. 1:4; Acts 2:22–26). The word *kurios* (Lord), used in the Greek translation of the Old Testament to translate the word *Yahweh,* now became one of the most frequently used titles for the man from Nazareth. In Philippians 2, Paul applied to Jesus the words from Isaiah which the monotheistic prophet had used for Yahweh. After mocking the idols, Yahweh insisted that he alone was God: "To me every knee shall bow, every tongue shall swear" (Is. 45:23). Paul took those words from the mouth of Yahweh and applied them to Jesus, declaring that "at the name of Jesus every knee should bow, in heaven and on earth and under the earth, and every tongue confess that Jesus Christ is Lord" (Phil. 2:10–11).

Since the crucified carpenter is now the Risen Lord of the Universe, the Christian will submit every area of his or her life—including economics and politics—to his Lordship. Since the Risen Lord is the one who proclaimed the radical socioeconomic reordering of the Jubilee, the Christian will demand fundamental structural change. Since the Risen Lord is the one who revealed most fully the fact that God is on the side of the poor and oppressed, the Christian will work for a radical restructuring of the present unjust relationships between scarred inner city and pleasant suburb, between blacks and whites, between rich and poor nations. Since the resurrection is a sure sign that the new messianic age has invaded this old aeon, the

Christian will exhibit a holy dissatisfaction with every evil and injustice of every status quo. And, since the resurrection has confirmed the fact that Jesus' nonviolent way of loving enemies is not naive utopianism but a realistic modeling of the *shalom* of the coming kingdom, the Christian will engage in a costly confrontation with systemic injustice which is as radically persistent in its demand for change as it is gently loving in its approach to oppressors. The Christian will demonstrate the courage to risk all for the sake of freedom and liberation for God's poor since the final word is not death but resurrection.

The resurrected Lord Jesus offers both inner strength for the weary struggle now and also a secure foundation for our hope of ultimate transformation. The rapid disappearance of student activism at the end of the sixties and the hasty rush to join the establishment underlines the need for something more than an ephemeral social mood as the foundation for commitment to fundamental social change. Nothing can more securely anchor a doggedly persistent commitment to the struggle for justice than the revolutionary regenerating presence of the Risen Jesus in one's life. Saint Paul says that Christians die to their old selves and are raised to a new life in Christ (Rom. 6:1ff.). The same supernatural power of God that raised Jesus from the dead now blows through our formerly timid, fearful personalities. It is in the power of the resurrection that we go forth boldly to join the oppressed of the earth in their costly confrontation with the oppressor.

The resurrection also anchors our hope. Repeatedly, the New Testament promises that what happened to Jesus at his resurrection will also happen to those who believe in him at the final resurrection (Phil. 3:20–21; 1 Jn. 3:2). Nor is this merely an individualistic hope. Saint Paul also indicates that, just as the individual Christian will experience the resurrection of the body, so the whole creation will be purged of evil and decay and injustice and will experience total transformation (Rom. 8:18–25). Because of the resurrection, we know that this whole fantastic creation will ultimately be freed from its bondage to decay and will obtain the glorious liberty of the children of God.

As long as one does not spiritualize it in a way foreign to the New Testament, the doctrine of the resurrection reaffirms the doctrine of creation. This earth is not an illusion to be escaped. It is a good gift which will be restored to its original splendor. The bodily resurrection rescues us from Gnosticism.

The resurrection, in fact, provides the best clue about the relationship between our work for peace and justice now and the perfect *shalom* of the coming kingdom. There is both continuity and discontinuity between our work now and the coming kingdom, just as there was continuity and discontinuity between Jesus of Nazareth and the Risen Lord Jesus. The continuity is crucial. It was Jesus of Nazareth who was raised on the third day. It was not some spiritual resurrection in the confused minds of befuddled disciples. It was the man from Nazareth who arose bodily from the tomb and appeared to talk and eat with his discouraged, frightened followers.[39] But there was also discontinuity. The Risen Jesus was no longer subject to death and decay. His resurrected body could do things we do not understand in our space-time continuum.

I believe there is the same continuity and discontinuity between culture and history as we know it and the coming kingdom. Certainly, there is discontinuity. We will not create more and more just societies until we awake some century and discover that the millennium has arrived. Dreadful imperfection will remain in persons and societies until our Risen Lord Jesus returns at the Parousia to usher in the final consummation. But there is also continuity. The New Age is best described, according to Scripture, as a new *earth* and a new *city* (Rev. 21:1ff.). It is *this* groaning creation that will be restored to wholeness. The tree of life in the New Jerusalem is for the healing of the *nations*. The kings of the earth will bring their glory and honor into the Holy City (Rev. 21:22–27).

So we work for justice and peace now, not with a naive optimism that forgets that faithfulness involves the cross, but with the solid assurance that the final word is resurrection. We have a secure faith anchored in the reality of Jesus' resurrection and a solid hope fixed on the Resurrected One's ultimate restoration of the broken beauty of creation. Anchored by that faith and hope and swept along by the pulsating power of the Risen Lord Jesus in our lives, we dare to submit ourselves to the Risen One who calls us to costly struggle for peace through justice.

What would happen if that kind of perspective permeated campus ministry in the 1980s? A holistic biblical approach would replace the one-sided perspectives and limited emphases that have tragically weakened all streams of campus ministry in the last few decades.

I dream of a new movement of campus ministry in the eighties— an evangelistic movement that gently and forthrightly invites non-Christians into a living personal relationship with Jesus Christ; a Spirit-filled movement that exhibits a radical dependence on the Holy Spirit; a praying movement that immerses all its activity in much prayer; a reconciled movement that has so visibly transcended the Old Age's sinful divisions of race, class, and sex that its common life is a powerful sign of the Risen Lord's coming kingdom; a radical movement of social justice that challenges every injustice of the status quo and dares to call for sweeping structural change because it knows that, ultimately, in God's good time, the kingdoms of this world shall indeed become the kingdom of our Lord.

NOTES

1. The following sketch of Oberlin and Wheaton depends largely on Donald W. Dayton, *Discovering an Evangelical Heritage* (New York: Harper and Row, 1976), chaps. 1, 2, 4, 5. See also Timothy L. Smith, *Revivalism and Social Reform* (New York: Harper Torchbooks, 1957). For additional works, see the bibliographies in Dayton and Smith. For a comparative study of Wheaton and Knox Colleges, see Thomas A. Askew, "The Liberal Arts College Encounters Intellectual Change: A Comparative Study of Education at Knox and Wheaton Colleges, 1837–1925 (Ph.D. dissertation, Northwestern University, 1969).

2. Quoted in Dayton, *Discovering an Evangelical Heritage,* p. 42.

3. Quoted in ibid., p. 39. For statistical analysis which demonstrates the effect of Finney's revivalism on social views, see John L. Hammond, "Revival Religion and Anti-Slavery Politics," in *American Sociological Review* 39 (1974): 175–86; and John L. Hammond, *The Politics of Benevolence: Revival Religion and American Voting Behavior* (Norwood, N.J.: Abley Publishing Co., 1979).

4. Quoted in Dayton, *Discovering an Evangelical Heritage,* p. 9.

5. Quoted in ibid., p. 10.

6. See David M. Moberg, *The Great Reversal: Evangelism and Social Concern,* rev. ed. (Philadelphia: J. B. Lippincott, 1977).

7. See Ronald J. Sider, *The Chicago Declaration* (Carol Stream, Ill.: Creation House, 1974), pp. 1–42, for the text and an analysis of the occasion. An ongoing organization, Evangelicals for Social Action (P.O. Box 4285, Philadelphia, PA 19144) has resulted.

8. For the Lausanne Covenant and the papers, see J. D. Douglas, ed., *Let the Earth Hear His Voice: International Congress on World Evangelization, Lausanne, Switzerland* (Minneapolis: World Wide Publications, 1975).

9. For the resurgence of evangelical social concern, see, in addition to the journals, *The Other Side* and *Sojourners,* Robert D. Linder, "The Resurgence of Evangelical Social Concern (19275–75)," in *The Evangelicals,* ed. David F. Wells and John D. Woodbridge (Nashville: Abingdon, 1975), pp. 189ff.; Richard Quebedeaux, *The Young Evangelicals* (New York: Harper, 1974); *Union Seminary Quarterly Review* 32, no. 2 (Winter 1977) and *Explor* 2, no. 2 (Fall 1976); Jeremy Rifkin and Ted Howard, *The Emerging Order: The Economic Transformation and the Second Protestant Reformation* (New York: Putnam, 1979), section 2.

10. See Ronald J. Sider, *Rich Christians in an Age of Hunger: A Biblical Study* (Downers Grove, Ill.: Inter-Varsity Press and Ramsey, N.Y.: Paulist Press, 1977), chap. 6. See also Mal. 3:5; Is. 5:8–24; Ezek. 18:5–9, 22:1–16; Am. 2:6–8.

11. José Miranda, *Marx and the Bible* (Maryknoll, N.Y.: Orbis, 1974), p. 44.

12. Ibid., p. 48.

13. The following section relies heavily on chapter three of my *Rich Christians in an Age of Hunger.*

14. See Richard Batey, *Jesus and the Poor: The Poverty Program of the First Christians* (New York: Harper, 1972), pp. 83–97; Albert Gelin, *The Poor of Yahweh* (Collegeville, Minn.: Liturgical Press, 1964). See, too, Carl Schulz, "'Ani and 'Anaw in Psalms" (Ph.D. dissertation, Brandeis University, 1973); Peter D. Miscall, "The Concept of the Poor in the Old Testament" (Ph.D. dissertation, Harvard University, 1972).

15. See Richard Batey, *Jesus and the Poor: The New International Dictionary of New Testament Theology,* ed. Colin Brown, 3 vols. (Grand Rapids, Mich.: Zondervan, 1976), vol. 2, pp. 822–23; and J. A. Ziesler, *Christian Asceticism* (Grand Rapids, Mich.: Eerdmans, 1973), p. 52.

16. James H. Cone, *God of the Oppressed* (New York: Seabury, 1975). pp. 199–200 (Cone's italics).

17. See nn. 29–32.

18. See for instance, Margin Hengel, *Victory over Violence* (Philadelphia: Fortress Press, 1973), chaps. 6 and 7.

19. Some portions of the following are taken from chapter 1 of my *Christ and Violence* (Scottdale, Penn.: Herald Press, 1979).

20. See for instance, John Howard Yoder, *Politics of Jesus* (Grand Rapids, Mich.: Eerdmans, 1972), chaps. 2 and 3.

21. Robert Sloan, *The Acceptable Year of the Lord* (Austin: Schola Press, 1977), pp. 43–44.

22. Ibid., pp. 168, 171.

23. E.g., W. G. Kummel, *Promise and Fulfillment* (London: SCM Press, 1957); George E. Ladd, *Jesus and the Kingdom* (New York: Harper, 1964).

24. Hengel, *Victory Over Violence,* p. 80.

25. Ibid., pp. 81, 112.

26. Ibid., p. 82.

27. See C. E. B. Cranfield, *The Gospel According to Mark* ("*The Cambridge Greek New Testament Commentary*") (Cambridge, Eng.: Cambridge Uni-

versity Press, 1963), pp. 441–42, for a discussion of Jesus' response ("I am") and the synoptic parallels.

28. Jürgen Moltmann, *The Crucified God* (New York: Harper, 1974), pp. 125, 132.
29. E.g., Paul van Buren, *The Secular Meaning of the Gospel* (New York: Macmillan, 1963), p. 100.
30. E.g., Rudolf Bultmann, "New Testament and Mythology," in *Kerygma and Myth,* ed. Hans Werner Bartsch (New York: Harper Torchbooks, 1961), pp. 1–44.
31. See the argument of C. S. Lewis, *Miracles* (New York: Macmillan, 1947), chap. 8.
32. This is true even of the best book on the subject, Van A. Harvey's *The Historian and the Believer* (New York: Macmillan, 1966). See my critique in "The Historian, the Miraculous and Post-Newtonian Man," in *The Scottish Journal of Theology* 25 (1972): 309–19.
33. See George Eldon Ladd, *I Believe in Resurrection* (Grand Rapids, Mich.: Eerdmans, 1975; Downers Grove, Ill.: Inter-Varsity Press, 1969); Hans von Campenhausen, "The Events of Easter and the Empty Tomb," in *Tradition and Life in the Church* (Philadelphia: Fortress Press, 1968), pp. 42–89; Wolfhart Pannenberg, *Jesus: God and Man* (Philadelphia: Westminster Press, 1968), pp. 66–105.
34. Reginald H. Fuller, *The Formation of the Resurrection Narratives* (New York: Macmillan, 1971), p. 2.
35. Robert Grant, *Historical Introduction to the New Testament* (New York: Harper, 1963), p. 376.
36. Wolfhart Pannenberg, *Jesus: God and Man* (Philadelphia: Westminster, 1968), p. 100 (Althaus's italics).
37. See C. F. D. Moule, ed., "The Significance of the Message of the Resurrection for Faith in Jesus Christ" in *Studies in Biblical Theology,* no. 8 (London: SCM Press, 1968), p. 9.
38. E.g., Fuller, *Formation of the Resurrection Narratives,* p.10.
39. Perhaps the weakest link in Jürgen Moltmann's brilliant book, *The Theology of Hope* (New York: Harper, 1967), is his failure to state precisely what he means by Jesus' resurrection. The theology of hope developed in the book requires a bodily resurrection and an empty tomb. But, at the crucial point (pp. 197–202), Moltmann's discussion is obscure, even though he has a helpful critique of others (pp. 172–97). See the pointed words in John Updike's "Seven Stanzas at Easter," in *Verse: The Carpentered Hen and Other Tame Creatures. . . .* (New York: Fawcett Publications, 1965), p. 164.

DESPITE ALL APPEARANCES TO THE CONTRARY

Beverly A. Asbury

I

A sort of agnosticism has marked my life since leaving for college at the age of seventeen. College challenged many of the religious assumptions which I had uncritically absorbed in a small Georgia town of the 1930s and 1940s. Not even the social gospel had penetrated the evangelical, pietistic, and fundamentalist churches of my childhood, to say nothing of the crisis theology then developing in both Europe and the United States. Consequently, it came as a shock to me to have such singularity of religious viewpoint challenged not only religiously, but also philosophically, scientifically, psychologically, politically, and economically.

One thing became clear early on: my religious outlook could never again be the same. I would never recover the certainty which had marked my earlier life. The challenges produced problems and doubts, many of which have never gone away and have occasionally come close to taking over my life completely. However, the thought behind each problem and doubt had its own difficulties, and none of them alone or all of them together persuaded me to give up my Christian faith. Perhaps Christianity was too deeply implanted in my life, and it often made better "sense" of human life and destiny than any of the alternatives. At least, I seemed "fated" to a life in which faith and doubt were in a dialectic, marked by a certain sort of agnosticism toward both. I could never again go "home" to the Christianity of my early life, but neither could I find a new home in any of the scientific and secular humanisms proposed in its stead. Rather, life has been a struggle to achieve an understanding of the Christian faith that did not require, on the one hand, a sacrifice of mind to a literalistic religious world view, or on the other, a sacrifice of spirit to the assumptions of the secular world.

No doubt, that explains why more than twenty years of my ministry have taken place in institutions of higher education. It may also explain my deep attraction to the following passage written by H. Richard Niebuhr, a passage which has shaped this essay:

The problem of man is how to love the One on whom he is completely, absolutely, dependent; who is the Mystery behind the mystery of human existence in the faithfulness of its selfhood, of being this man among these men, in this time and all time, in the thus so-ness of the strange actual world. It is the problem of reconciliation to the One from whom death proceeds as well as life, who makes demands too hard to bear, who sets us in the world where our beloved neighbors are the objects of seeming animosity, who appears as God of wrath as well as God of love. It is the problem that arises in its acutest form when life itself becomes a problem, when the goodness of existence is questionable, as it has been for most men at most times; when the ancient and universal suspicion arises that he is happiest who was never born and he next fortunate who dies young.

Reconciliation to God is reconciliation to life itself; love to the Creator is love of being, rejoicing in existence, in its source, totality and particularity. Love to God is more than that, however, great as this demand and promise are. It is loyalty to the idea of God when the actuality of God is mystery; it is the affirmation of a universe and the devoted will to maintain a universal community at whatever cost to the self. It is the patriotism of the universal commonwealth, the kingdom of God, as a commonwealth of justice and love, the reality of which is sure to become evident. There is in such love of God a will-to-believe as the will-to-be-loyal to everything God and his kingdom stand for. Love to God is conviction that there is faithfulness at the heart of things: unity, reason, form and meaning in the plurality of being. It is the accompanying will to maintain or assert that unity, form and reason despite all appearances. The dark shadow of this love is our combative human loyalty which in its love of gods—principles of religion, empires and civilizations, and all partial things—denies while it seeks to affirm the ultimate loyalty and so involves us in apparently never-ending religious animosities which at the same time unite and divide neighbors, as they forge close bonds of loyalty to each other in a common cause among closed societies disloyal to each other.[1]

II

As Niebuhr says, the problem arises in its acutest form in those times when life itself becomes a problem and the goodness of existence is questionable. The times in which we live seem to be pre-

cisely such times when there does not appear to be faithfulness at
the heart of things.

Of course, the problem is not a new one. The following meditation on the First World War was written in 1916 by the Russian poet
Zinaida Gippius.

> *My window is low over the street,*
> *Low and open wide.*
> *The blood-colored, sticky wooden cobbles so close*
> *Under the window that's open wide.*
>
> *On the cobbles there are spots of light from the street lights,*
> *On the cobbles there are people, people. . . .*
> *And the sound of running feet, wails and cries,*
> *And confusion of people, people. . . .*
>
> *Like the blood-colored, sticky cobbles are their clothing and*
>   *faces.*
> *They—the living and the dead—are together.*
> *It has lasted for years and years—*
> *That the living and the dead are together.*
>
> *I won't shut the window against them.*
> *I myself—am I living or dead?*
> *No matter. . . . I wail together with them,*
> *No matter, whether living or dead.*
>
> *There is no blame, and no one to answer.*
> *No one answers for hell.*
> *We thought we lived in the world. . . .*
> *But we're wailing, wailing. . . . in hell.*[2]

The reign of death has become for me a major problem. Alvarez,
using Browning's phrase, has called it the coming of the Savage
God,[3] and his view of things is shared by many others. Richard Ru-
benstein sees the Savage God to be the bureaucratized violence of
our century, an expression of contemporary Western civilization,
and not an aberration from it or a rebellion against it. It is civilization become Necropolis, the city of anti-life and anti-nature. The Savage God is an earth-bound god—a god experienced as ferocious,
malicious, barbarous, capricious, cruel, and not as a God providen-
tial, caring, loving, redeeming. The Savage God as absent, uncaring,

unresponsive has challenged and threatened our very understanding of human existence as good.

Our lives have been immersed into meaningless, absurd death, randomly delivered, robbing both life and death of personal meaning and significance. The resulting deformations, dislocations, and imaginative impediments not only produce what Robert Jay Lifton calls "psychic numbing," but also an inability to express a hope in immortality through any of the "symbolic modes" previously used in human history. Hell has replaced heaven as the metaphor of our existence. Holocaust, the threat of nuclear destruction, racism, environmental disaster, and more seem to offer evidence that faithfulness is not at the heart of things, but that the bloodthirsty Savage God *is.*

If the times in which we live pose enormous problems to Christian faith and life through the events of history, they do so as well in the realm of ideas. The prevailing assumptions of the modern university hold it illusory to believe that there is "unity, reason, form, and meaning in the plurality of being." Many contemporary scientists, particularly in molecular biology, microbiology, biochemistry, and astrophysics, go far beyond Darwin in holding that the emergence of intelligent life on the planet earth through the evolutionary processes is a meaningless accident. Human life appears to them, in the light of their "evidence," to have no ultimate or transcendent purpose. Humans are reduced to giving life what meaning they can, as rational, intelligent beings, within the framework of the evolving chemical and biological order of things. And there is certainly no mystery in such views of reality.

Similar assumptions are held equally strong by others who arrive at them by different routes. For many Freudians, religious belief is based on illusion. For behaviorists, the imperative is to get beyond traditional notions of human "freedom and dignity." Marxists and other materialists see religious faith as a diversion, at best, from the pressing agenda of creating a just world order. And those are mere examples of the secular assumptions prevailing in the modern university and, often, in modern society.

It is worth noting the irony that many who make such assumptions still seem more fearful of the God of our faith traditions than they are of the Savage God. On nearly any campus, secular academ-

ics continue to do battle against Christianity, often stereotyping and
caricaturing it in the process. But one rarely hears similar polemics
against the Savage God or contemporary ideological assumptions. It
is my sense that many academics still see religious faith as an
enemy. If that is so, then it seems to this observer, who is in the liberal religious tradition, that they are woefully anachronistic. Many
in my tradition are convinced, as Professor Edward Farley of Vanderbilt Divinity School has put it, that the "House of Authority"
and its "Scripture Principle" have fallen, and many Christians have
suffered a crisis of belief, identity, and purpose, not unlike my own,
as a result. It has been in that climate that many liberal Christians
have both consciously and unconsciously gone about collapsing the
concepts and categories of the gospel into humanistic psychology or
social activism. At the same time, the neoevangelicals reassert those
concepts and categories as though the Savage God had never loosed
itself upon us and as if Darwin, Freud, and Marx had never lived at
all. With religion in so sad a state, one would have thought that the
secular and humanistic reductionists in our universities would have
moved with consciousness and clarity away from their preoccupation with absolutizing relativity to the task of constructing new systems of viewing and reordering reality. Alas, few even seem to make
the attempt even at a time when astrophysics seems to be opening a
new basis for metaphysical constructs and religious hypotheses
about the origin and nature of human life.

Rather, academics represent principalities and powers caught up
in what Christopher Lasch has termed "the culture of narcissism."[4]
Lasch sees narcissism as the spiritual malaise of our times, wherein
society does not produce free, productive, and loving persons. The
culture of narcissism is another form of the Savage God—a form
which dispenses with wisdom and knowledge in favor of expertise
and information. The narcissist is, at the core, one who "depends on
others to validate his self-esteem," and can there be a better definition of many modern academics, who, holding to the the world of
appearances, cannot believe that there is faithfulness at the heart of
things, and hence no affirmation available elsewhere? Little wonder,
then, that our institutions of higher education rarely produce a community of mutual respect and trust; they embrace the culture which,
in Lasch's view, is "terrified of aging and death." They go on about
their "work," but they have lost their heart and soul. They offer no

new mythos, no system of symbols and meaning, no faith to live our days in the face of the Savage God.

Such insights have been expressed previously. As Ernest Becker said in *The Denial of Death*,[5] Kierkegaard anticipated Freud in all that he saw. Alan Lacy makes the same point about Kierkegaard in reviewing Lasch's book.[6] Lacy pointed out that, in *The Present Age* (1846), "Kierkegaard harshly surveyed [his] culture, pointing out its lack of ultimate seriousness, its empty and manipulative relationships, its trivialization of intellect, its substitution of flirtation or seduction for love, its violation of the distinction between public and private life." Or, to put it another way, Niebuhr's way, the problem of believing in and loving God is not new. It is however, a problem which has been compounded by the experiences and appearances of life in this century.

As I said earlier, I have often been tempted to give in to the problems and the doubts attending them and produced by them. I have been led from such temptation partly because the alternatives to Christianity seem so bleak and unpromising, if not downright bankrupt. On the more positive side, my continuing attraction to Christian faith is closely akin to what Emil Fackenheim expressed in his essay, "The Commanding Voice of Auschwitz."[7]

What does the Voice of Auschwitz command? Jews are forbidden to hand Hitler posthumous victories. They are commanded to survive as Jews, lest the Jewish people perish. They are commanded to remember the victims of Auschwitz lest their memory perish. They are forbidden to despair of man and his world, and to escape into either cynicism or otherworldliness, lest they cooperate in delivering the world over to the forces of Auschwitz. Finally, they are forbidden to despair of the God of Israel, lest Judaism perish. A secularist Jew cannot make himself believe by a mere act of will, nor can he be commanded to do so.... And a religious Jew who has stayed with his God may be forced into new, possibly revolutionary relationships with Him. One possibility, however, is wholly unthinkable. A Jew may not respond to Hitler's attempt to destroy Judaism by himself cooperating in its destruction. In ancient times, the unthinkable Jewish sin was idolatry. Today, it is to respond to Hitler by doing his work.

III

Going back to Niebuhr now, what I wish to reaffirm is that faith is "loyalty to the idea of God when the actuality of God is mystery; it is the affirmation of a universe and the devoted will to maintain a universal community at whatever cost to the self." And "Love to God is conviction that there is faithfulness at the heart of things: unity, reason, form and meaning in the plurality of being. It is the accompanying will to maintain or assert that unity, form, and reason despite all appearances."

For me, that is the definition of prophetic religion: the will to maintain or assert faithfulness being at the heart of things despite all appearances to the contrary.

Negatively, it is the refusal to be held in and by the world of appearances and to absolutize the human experiences of any time and place. It refuses to hand either Hitler or the Savage God a victory.

Positively, prophetic religion arises out of the conviction that God has acted and disclosed his/her being in certain particular, distinctive moments in human history. The memory of Abraham, the exodus, the deliverance from captivity remain alive. The memory of Jesus who was crucified, dead, buried, and raised to new life remains alive. The hope of a "universal commonwealth, the kingdom of God, as a commonwealth of justice and love" remains our vision and, indeed, our expectation—a "reality which is sure to become evident," despite all appearances to the contrary.

Those appearances to the contrary we take to be part of the process of faith which disillusions us as means of opening us anew to the reality of the One beyond our experiences and idolatries. It is the faith that requires that we take a "leap" in the face of appearances; a "leap" which, in Niebuhr's words, "makes hope possible, encourages new desire and arouses [human beings] to anticipated attainments of future possibility." Again, such a "leap" is loyalty to the idea of God and the conviction that God has been distinctively and uniquely present in the exodus and the resurrection of Jesus Christ from the grave. And such a leap allows us "to see" a reality beyond appearances and despite them.

To speak of "coming to see" is to speak of contemplation. The very word *contemplation* means "to look at thoughtfully," to ponder or consider, to anticipate, to regard as possible, to take seriously. All that is involved in "coming to see" because it has to do with how our awareness happens.[8] Coming to see (or contemplation) happens as the sensing of the relations of things, and as a feeling about those relations—a sense of wholeness or rupture or bifurcation. We come to see, to be aware, in concrete situations and events, at particular times and places, and our "seeing" or awareness is always an event of meaning.

As a result of seeing, we become events of meaning ourselves. We do not stand apart from all the relations and meanings we see. We are our own relations of drawing close or withdrawing; we are our blindness and our insight. When we are deceived by appearances, that becomes a part of our "seeing," and the same is true when we are unnoticing or ignorant. What we mean and what meaning we profess are directly related to our "seeing," our awareness.

When we come to see, we experience an intensification of self-awareness and world-awareness. Coming to see seems to mean open acceptance of myself and others, and openness to separation as well as closeness, to dying as well as continued life, to pain as well as pleasure, to being unfulfilled as well as satisfied, to disappointment as well as happiness. These realities reveal to me that being a stranger is a part of being familiar, that union always involves separation, that our place in the scheme of things is always indicated by death, regardless of courage or cowardice. And as a result of seeing all that, I may choose to deny those experienced insights—by a thousand means. Or I may choose to seek a new sense of how the world and I are together and get attuned to that sense no matter how much that hurts or how many of my beliefs I must change. Coming to see has much to do with our faith and what it and we mean.

Prophetic religion "sees" through the events of Exodus and Easter. It "sees" because it takes the "leap of faith." It "leaps" because it must—because it must not hand Hitler or the Savage God or any idol, however respectable, the victory. And it maintains or asserts that faithfulness is at the heart of things despite all appearances to the contrary. Prophetic religion, in this sense, calls one to live what one "sees," as if it and not the appearance were the clue to ultimate reality.

Such faithfulness, combining "seeing" and acting, will and does surely seem suspect in many institutions of higher education, which generally "see" through other modes and events and often make no effort to act out what is "seen." Moreover, academics also suspect that religious faith simply refuses to "see" what they take to be "evidence."

It is, therefore, important to insist that those in the prophetic religious tradition do not deny the "evidence," or the "appearances." Persons in the prophetic tradition must, indeed, go even further by insisting that "evidence," and "appearance," be taken seriously, and that the acts of faithful people be informed by them. God did not call his people to be "know-nothings," and surely God's people can be informed in their minds, qualified in their beliefs, and opened in their souls not only by the "evidence" but also by critical analyses and interpretations characteristic of academic institutions. As we have repented of the church's other sorry history of fighting, resisting, and ignoring the discoveries and insights of those such as Darwin and Freud, Christians must continue to resolve to be open to new findings and developments. To be sure, academics may "see" one thing in them while we "see" another. And, often enough, what academics "see" leads them to form "religious hypotheses," formulations or interpretations beyond the scope of "proof." Their way of seeing must be taken seriously, but it does not have to be regarded as a better or superior one. Once we are confident of that, we can live more easily with a natural and mutual respect and skepticism of each other.

Given both our own history and academe's suspicions of religious traditions, we openly and willingly reaffirm that faith in God does not require that we ignore or deny the appearances even while insisting that there is unity, reason, form, and meaning in the plurality of being. Rather, a faith informed by Exodus and Easter seeks to grasp such "evidence" and "appearances" and render them significant in the light of its own "seeing." For example, prophetic faith recognizes the presence of the Savage God in our times; it "sees" the Holocaust as a supreme incident of the Savage God's presence, and it accepts the risks in "seeing it." Prophetic religion records the experience of the Savage God, enters into that experience in order to learn a truth about human life. It gives the Savage God and its Holocaust of death dealing to the Jews a place in our religious, moral, and aesthetic imaginations. It connects the history of our times to our lives as a people seeking to be faithful. And it does so because it is loyal "to the idea of God when the actuality of God is mystery" and in order to affirm and maintain "a universal community at whatever cost to the self."

Yale research psychiatrist Robert Jay Lifton "sees" much the same thing, coming albeit from a different starting point. In *The*

American Poetry Review,[9] Lifton recalls that, in his study of Hiroshima, he defined the survivor as "one who has come into contact with death in some bodily or psychic fashion and has himself remained alive." He then goes on to say:

I spoke of a survivor ethos, thrust into special prominence by the holocausts of the twentieth century, imposing upon all of us a series of immersions into death which mark our existence. I would go further now and say that we are survivors not only of holocausts which have already occurred but of those we imagine or anticipate as well . . .

Lifton holds that, by "coming to see" through this death immersion, the survivor can "cease to be immobilized by this death imprint, his death guilt, and his psychic numbing." That is, if we reorder our own experience on the personal and individual level, we may also contribute to a more general reordering of the world in which we live. All of us have been or can be "touched" both by actual and anticipated holocausts, and out of being "touched" we can come "to see"—to hold a new vision of life. Lifton's view, which is in accord with my own, is that those of us who have "touched death" potentially have a source of insight and power that can serve to renew life. That is, the experience of death, on whatever level or scale, may give us not only a vitality to renew life, but also a "special wisdom" in doing so. To be "touched" by death can animate the human imagination to work for life, for justice and peace and reconciliation.

Of course, Lifton knows full well that such intimacy with death can also lead to denial, numbing, disintegration, and passivity. Yet, in his view it does not have to do so because of the human capacity to bring imagination to bear upon our plight in order to survive. The purpose of confronting the imagery of the Savage God as nuclear holocaust is, as Lifton sees it, "to deepen and free our imagination for the leaps it must take. In the words of Roethke: 'In a dark time the eye begins to see.' The vision of death gives life. The vision of total annihilation makes it possible to imagine living under and beyond that curse."

Dr. Lifton would not have me co-opt him for Christianity and prophetic faith, and it is not my intention to do so. However, I have found his books to open my own "seeing" as few others have. The themes of life and death, of death in life, and of the "seeing" necessary for the reordering of our lives and societies receive compelling expression. Lifton has given me the concepts and words for much of what I "see" and of what it "sees" as a result. Where Lifton hopes for a reordering of personal and societal life based on "the painful wisdom of the survivor," prophetic religion extends the definition of survivor to include Exodus and Easter. It, therefore, expresses its hope based on those disclosures of reality which are, in Niebuhr's words, sure to become evident again as a commonwealth of justice and love. That is, prophetic faith, out of its contemplation, foretells a future in which God will act anew in human history to break the kingdom of God in upon us and the world of the Savage God.

In the meantime, before the endtime, prophetic faith calls us to live now in the expectation of that event. That living of faithfulness is not and will not be easy. For one thing, there are all the appearances to the contrary. For another, there is what Jacques Ellul has called "the political illusion," which is not unrelated to what I earlier referred to as collapsing the concepts and categories of the gospel into those of political activism. Indeed, that may be our greatest temptation; namely, "to see" salvation coming to our world, the world of the Savage God, through politics.

Ellul warns us against that temptation and course of action. The world sets the agenda which prophetic faith must address, but he cautions against Christians allowing politics, as defined by the modern state, to tell us what our response should be. In his book, *The Political Illusion* (Vintage, 1972), Ellul argues that Christians should seek to view life, its problems and solutions, through the prisms of the gospel. To see life through such prisms produces a very different vision from what one sees when looking through the lenses of what politics has already defined as "possible" or "necessary." Ellul believes that Christians have become so accustomed to accepting political definitions and solutions that it is no easy matter for us to learn again to see through the prisms or perspectives of the gospel. And that is why he advocates a strategic withdrawal from politics. Politics today is illusory. It focuses our eyes on false problems and fake solutions. It solves nothing. Therefore, says Ellul, if we withdraw and try to see as Christians, we may gain a better grasp on what are the real problems facing humankind and how to address those problems at a deeper and more decisive level than can the present political system.

When that has been done, we can return to politics. However, that work lies ahead of us, and, in the meantime, Christians should be busy creating "poles of tension" to the modern political state. Otherwise, Christians are simply swept along in the tides of the political illusion, unable to resist the state's intrusions into private life and its rationalized acceptance of injustices, inequities, and violence. Ellul sees such "poles of tension" not only as necessary for resistance but also as the prerequisite for arriving at a new vision for reordering human life and societies. He has a keen awareness that such a course runs the greater danger of being disloyal to the requirements of the gospel.

It is important to remember that Ellul is a Christian, a contemplative Christian. He speaks out of the prophetic religious tradition, and, in accordance with that tradition, his words of what he "sees" are addressed to others within it, who may and can "see" what he "sees." He is not calling for abdication from the world and its politics, and he surely is not calling for us to be irresponsible. Rather, he is asking Christians in the prophetic tradition to address the problems of faithfulness on the basis of the gospel and what it "sees" rather than be totally dominated by politics and what it "sees."

Only so, according to Ellul, are we likely to address the issues of human life and destiny at that deeper level required by "loyalty to the idea of God when the actuality of God is mystery." Or again, out of the conviction that there is faithfulness at the heart of things, Christians must create "poles of tension" confronting the state (and, I add, higher education), forcing the latter to "think again [to 'see' in ways other than their usual ones] and limit [themselves] to considering real political problems without being in a position of omnipotence." It is, after all, that assumption of omnipotence that has loosed the Savage God upon us.

Here I am reminded of what Joseph Tussman says of docility in his book, *Experiment in Learning.* Tussman speaks of docility, not in the usual sense of passivity, but in the sense of beatitude: "Blessed are the meek, for they shall inherit the earth." Following Tussman, that might read, "Blessed are the docile," the ones who are open to learning. Blessed are those lacking in the arrogant belief that they already have all the answers or the means to getting them. Docility implies a certain humility, a willingness to see what one has not seen before. A docile person is blessed because he or she has a willingness to consider what another may know, to appropriate "the painful wisdom of the survivor" or "the good news of God in Jesus Christ." And to them will belong the earth, to set it right, to reconcile it to the universal commonwealth which is the kingdom of God.

Ellul asks us to cultivate such a docility, to develop such a contemplative spirit, in order to see not only the problems facing us, but, more importantly, to discover how to live in the conviction that faithfulness is at the heart of things, to act more decisively than the modern state can or will act. In order to do so, we must, in Ellul's view, first "re-invent private life," a situation in which life's true problems are not posed in political terms.

To speak of reinventing private life may sound like a sure prescription for personalistic escapism. That is not Ellul's meaning, and it certainly is not mine. Rather, such a reinventing of private life insists that involvement and action lead to contemplation and that contemplation and seeing are prerequisites to further action. The problem today is that, on the one hand, we are absorbed and preoccupied with spectacles, nonevents (such as sports), and the constant bombardment of news and information. And, on the other hand, modern life rather than the gospel has defined for us what actions are "necessary" and "unnecessary." Consequently, the purpose of reinventing private life lies in creating the time and space to see what God requires of us, what the gospel imposes on us as "necessary," and how the Christian community of prophetic faith can provide a pole of tension to the state and its political illusions. Ellul's point is that, in order to do that, those believing in a faithfulness at the heart of things must first get in touch again with what that faithfulness means. They must strategically withdraw from the present solutions of political life in order to "see" politics in a new light. Ellul believes that "the only way to hold the state within its framework and function, to return true reality to the conflict of 'private versus political life,' to dissipate the political illusions is to develop and multiply tensions." And that we cannot do unless we first reinvent private life.

IV

At this point, I am compelled to add that I have not found it easy to follow Ellul's advice. My life in ministry has been marked by engagement in many causes and issues and it remains difficult for me to disengage completely from them. Moreover, I have lived a good many years in institutions of higher education, and I have reason enough to fear, as a result, that disengagement would simply be a capitulation to academe's entrenched dichotomy between thought and action. In fact, it has been the willingness of campus ministers to *act* that has often created the tensions which Ellul regards as necessary. On the other hand, I have an equal fear of being stereotyped as being "predictable," and of simply patterning my actions after those prevalent in the secular society. Consequently, Ellul's counsel has proven for me a valuable corrective. I take him seriously, if not literally, and I have found myself more effective (and perhaps more diligent in seeking patterns of faithfulness) as a result. That is, I have sought to reinvent a private life of my own without yielding to the privatism that prevents action. And the reinvention of such a life has, indeed, enriched my being and, I believe, made my actions more imaginative and less predictable. In short, it has helped me to "see" and in "seeing" to act more creatively, if not more decisively.

However, in saying this, I do not mean to minimize the risks. They are enormous. Here too, Kierkegaard preceded us in making that clear, but so does the gospel in calling us to be in but not of the world. Such risks may put us in the position of seeming always to be waiting when action is required, and anyone familiar with the history of Christian silence in the face of the Holocaust finds such a thought unbearable. As Thomas Mann said, "waiting is hell," and waiting may lead us to hell. Yet, if we do not risk waiting, our hell may have all the trappings of Christianity but without the substance of "the universal commonwealth, the kingdom of God."

If these words from one in the tradition of "liberal Christianity" sound strange to you, you can be sure that they first came strange to his own ears. They may sound as if I had joined those evangelical Christians who have never seen the connection, the unity, between faith and action. They even make me wonder if the "evangelicals for social action" are not mistakenly following the path of liberal Christians which will eventually lead them, too, to replace faith with ethics and action. Perhaps it will suffice to say in the face of such "strange words" that evangelicals have waited long enough, too long; and that it is time or past time for them to act, assuming all the risks in doing so. On the other hand, it is time for the liberals to wait so that they do not further confuse their Christian action with "political illusion."

As I have already said, there are great risks involved in following such a course, and I see no way to avoid them if we would learn anew what it means to be a faithful people. The risks seem far preferable to continuing to drift with illusions and to surrendering to narcissistic religion, or to "religion in its place," or even to religion predictable in its "liberal actions." The risks at least hold possibility for the renewal of prophetic religion and its promise of a "commonwealth of justice and love," which, despite all appearances to the contrary, may become evident again in human life.

I am disposed to take those risks. Indeed, I believe that the gospel requires that of all Christians, no matter the cost to ourselves.

NOTES

1. H. Richard Niebuhr, *The Purpose of the Church and Its Ministry* (New York: Harper, 1956), pp. 36–37.
2. Translated from the original metered, rhymed verse by Professor Nina Gove of Vanderbilt University.
3. A. Alvarez, *The Savage God* (New York: Bantam Books, 1973).
4. Christopher Lasch, *The Culture of Narcissism* (New York: Norton, 1978).
5. Ernest Becker, *The Denial of Death* (Boston: Free Press, 1973).
6. Allen Lacy, "Visions of Narcissus in a Decadent World," in *The Chronicle of Higher Education,* Fortnightly Supplement, January 22, 1979, pp. 11–12.
7. Emil Fackenheim, *God's Presence in History* (New York: New York University, 1970), p. 84.
8. These thoughts on "coming to see" are drawn from lectures given by Dr. Charles E. Scott of the Vanderbilt philosophy department. However, he is not to be held responsible for the limits of my own understanding of his words and concepts.
9. Robert Jay Lifton, "The Survivor as Creator," in *The American Poetry Review* (Philadelphia: World Poetry Inc., January/February 1973), pp. 40–42.

IV

The Ministries of Faith Communities

THE MINISTRIES OF FAITH COMMUNITIES
An Interpretation

Myron B. Bloy, Jr.

The biblical vision of reality is dominated by a concern for community: humankind was originally created for existence in communal innocence; we are destined to be restored to our appropriate communal identity in a New Jerusalem; now, with the support of God's Holy Law and Holy Spirit, we are to bear witness in community to our origin and destiny. The terms which most nearly express our vocational goal—*justice* and *love*—point to the restoration and enlargement of life as community. But our society and culture are largely determined by an ideology of predatory individualism, an ideology which is especially deep-rooted in the academic world. Thus, Jews and Christians in the academic world have the dilemma of being in an environment which is especially subverting of their life together and, hence, especially and poignantly needful of their witness to life as community. Each of the writers in this section addresses that dilemma from the perspective of his or her own particular tradition.

We decided, during the first meeting of the writers, that illuminating relations among their several perspectives would be more apparent if the essays had a common structure or argument. So we determined that each essay would begin with a historical and theological description of the normative idea of community in this particular tradition; that a second part of each essay would describe the factors, both internal and external, which seem today to inhibit the actualization of such community; and that, finally, each essay would conclude by setting out real examples or ideal projections of how those inhibiting factors are or can be overcome and faith community accomplished. Needless to say, no one of these essays follows that format in every regard, but the pattern is more or less there in each one and knowing it will, I hope, help readers to see the implicit dialectic among them.

It was Joseph Williamson, in an early version of his essay, who helped us to see and to play more deliberately on the dominant, distinguishing basis for establishing and nurturing community in our several traditions. He argues that "the dominant Protestant model for faith community in the United States is . . . conversionist. . . . It is through the conversion experience that one enters the faith community which is called into being by all those who share that experience." He says that "the second model for faith community is more objective than it is subjective in character. Its objectivity is set primarily by the sacraments as a means of grace." (Elaine Prevallet, S.L., sees "the sacrament as both expressive and formative of faith community" in the Catholic tradition.) Finally, Williamson adduces the model of his own tradition: "The covenant model insists that it is the covenanted people in their corporate reality who are indeed the means of grace. Grace is mediated precisely by those persons who are bonded together in covenant with each other and with their God. So salvation is appropriate through the life of the congregation." It seems to me that Payne, Prevallet, and Williamson do, indeed, use the ideas of conversion, sacrament, and covenant as theological touchstones in their discussion of community in their respective traditions.

It also seems clear enough that the Jewish model of community as Richard Levy explicates it includes, not surprisingly, elements of all three of those models: "davening," in some measure expressive of the affective and ecstatic in worship, is akin to the conversionist model; the Passover meal, a powerful event of anamnesis, is sacramental; and the idea of chosen people is, of course, based on covenant. But if I were to choose a dominant idea in Levy's essay which distinguishes Jewish from Christian models of community, I would say that it is *cognition:* study of the Torah is certainly a primary way by which Jewish community is established and the people brought into the numinous, transforming presence of God. Again, it may help readers to see the implicit dialectic in these essays by keeping these paradigmatic ideas of conversion, sacrament, covenant, and cognition in mind when reading them.

I want, also, to underline a fact which is both implicit and explicit in these essays, namely, that their authors have continuing, first-hand involvement in building the kind of communities they describe. They have a certain palpable "authority." Eric Payne, a former staff member of Tom Skinner Associates, is now a student and advisor to minority students at Gordon-Conwell Theological Seminary near Boston; he struggles daily with the awesome task of racial reconciliation. Richard Levy, former Hillel director at UCLA and now executive director of the Hillel Council in the Los Angeles area, continues to nurture the kind of Jewish communities he describes in his essay. Joseph Williamson works at the difficult task of including students in the ongoing life of an inner-city congregation of heterogeneous makeup. And Elaine Prevallet, who recently completed two years on the staff of Pendle Hill, the Quaker Center, has responsibility for the development of community life in the Sisters of Loretto Retreat Center in Kentucky. They all know whereof they speak when they discuss the norms, the problems, and the possibilities of faith community in their traditions. Finally, as my own contribution, I have attempted a kind of taxonomy of community in biblical tradition, broadly conceived.

The story of humankind can be told as our struggle, through the ages, to achieve communion with each other; we know that, in the deepest sense, what it is to be human is to live in community, as brothers and sisters, and our lifelong task is simply to realize that creaturely calling as fully as possible. Some persons, called saints, achieve this human calling more fully than others; some ages, called golden, provide more supportive political, economic, social, cultural, and religious contexts for the realization of our humanity in community than do other ages—perhaps called dark, and perhaps like our own.

The best contemporary statement I know of the essentially communal character and calling of the human creature is provided in Ignazio Silone's essay, "The Choice of Companions." Silone, whose life of underground resistance in Fascist Italy and, later, against Stalinism, and whose literary art in novels like *Fontamara* and *Bread and Wine* celebrate the struggle for human community against oppression, was concerned in this essay with the deep despair which had overcome the Western intellectual and literary world after World War II. Here is the way he succinctly describes the problem:

Post-Nietzschean and existentialist literature has portrayed for us man's well-known present predicament. It can be reduced to this: Every tie be-

tween man's existence and his essence has been broken. Existence is
bereft of every meaning which transcends it. The human is reduced to
mere animal energy.[1]

After describing the ravaging despair of meaninglessness among
contemporaries like Orwell, Malraux, and Camus, Silone concludes
with this poignant question: "In spite of everything then, is there
anything left?" Here is his reply:

Yes, there are some unshakable certainties. These, in my belief, are
Christian certainties. They seem to me to be so built into human reality
that man disintegrates when he denies them. This is not enough to constitute a profession of faith, but it will do as a declaration of confidence. It
is a confidence which rests on something more stable and more universal
than the simple compassion of which Albert Camus speaks. It is supported by the certainty that we are . . . free and responsible beings; it is
supported by the certainty that man has an absolute need of an opening
into the reality of others; and it is supported by the certainty that spiritual
communication is possible. If this is so, is it not an irrefutable proof of the
brotherhood of man?[2]

Silone then goes on to draw the necessary *moral* conclusion from his
"declaration of confidence" in the essentially communal identity of
humankind. He says:

This certainty also contains a rule of life. From it is born a love of the
oppressed which no historical failure can put in doubt, since no vested interest is involved. Its validity does not depend on success. With these certainties how can one resign oneself to witnessing man's potentialities
snuffed out in the most humble and unfortunate? How can one consider
moral a life that is deaf to this fundamental commitment?[3]

While Silone belonged to no church (he called himself a "Christian
without a church and a socialist without a party"), this is one of the
purest summaries of biblical anthropology I know.

But the fact that our human identity *is* essentially communal and
our consequent task to make sure that *all* share fairly in that reality
does not mean, of course, that we will accept our identity and task.
We can, like Faust, deliberately choose not to do so. Or the contexts,
in various aspects, of our daily living can subtly lead us away from
our essential identity in communality. In fact, those cultural stratagems painfully built up over the ages—the family, the tribe, the vil-

lage and town, the religious order, the guild, the neighborhood, etc.—to help us to learn how to enter into the reality of others and to engage in spiritual communication are not as tough and durable as we tend to think.

An example of the massive breakdown of the cultural norms of community in one people is the story of the Ik. The Ik are a small group of hunters, isolated in the mountains separating Uganda, the Sudan, and Kenya, who have been driven from their natural hunting grounds into these barren wastes by the creation of a national game reserve; without the appropriate culture, tools, and experience to become farmers, they have been told nonetheless to do so in this land without rain. Anthropologist Colin Turnbull, in his book, *The Mountain People,*[4] describes how, in less than three generations, the Ik have deteriorated from a community of prosperous and daring hunters to scattered bands of hostile people whose only goal is individual survival, and who have learned that the price of survival is to give up compassion, love, affection, kindness, and concern—even for their own children. The Ik can and do steal food from the mouths of their parents, throw infants out to fend for themselves, abandon the old, the sick, and crippled to die without a backward glance.

I cite these horrifying details because I think we are all too sentimentally idealistic about the capacity of human beings under pressure to maintain their capacity for community, for empathically entering into the reality of others for love; our naive idealism as a means of withstanding the *real* powers of chaos is about as effective as whistling in the dark against the dangers of the night. I want also to suggest that each one of us is far more ready, under similar pressures, to adopt the behavior of the Ik. Remember the private back yard bomb shelters, equipped not only with food, but with shotguns to keep the neighbors from trying to get in, which were built a few years back under the threat of imminent nuclear attack. What will happen to our vaunted community spirit when there is too little fuel to heat all of our homes? We have witnessed the predatory selfishness and violence which erupted in gasoline lines. What about current popular theories of triage which have it that we should abandon the weaker segments of the world population when world hunger hits? That is simply the Ik solution writ large. While, as Silone says, "man disintegrates when he denies" his communal identity, we nonetheless find our ability to realize and maintain that identity fragile indeed.

We find ourselves, I expect, in the same situation which Saint Paul recognized: "I do not understand my own actions. For I do not do what I want, but I do the very thing I hate" (Rom. 7:15). While the biblical tradition—with answers like "hardness of heart" and "sin" and "pride"—begs the question, along with every other system of thought about the ultimate *cause* of our suicidal tendency to deny our communal identity, that tradition *does* recognize its danger more clearly and describe the way it works more subtly than any other tradition I know. Let me trace some of the highlights of that tradition, beginning with the story of the creation and fall in Genesis. The story has three acts: In the first act of the older account, after man has been created and put in the Garden, it is apparent to God that this new creature remains incomplete: "It is not good that the man should be alone." The "other" is created that humanity might be fully realized as community; the man and woman cleave to each other so that they become "one flesh," and—so the account says—although they were both naked, they "were not ashamed." That is, their opening into the reality of each other was so total that they became as one, their spiritual communication so deep that they were totally unself-conscious: their fellowship represents human identity in its basic, underlying *communal* character.

In the second act, under the symbol of the tree, they rebelled against the empowering source of their life together, claiming that power for themselves, to be as God. Milton names the source of their rebellion "pride," and while that, of course, doesn't advance our understanding of its cause one wit, the suicidal character of the act is perfectly familiar to anyone who, like Saint Paul, has been honest with himself: "I do not understand my own actions. For I do not do what I want, but I do the very thing that I hate." There is that itch to be God in all of us.

In the third act, we see the devastating result of their rebellion against the empowering source of their communal life of, as Tillich calls it, "dreaming innocence."

Now the most immediate result of their willed separation from God, from the creative and sustaining source of their life, is separation from each other, most tellingly revealed in the symbol of nakedness. When the attention of the self is totally on God there can be no self-regarding and, hence, no shame—no barrier to becoming "one flesh." But when the self in effect sets itself up as God, then it is, *ipso facto,* separated from every other self and implicitly assumes its presumptive hegemony *over* every other self. No wonder Adam was ashamed when God appeared in the cool of the evening. While the shame of nakedness is the sign of separation, first from each other and then from God, the self-righteous character of the new God-presumptive self is revealed in Adam's and Eve's responses to God's question about the fruit of the tree: Adam tries to shift the blame to Eve, and she, in turn, tries to shift the blame to the serpent. Another consequence of their rebellion, a fact which tends to reinforce their isolation, is the condition of meaninglessness which now infuses their lives: there is a dizzying nausea, to use the existentialist's term, in contemplating the fact of death, that we are dust and to dust shall return, and in the realization that our situation is hopeless, that the angel with the flaming sword will not permit us to return to the tree of life.

This myth of creation and fall captures, with breathtaking insight and poignancy, the tragic irony of our situation. The deepest thing that we, each of us, know about ourselves is that our creaturely fulfillment lies in being so open to the empowering source of our creation that we can unself-consciously, unashamedly, for the sheer joy of it alone, enter into the reality of others and achieve "spiritual communion" (to use Silone's term); we have all experienced enough, usually brief, moments of such communion—in parental compassion received and given; in the self-forgetfulness of romantic love; in the sudden, surprised opening to and from one another, usually a friend but often a stranger too—to know that our deepest heart's desire is to live permanently in such communion with others. We have all glimpsed the Garden of Eden; we remember it nostalgically at the deepest level of our being. But, and this is the irony, we also know that our lives have assumed a habitual pattern of betrayal of our heart's desire: our own God-itch and our defensive fear of it in others tends to commit us to a life of lonely separation under the constant threat of meaninglessness. We despair that our own perverse wills will ever allow us to live the real life which we know only in momentary snatches—that we will ever get back behind the angel with the flaming sword. The fall, and its inevitable consequences, is also our daily, chosen experience. We are, in fact, Adam and Eve.

For biblical people, the tragic irony of our endless betrayal of our Creator and, hence, of our created, communal selves which inevitably plunges us into isolation and loneliness, into meaninglessness and despair, is *the* dilemma of the human condition. The rupture of human community caused by the many different languages is understood to be the result of an attempt to build a Tower of Babel high enough to threaten God. When Amos sees the people plunged into faithless idolatry, he understands God's direst threat to be "a famine not of bread, a drought not of water, but of hearing the word of the Lord. They will stagger from sea to sea, wander from north to east, seeking the word of the Lord and failing to find it. That day, delicate girl and stalwart youth shall faint from thirst" (Am. 8:11–13). That is, without the sustaining and nourishing Word of God, meaninglessness and aimless despair is humankind's lot. In Christianity's greatest literary myth, the *Divine Comedy,* Dante reserves the deepest circle of hell for traitors, those who have betrayed human community, who are embedded separate and silent in a lake of ice, a cold isolation which Turnbull saw in the daily life of the Ik.

If, then, the tragic irony of creatures created for community and life who nonetheless constantly betray it for isolation and death defines the basic dilemma of humankind, then the basic business of human culture is to devise stratagems, like the family or like the tribe, to help us mitigate that dilemma. All of the Ik's stratagems crumbled under the threat of their physical survival. I indicated earlier how that kind of external threat begins now to impinge on us: when the living is easy we can indulge in delusions about human nobility, but when things get tough such delusions must give way to a chancier—and more real—version of our identity.

But the deeper, internal threat, which has been growing in the West over the last several hundred years, is the idea or ideology of radical individualism. Paul Ramsey, in describing what he believes to be the basic "value-conflict in all modern societies," puts it well:

The key is atomistic individualism versus the tattered fragments of community that still remain. Since the eighteenth century, church and synagogue have been under massive assault from individualistic rationalism. So has a proper sense of political community, of education, of marriage, and of the family. The family was seen as a community in which fully human life is transmitted. In the atomistic view the state is merely an instrument for aggregating interests; marriage becomes contract and the family an amalgam of perfectly interchangeable roles or relations that reaches perfect expression when children call parents by their first names.[5]

It is difficult, perhaps impossible, to determine how we have become so overcome by this ideology of individualistic rationalism which Ramsey describes, but I think it is indisputable that today our *primary* self-identity is hardly communal at all, that we have in fact managed to make something of a heroic virtue out of that terrible isolation of the self which has constituted the dilemma of the human condition for biblical people in the past. Certainly, the Protestant ethic (as Max Weber defined it), Cartesian rationalism, the factory system, and the economics of consumerism have all contributed to that ideological condition, a condition which we have tried to hide from ourselves under the old communal ideals of the past. We still see our nation as a secure community, despite the recent spectacle of its leaders using it for their personal aggrandizement; the family has never been more fulsomely praised, as it clearly shows increasing signs of collapse; the prolegomenon of every college catalogue proclaims it to be a *community* of learning, but it has in fact become increasingly a training ground for predatory individualism, e.g., through grading on a curve which pits every person against every other person.

In *The Culture of Narcissism,*[6] Christopher Lasch describes our time as "the dotage of bourgeois society" in which the psychological condition of narcissism, of individualistic preoccupation and self-indulgence, has become increasingly our covert cultural norm. Even the characteristic symptoms of psychological illness are, according to Lasch, changing from those associated with guilt, which presumes some communal norms about right and wrong, to those of a kind of free-floating anxiety, presuming a self caught, as Arthur Miller said about his character Willy Loman, "between galaxies of promise and the fear of falling." While social scientists, our institutional leaders, and even the popular media in their discussion of the new "me-ism" are increasingly recognizing the *deepening* isolation of the self, our *decreasing* capacity for communal life in every form, I think it is important to note finally that this theme of the isolation of the self has been a persistent theme in American literature, at least since Hawthorne and Melville.

In summary, so far, I have sought to make the point that both Silone's perception that our communal identity is an ontologically given fact of our human identity *and* the Ik's demonstration that the apparent solidity of the basic forms of human community is illusory are true, that both truths are comprehended in the tragic irony of the Genesis myth and in biblical anthropology generally, and that today in America our own forms of communal identity have been so weakened by a culture of narcissistic individualism that we are dangerously open to the fate of the Ik under the pressure of any major social disruption at all.

AMERICAN HIGHER EDUCATION

I can only sketch the devolution of American higher education from community to competitive individualism, but the turning points are clear enough. American higher education was, of course, modeled originally on the English college (particularly Emmanuel College at Cambridge University), which was, in turn, rooted in the monastery. The great continental universities, like those of Paris and Bologna, were set in cities and focused on the scholarly productivity of their faculties, with students, living usually in rooming houses nearby, paying for the privilege of being intellectual apprentices. The English college, set in the country in self-contained living-learning compounds, was focused, like the monastery, on the communal *formation* of the students. The chief end of the English— and, hence, of the American colonial—college was the moral and spiritual, as well as intellectual, transformation of the young through a total community life into persons fit to participate usefully in serving the ends of the larger community.

Thus, a 1643 promotional tract designed to raise money for the new Harvard College advanced this argument:

After God had carried us safe to New England, and wee had builded our houses, provided necessaries for our liveli-hood, rear'd convenient places for God's worship, and settled the Civill Government: One of the next things we longed for, and looked after was to advance Learning and perpetuate it to Posterity; dreading to leave an illiterate Ministry to the Churches when our present Ministers shall lie in the dust.[7]

"Learning" is here understood to constitute one of the necessary, but not first, functions of this new exodus community within the biblical dispensation, part of a faithful response to the call of God to build a new Canaan. Cotton Mather, emphasizing in 1672 the need for ministerial leadership to fulfill this covenantal mandate in founding Harvard, said, "Without a nursery for such Men among ourselves *darkness must have soon covered the land, and gross darkness the people.*"[8] And a kind of "nursery"—a controlled communal environment for the intellectual, moral, and spiritual formation of the young—is precisely what the colonial colleges were. When one reads the first statutes of Harvard (1646), which were closely modeled on those of Cambridge, and of the other colonial colleges, one sees just how meticulously ordered their total community life was for the formation of leaders who would be able to extend the reign of God over this dark continent. In fact, the belief then was that formal learning began, as Jonathan Mitchell put it in 1663, in "Sundry Schools or Colleges in Israel wherin scholars (or sons of ye prophets) were trained up."

After the Revolution, the hard transcendent focus of the colleges was softened to a somewhat more moralistic and nationalistic purpose, but that the purpose of learning was to help the young to serve the larger community remained firm. In 1802 Joseph McKeen, president of Bowdoin College, said about that purpose:

It ought to be remembered, that literary institutions are founded and endowed for the common good, and not for the private advantage of those who resort to them for education. It is not that they may be able to pass through life in an easy or reputable manner, but that their mental power may be cultivated and improved for the benefit of society.[9]

The college was a community for the formation of effective citizens, men endowed not only with the skills for serving the common good, but also spiritually formed and motivated to that end. The college president's first responsibility was the maintenance of a total community environment for that purpose, and he generally taught a course in moral philosophy, usually in the senior year, which explicated that purpose carefully.

But after the Civil War—when industrialization and an attendant bourgeois individualism developed rapidly and when the educational influence of the land-grant colleges and the German university became paramount—the idea of higher education as the communal formation of the young for service to the larger spiritual or moral purposes of the nation became attenuated. Daniel Coit Gilman—first president of Johns Hopkins—put this new purpose in the following terms: "The university is the most comprehensive term that can be employed to indicate a foundation for the promotion and diffusion of knowledge—a group of agencies organized to advance the arts and sciences of every sort, and train young men as scholars for the intellectual callings of life."[10] Knowledge, which had in the earlier college been a means to larger moral and spiritual ends, has now become the *end* of education; the young are to be trained to become votaries of knowledge, and what Gilman and his allies primarily meant by that was the knowledge of scientific rationalism. Similarly, the communal character of education was rapidly undermined by the new individualism: this is the time when, for example, under the aegis of Charles Eliot (elected president of Harvard in 1863), the so-called "elective principle" swept higher education (by 1897 Harvard's *only* required course was freshman rhetoric) and the idea of preparation for an individual "career" took hold. Neither the purpose nor, *ipso facto,* the means of higher education had anything like its formerly strong communal character by the end of the nineteenth century. Thus, higher education today is still largely in thrall to the ideology of individualistic rationalism gestated in the last third of the nineteenth century.

And higher education today is not merely empty of its formerly communal purpose and character, but it also serves as one of the great socializing instrumentalities for the atomistic individualism which has deeply undermined all of our traditional forms of community and even our primary cultural and spiritual capacities for knowing ourselves as communal beings. The massive, continuing fragmentation of knowledge in higher education, beginning with the first academic departments at Johns Hopkins a hundred years ago, and the intense struggle for careerist security combine to witness to no purpose larger than predatory individualism. That is the real socializing force of higher education, not the typical college catalogue claims nor commencement rhetoric about a community of learning which, in fact, are revealed more and more to be abstractly self-serving against that foil of reality. The "new careerism" in higher education, which rests on the Ik-like assumption of all against all, is not "new" at all, but simply the emergence of a process which has been at work for at least a hundred years—a process which, moreover, is common to our whole society.

If, then, institutions of higher education are, as instrumentalities for socializing the young, aiding and abetting the general drift of our society away from traditional communal forms and identities and into forms and identities which radically isolate the self, pitting one against the other, then Jews and Christians in those institutions should recognize the familiar tragedy that is taking place. Humankind, made in God's image for community—for love and justice—is once again caught up in a suicidal idolatry of the isolated self. Furthermore, a concomitant of that recognition will precipitate biblical people in academic institutions into a ministry of communal witness and action, for the fact is that God has not left humankind stuck in its tragic and suicidal dilemma, but has provided means for growing more deeply into our created identity as brothers and sisters of each other. We will now turn to look at those means, in biblical tradition, and then speculate on how they might be realized in and for the academic world.

COMMUNITY AS A SIGN OF SALVATION

God's fundamental purpose, according to the Bible, in entering into our history is to help us so to recover our right relation with Him/Her that we can again know ourselves as brothers and sisters of each other. The most crucial events in this community-making mission of God's are the Exodus, particularly in its culmination at Sinai, and the ministry of Jesus, particularly in its culmination in the coming of the Holy Spirit at Pentecost.

At Sinai the Lord said to Moses:

Thus you shall say to the house of Jacob, and tell the people of Israel: You have seen what I did to the Egyptians, and how I bore you on eagles' wings and brought you to myself. Now, therefore, if you will obey my voice and keep my covenant, you shall be my own possession among all peoples; for all the earth is mine, and you shall be to me a kingdom of priests and a holy nation. (Ex. 19:3b–6a)

First, God points to the palpable demonstrations of his love for this ragtag group of ex-slaves: God is clearly seen to be the initiator of this burgeoning relationship. Then, God tells them the appropriate response to that initiative—"obey my voice," i.e., remain constantly ready to hear and respond to my *continuing* initiatives in your future history, and "keep my covenant," i.e., remain steadfast in keeping the *fixed* conditions of our relationship. That consequentially "you shall be my possession . . . a kingdom of priests and a holy nation" has the meaning not of a prize for good behavior, but, rather, of an inevitable, spiritually organic result of such obedient attentiveness and steadfast keeping. What emerges, as the flower does from the seed, from the restoration of an authentic human relation to God, according to the means given by God, is precisely the restoration of human community.

The terms of the biblical drama of this people have now been set: despite the efforts of prophets to help the people to hear and respond to God's voice in every present moment and of the priests to help them to be steadfast in keeping the ritual law, the fixed terms of the covenant, they nonetheless become periodically possessed of the God-itch, of "hardness of heart," and the first sign of this inner defection is the outward breakdown of community, of "the holy nation." Then God, ever faithful to the covenant, provides means in person or historical event to recall the people to himself and, therefore, the people to *them*selves as community, and the stage is set for some further defection.

This struggle, it eventually becomes apparent, is crucial not only for Israel, but for all humankind. The Lord says to Israel, "It is too light a thing that you should be my servant to raise up the tribes of Jacob and to restore the preserved of Israel; I will give you as a light to the nations, that my salvation may reach to the end of the earth" (Is. 49:6). The promise is that God, like a shepherd, will finally guide the people of Israel and call all the nations to a restored Jerusalem where all will live together in a community of justice and mercy. Israel, as a community, bears witness to the promise that all humankind will be restored to each other as brothers and sisters.

The event of Pentecost is, in many ways, parallel to that of Sinai. God has decisively demonstated his love for humankind in the life, death, and resurrection of Jesus; but what can that mean—in a practical, here-and-now sense—for his friends who have witnessed these events? It is certainly a cause for exaltation that, in the resurrection of their friend, death itself has most awesomely been defeated; but what can that mean for them and the rest of humankind? The answer is given in the coming of the Holy Spirit who, like the voice of God at Sinai, empowers the people to enter into the restoration of their relationship with God, the outward and visible sign of which is their restoration to each other in a new community. Thus, the ability of those filled with the reconciling power of the Holy Spirit to understand each other despite the barrier of linguistic diversity, signals the restoration of the community which was destroyed at Babel because of our God-presumption.

As at Sinai, obedient attentiveness to God is the ground of their life together as they "devoted themselves"—in teaching, fellowship, sacrament, and prayer—to God in Christ. What flows from this restored and disciplined relationship with God is, of course, the restoration of human community in truly radical form. It is charged with numinous power, its members freely share their goods in a time when existence is precarious indeed, and they do so with élan— "with glad and generous hearts"—that inevitably attracts others to their community. No wonder that the writer of 1 Peter (as well as of Titus and Revelations) uses the language of God's earlier promise to Israel to describe this community: "But you are a chosen race, a holy nation, God's own people, that you may declare the wonderful deeds of him who called you out of darkness into his marvelous light" (1 Pet. 2:9). And while this community, too, is immediately attacked, both from within (by Ananias) and without (by the religious authorities who had its leaders jailed and beaten), it similarly knows the promise of eventual salvation in a new Jerusalem with God. This hope is what enlivens them to persist in the struggle for their life together as a witness to God's "wonderful deeds."

Now, while there are indeed some important differences between Jews and Christians about the ground and nature of the communities to which God has called them, the fact is that both assert that the primary constitutive and continuing evidence of God's love for them is precisely their life together in a community of justice and mercy, of generosity and gladness. (Historians of the church have, I fear, made far too much of heroic individuals and not enough of this life together as its primary enlivening event.) Furthermore, Jews and Christians share a similar understanding of the rich and complex dimensions of the communities which are the essential medium of their life with God. In the first place, Jews and Christians require rootedness in here-and-now communities of the faithful both as a necessary means for being nurtured in that obedient attentiveness and steadfast keeping which God requires, and also as the joyfully inevitable fruit of such nurturing.

But, of course, such here-and-now communities do not, simply in themselves, provide the fullness of life in community for biblical people. To begin with, such an expectation would be unrealistic; we, too, despite the favor God has shown us, and despite the fact that we know better, become possessed by the same ironic "hardness of heart" which causes human beings to betray repeatedly that obedient attentiveness and life together which is their authentic existence. While our life together in proximate communities is indeed the very sign of and witness to God's love for the world, we also, willy-nilly, provide in the checkered history of every such community a witness to the lingering power of chaos and death. The fact is that, while local faith communities provide us a necessary, albeit ambiguous, context for our life with God, they are also gateways to the discovery of our deeper rootage in the historic community of the people of God in history, a pilgrim community which begins with Abraham, Isaac, and Jacob and will only end when "God will wipe away every tear from their eyes" at the end of history. Each here-and-now community both receives and gives nourishment to this more abiding community.

The most important means for the realization of our continuing existence in that deeper community is a kind of transmogrification of time. In Catholic Christian communities, the calendar of saints, concretizing as it does that "cloud of witnesses" of which we are a part throughout time, is an important aspect of that incorporation. But the habit of mind which might be called *anamnesis*, remembrance, is common to all biblical people.

When that command to *anamnesis* is incarnated in liturgical form—in the celebration of the Passover or the Eucharist, for example—what is understood is not that a past event is nostalgically reenacted in the present for each participant individual's edification, but, rather, that the celebrant community is drawn by the rite into the original, constitutive event and is, thus, incorporated into the historical community of faith, a community of all who have, do, and will share that incorporation. Local communities in the biblical tradition can only achieve their fullest identity through deep rootage in this historical community of pilgrim people; otherwise they become isolated, quirky, self-indulgent, and anxious seekers after continual emotional highs from groovy worship or instant gurus.

A third dimension of community in the biblical tradition—besides the here-and-now congregation and the historical communion of saints—is that which includes all humankind. One of the most radical statements of it is in the often-repeated Mosaic statement, "There is to be one law only, and one statute for you and for the stranger who lives among you" (Num. 15:16). This inclusiveness is a radical departure from the normally exclusive nationalism or tribalism of the Middle Eastern people at that time. That theme is, of course, developed further in the universalism of some of the prophets and, for Christians, reaches its fulfillment in Jesus' parable of the Good Samaritan and Paul's assertion that "God was in Christ reconciling the *world* to himself, not counting their trespasses against them, and entrusting to us the message of reconciliation" (2 Cor. 5:19). Indiscriminate neighbor-love is, of course, the logical moral consequence of the knowledge that we have already been made one human community by God's own act; we gain *that* knowledge by anamnesis—by immersion in the pilgrim community of the people of God in history, in all the revelatory events of our communal and continuing relation with God; and, finally, we are enabled to immerse ourselves in *that* historic community only by sharing deeply, day by day, in a here-and-now congregation of believers. Thus, biblical people know themselves to be living in a richly complex community of three dimensions—here-and-now life together, the communion of saints through all of history, and the family of all humankind—each dimension presupposing the other two in a mutually reinforcing dialectic.

Faith Community in Academic Life

It is precisely the presence of faithful Jews and Christians in academic institutions, openly living the richly communal life God has given them, which can bring a steady, healing challenge to the demonic forces of atomistic individualism which more and more possess academic life. What programmatic strategies, organizational structures, professional skills such faith communities ought best to employ are strictly secondary and derivative questions, and the fact that we generally accord them primary, even exclusive, attention only demonstrates how profoundly we too have become possessed by the very demonic powers we are called to exorcise. Only as a given collectivity of persons begins to live more deeply into its richly dimensioned calling as a community of the people of God will it discover the appropriate proximate and technical means for its life and witness and, also, only then will *any* such means possess effective spiritual weight. The fact is that our situation is as serious, as perennially desperate, as Saint Paul recognized in giving the following advice:

Finally, be strong in the Lord and in the strength of his might. Put on the whole armor of God, that you may be able to stand against the wiles of the devil. For we are not contending against flesh and blood, but against the principalities, against the powers, against the world rulers of this present darkness, against the spiritual hosts of wickedness in the heavenly places. Therefore take the whole armor of God, that you may be able to withstand in the evil day, and having done all, to stand. (Eph. 6:10–14)

Only, hence, as we consciously and decisively live and grow together in the communal spiritual reality of God's new creation will we have any vision or strength at all to counter the powers of chaos which, in the form of atomistic, predatory individualism, increasingly hold our world, including the academic portion of it, in thrall.

But when one does discover such communities of faith in the academic world, communities whose very life is a rebuke to the powers of chaos and a celebration of the power of God in that world, they seem to have four distinguishing marks. In the first place, they are spiritually disciplined. That is, knowing full well that their life is sustained and their mission focused only through obedient attentiveness to God, they follow Saint Paul's additional advice in Ephesians: "Pray at all times in the Spirit, and with all prayer and supplication. To that end keep alert with all perseverance, making supplication for all the saints ..." (Eph. 6:18). The embarrassment among some Jews and Christians about prayer which inhibits the lively communal and individual engagement in it and prevents mutual support for growing in spiritual discipline bespeaks a lack of faith—certainly in Saint Paul's counsel and probably in God's empowering presence in prayer. No amount of moralistic word and work can cover up or compensate for that lack.

In the second place, such communities are morally engaged. That is, they know that the new life as brothers and sisters which they experience in their proximate and historic life together has its deepest rootage in the community of humankind, that they will remain ever restless until all human beings share in the justice and mercy which brothers and sisters deserve. Some Jews and Christians seem to stop short of this fullest realization of our life in community and, in so doing, they too bespeak a lack of faith; they imagine that God's salvation is intended for a religious club rather than for the world. No amount of effusive piety can cover up or compensate for that lack. In mature and faithful Jewish and Christian communities, spiritual discipline and moral engagement become such necessary concomitants of each other that it is difficult to see where one leaves off and the other begins.

Two other marks of the mature faith community which seem especially crucial in the academic world are that they are theologically reflective and collegially led. Because, contrary to Marx, ideas *do* have power, because academic institutions have become primary gestating places for the ideas which shape our common life, which determine our primary self-identity, and because in such institutions human beings in the most formative stages of their lives are grappling with those ideas, mature faith communities will reflect on and engage those formative ideas out of the experience of their life with God. Communities of faith in the academic world have, thus, a specific role to play on behalf of the whole people of God.

They are also collegially led. That is, while they may recognize that certain specific formal functions are reserved for ordained persons, they know that God is no respecter of persons (David was the youngest son, Jesus from a no-account village), that the community must remain always open to the leading of the Spirit concerning its own leadership. Thus, students, faculty, administrators, staff, spouses—whoever is joined to the community—are all looked to for the insight and leadership they are given on behalf of the whole community.

Such communities of Jews and of Christians—living in all the dimensions of the communal existence God has called them to, spiritually disciplined, morally engaged, theologically reflective, and collegially led—do indeed exist and carry out significant ministries in the academic world. They do so, of course, only "more or less," for we all always have a good deal of growing in grace to do in this world before we are finished. Nonetheless, these are the communities which we Jews and Christians must celebrate and hold up for our mutual edification, which we must attend to and learn from if our presence in the academic world is to account for anything in the providence of God, if we are to be able to accept God's commission in the academic world to be "a light to the nations, that my salvation may reach the end of the earth."

NOTES

1. Ignazio Silone, "The Choice of Companions," in *Emergency Exit* (New York: Harper and Row, 1968), p. 144.
2. Ibid., p. 126.
3. Ibid., pp. 126–27.
4. Colin Turnbull, *The Mountain People* (New York: Simon and Schuster, 1972).
5. Paul Ramsey, "Observations," in *Worldview,* October, 1977, p. 33.
6. Christopher Lasch, *The Culture of Narcissism* (New York: W. W. Norton, 1978).
7. "In Respect of the College, and the Proceedings of 'Learning' Therein," in *American Higher Education: A Documentary History,* ed. by Richard Hofstadter and Wilson Smith, vol. 1 (Chicago: University of Chicago Press, 1961), p. 6.
8. Cotton Mather, *Magnalia Christi Americana,* in Hofstadter and Smith, vol. 1, p. 13.
9. Joseph McKeen, quoted in Frederick Rudolph, *The American College and University* (New York: Vintage Books, 1962), p. 58.
10. Daniel Coit Gilman, in Rudolph, p. 333.

TIME, SPACE, AND PURPOSE
The Struggle for Jewish Community

Richard N. Levy

PROLOGUE: THE IMPOSSIBILITY OF SOLITUDE IN JEWISH TRADITION

It is hard to be a Jew alone. It is not only hard, it is discouraged. While some of the prayers originally said privately upon awakening in the morning are couched in the first person singular (e.g., "my God, the soul You have placed in me is pure"), they are surrounded by prayers in the first person plural ("our God and God of our ancestors"), a continual reminder that the individual generally approaches God through the shared experiences of the Jewish people. There is one God of all the universe, but the proper way for each Jew to encounter God is as a member of the Jewish people, standing with that people at all the periods in its history, from Sinai to the Holocaust, from the call of Abraham (when one human being was all the people) to the coming of the Messiah (when the people will become one with all human beings).

Not only the language, but the stance of prayer reflect this avoidance of solitude. Jews praying alone or in a group traditionally turn in the direction of the site of the Holy of Holies in the Temple in Jerusalem, the place where, it was believed, Jews could come as physically close to God as humans could. It is as though, praying alone in one's room, the eastern wall marked by a decorative *mizrach* pointing the way, one really stood amid a vast invisible congregation of the Jewish people, all directing praises and petitions toward the universal Ruler standing, during the period of Jewish prayers, in Jerusalem.

It is instructive that, when traditional Jews pray the prescribed prayers in silence, they wrap the *tallit*, the striped, fringed prayer garment, around them, enveloping themselves symbolically in a universe created by God and knotted with reminders of the Torah's commandments hanging from each corner. For the traditional Jew, to be alone with God is to feel oneself surrounded by a universe laced with *mitzvot,* the commandments that flowed from the Jewish people's encounter with God at Sinai.

And so, the Jew is never really alone at all. It is traditional to wear the fringes all day long, usually under one's regular garment, and to live and work in buildings whose every doorframe is crowned with a *mezuzah,* the ornamental container of biblical verses proclaiming the unity of God and the importance of our actions in furthering the natural course of the universe. Some of the same verses are inscribed in the *tefillin* even solitary Jews bind around the arm in prayer, close to the heart, so that one lives—in prayer, study, or work—in a world surrounded by the Torah's reminders of the interplay between God and the Jewish people in the upholding of the world. One is reminded of the gatherings of Israelites into their houses on the night of the Exodus, the blood of the newly slaughtered lamb crowning the doorpost, aligning those inside who are consuming the Lord's Passover with the forces of life in the world, opposing the forces of death. Even on Yom Kippur, the Day of Atonement, on which one encounters most awesomely the possibility that the consequences of one's yearly failings may be fatal, one does not confess one's innermost sins privately, but in the first person plural, with everyone standing: "*We* have erred thus before you." Each individual takes up all the sins which might possibly have been committed by some Jew somewhere and confesses them as a personal failing. If the covenant between God and the people is the instrument through which we shall be forgiven our sins, then it equally behooves us to feel responsible for the acts of other Jews, in whose common destiny is our atonement.

It is hard to be a Jew alone; at every step of the path of life one is surrounded by the Jewish experience of God. The challenge is to feel its presence.

THE "FAITH COMMUNITY" OF THE JEWISH PEOPLE

Even before considering the individual examples in text and ritual of the omnipresence of a religious community, it is necessary to look upon the existence of Jews in one's own community and in the world as a fact with theological significance. That the Jewish people is still alive, thriving in its own land and in many diaspora communities throughout the world, able to assist its members in countries where they are beleaguered, is evidence that God is keeping the promise made to Abraham that we would remain alive, one day to be as numerous as the stars in heaven, heirs of the space determined by God in the land of Israel. The existence of other Jews in the world is thus de facto evidence of the existence of a Jewish community, however attenuated the majority of its members may be—those isolated Jews are bound to each other through the fact of their existence, which given the ferocity of the assaults on their existence throughout time must, I believe, be attributed at least in part to the working of the hand of God in the world.

A second contributor to the a priori existence of a Jewish community, as distinguished from a finite number of individual Jews, is the attitude toward us of the non-Jewish majorities in the world, which regard Jewish individuals as members of a community of stereotypes if nothing else, whether we wish to be counted in or not. Thus, both on the basis of our own theology as well as the attitude of the world outside, the very existence of Jews contributes to the feelings of Jewish individuals that their mere presence in the world bears witness to the existence of a Jewish community.

Within that a priori unintentional community, however, there are many forces which strengthen the importance of intentional community among Jews. We have just noted how even the solitary Jew immersed in the seeming privacy of prayer or spiritual stock-taking is enveloped by the God-related community of Israel. But private religiosity is discouraged by requirements that certain prayers and religious actions can take place only in the company of a set number of Jewish companions. Psalm 82:1 declares that God stands in the congregation of God (*Elohim nitzav ba-adat El*), which the rabbis took to mean that prayer requires a "congregation" for God's intimate presence, the *Shechina,* to attend. What constitutes a "congregation"? Its Hebrew equivalent, *edah,* occurs also in Numbers 14:27, where the rabbis understand it to refer to the ten scouts who brought back a negative report on the land of Israel; hence a congregation, or a *minyan,* requires ten. It is useful in this regard to recall that ten was also the minimum number of righteous people God required in

Sodom and Gomorrah before their presence could save the cities—
Abraham (Gen. 18:32) did not dare ask for God to spare them for a
smaller number of the righteous.

What are the consequences of praying with a smaller number
than ten? Certain prayers may not be said: the responsive call to
worship (*Barchu*), the elongated praises of God's holiness, whether
incorporating the "trisagion" of Isaiah's vision, or the doxologies
concluding major portions of the service (*Kaddish* in its various
forms). The latter exclusion is based on the rabbinic understanding
of Leviticus 22:32, *V'nikdashti b'toch bney Yisrael,* "I shall be sanctified amid the Israelites," suggesting powerfully that God's holiness is
too awesome for an individual to approach alone; only fortified by
the community can the individual both experience it and survive it.

The same Psalm verse which requires a congregation for the
standing presence of God also establishes that God's presence is felt
when judges (which the rabbis in Mishna Sanhedrin 1:1 set at a
minimum of three) decide cases. Even the study of Torah, while
permissible by an individual, is less praiseworthy than when done in
the company of others, preferably with a steady companion
(*chaver*), in whose presence the divine dialectic begun at Sinai with
Moses and passed down through the prophets to the rabbis can be
continued. Traditional learning in a yeshiva is not the grimly silent
affair one encounters in great university libraries, but a noisy confrontation of the text and its implications by students reading, questioning, and challenging over against each other. As Moses did with
God, so does the littlest yeshiva *bochur* with his *chaver* to this day.

Do three people make up a community? Do two? When God
spoke with Abraham, all Israel was present with them *in potentia;*
when Moses came up to God and God came down to meet him, all
Israel was present in the flesh. The destiny of all Israel is at stake
when three judges decide a case which becomes a precedent for the
people; it is at stake when two students of Torah carry on the learning of the past into the next generation.

In addition to prayer and study, holiday celebration also requires
a community. Here the primary focus is the family, so important in
Israel's first communal worship at the first Passover. The family
around the Seder table is the community of Israel writ small, but that
community is summoned forth every Friday night to accompany the
Sabbath queen and even at such humble occasions as the daily meal,

when a cup of water to wash and a small loaf of bread to bless and cut evoke the altar of the Temple in Jerusalem. By transforming its table into the common altar, each family does its part to keep the reality of that intimate experience of God alive until the Messiah will bring it fully into reality again with the rebuilding of the Third Temple.

In short, the opportunity for ideal community proferred by Jewish tradition is a common sense of purpose, fulfillment of the covenant between God and Israel; a common experience of the holiness of time, sensed by the presence of other covenanters and by the connections between their time and the original moment they are celebrating—Creation, the Exodus, the Messianic expectation; and a common use of space which transforms the ordinary walls and objects which support their meeting into the instruments of an encounter with God and the people of God.

All these communal elements—prayer, study, holiday celebration, commensality—were combined in the early centuries of this era in the utopian communities called *chavurot* which some of the Pharisees formed to preserve strictures of tithing, of the purity of food in their homes and garments on their bodies. Unlike the communities of Qumran, the *chavurot* did not isolate themselves physically, but moved among the less observant members of their society as preservers of a more intense observance of the *mitzvot*. Some of the rules and degrees of membership have been preserved in the literature, and the ideal of an observant minority sharing the same outward life as the majority has reappeared in our own time, as we shall see later on, as a model for the renewal of Jewish life in the midst of a non-observant, materialistic society.

FORCES INHIBITING COMMUNAL FULFILLMENT

If community is so widespread in Jewish life, why is there so much uninvolvement of Jews, so much mixed marriage, so much that goes by the general title of "assimilation"? It is difficult to embrace the community that surrounds you when you live in a Western society that believes that religion is a matter of individual conscience, and so does not recognize communities, only individuals. The obstacles to the realization of community among Jews are manyfold: they lurk within the Jewish world and the non-Jewish world, and they strike at the possibility not only of communal identification, but particularly of identification with a faith community.

Paradoxically, one of the chief factors within the Jewish world that inhibits the formation of Jewish communities is the very continuity of Jewish existence through these centuries. There is a phenomenal number of Jews who believe that just because one identifies oneself as a Jew one is participating in the shared destiny of Jewish existence, and any conscious acts of observance, study, worship, membership, or monetary contribution is unnecessary. Such people seem almost to be saying, "Look at the terrible decimations of the Jewish people that have taken place over the centuries. Isn't it enough that there are still individuals willing to call themselves Jews in the face of so much virulence? Just to be called Jewish is to share a destiny."

Such people frequently prefer to live in areas inhabited by other Jews, may choose only Jews for friends, enjoy a diet of foods generally considered "Jewish," but when asked why they do not formally identify with Jewish organizations or rituals, they will respond with a reply that is popularly known as "cardiac Judaism": "It's enough that I feel Jewish in my heart." A variety of this response is found among Israeli Jews who insist that it is a Jewish enough thing to do to live in Israel without having to study traditional texts, attend synagogues, observe *Shabbat*, etc. This pattern frequently changes, however, when these Israelis move to the diaspora for any period of time and find that such external evidences of their identity as universal use of Hebrew and an economy based on the Hebrew calendar have disappeared. In their absence, many of these Israelis find they have to affiliate lest their identity be swallowed up by their new environment.

The common sense of purpose, time, and space which I have suggested forms the basis of the Jewish promise of community requires for its preservation the externals of prayer book and texts, like-minded people, ritual objects and blessings at table and holiday celebrations. Jews who have overthrown these *materia* for an invisible internal awareness of their Jewishness run the grave risk of finding more and more of their identity determined by the *materia* of the majority culture, which has no dearth of its own texts, like-minded people, objects, and contemporary expressions to share an identification with the larger culture.

Even more insidiously, when Jews lose the confidence of their own intimate relationship with the *materia* of Jewish life, when they feel inhibited by the presence of observant Jews whom they feel will not consider them sufficiently worthy or informed, they will seek refuge in institutions which promise to offer them Jewish involvement ready made, often on an assembly-line scale. Too many synagogues have substituted unison readings and community singing for real prayer, seducing their members into believing that mere attendance, mere following of the rabbi or cantor is sufficient to enable them to feel part of "the Jewish community." When a synagogue is devoted to the elevation of the rabbi through sermons or a commanding presence, or of the officers through their money or power, the congregant lacking all those attributes tends to feel that only Jews possessing them can enter into a religious community. Too often the early spontaneity and enthusiasm in the synagogue's founding days that brought a bright glimpse of the spark of holiness that connects God and Israel turns merely to pomp and formality when the synagogue begins to grow and needs to enshrine itself in bricks and concrete which no one knows how to shape into a place where holiness can be encountered.

Spontaneity and earnestness are rare commodities in home observance as well. Jews raised by parents who used tradition as a whip often flee from observance in the homes they found with their own families, shuddering at what they remember of table celebrations until they have forgotten even the positive remnants of their upbringing. When duty calls them to conduct a Seder they pretend that the service must be rushed through to get to the "real" purpose—the meal—as though tradition were still an obstacle to bodily enjoyment, as it was when they were young. Other Jews, raised less traumatically, who might have been able to create their own observance, come under the influence of institutional propaganda and believe that there are certain "correct" ways of doing things that only rabbis or "knowledgeable Jews" know about, and so lest they make an error which may have some kind of terrible consequence—or lest someone laugh at them and betray their ignorance—they seek shelter in rote reading from a printed page. That the once impregnable Jewish family is falling victim to the same strains and attenuations of non-Jewish families does not help either. When family is something to be tolerated or escaped from, it is hard to see it as an instrument of holy celebration.

But it would be a mistake to see the established institutions of synagogue and family as the sole internal forces undermining Jewish community. The alternative structures that have arisen in the past decade to complement or replace those institutions have weaknesses as well. The ideal components of community which are shared time, space, and purpose find their obstacles in these informal structures as they do in formal ones. A decade ago, independent groups of students or synagogue members adopted the name and sometimes the model of the *chavurah* to symbolize their desire to conduct a more intensive and intimate Jewish life than the institutions allowed. Like the Pharisaic *chavurot,* the groups that developed within synagogues did not want to separate themselves physically from the synagogue, and even the independent *chavurot,* most of whose members were students, saw themselves as participants in the wider community, influencing it by the public presence of their *chavurah* in its midst. Many of these independent and synagogue *chavurot* have been successful in their efforts to deepen the Jewish experience for their members, but many have also failed because they lacked a clear sense of purpose in being together.

Synagogue *chavurot* have usually been intent on developing their own Jewish experiences without the guidance (or interference) of rabbis or other "professionals." But they have often found that they lacked the resources to do so, and frequently have taken refuge in primarily social gatherings which, paradoxically, have often merely strengthened their sense that being Jewish and being together were enough of a commitment to make. Study *chavurot,* another product of this decade, have often been bedeviled by the anxiety over ignorance mentioned above, and so have unconsciously devised many sorts of schemes to sidetrack them from study. Members announce they have not done the self-assigned reading, the discussion leader for the evening suddenly gets a cold and cannot come, a particularly ambivalent member frustrates the plan of the evening's well-prepared leader by diverting the discussion to extraneous and nonintellectual topics. Jewish women seem to have suffered most from this syndrome of "text anxiety," just as women have sometimes been the most ardent in establishing study *chavurot,* since even the most liberated Jewish women labor under the burden of a tradition which suggests that women should place first priority on home and scholar-husband and that teaching Torah to women may even encourage them to make the wrong choice.

Groups which form themselves into a *Shabbat minyan* are often more successful in forging a common purpose, since they arise with the limited goal of *davening* (praying) together on *Shabbat* and holidays, and perhaps studying the Torah portion at some time in the service. While these *minyanim* are often egalitarian in intent, giving women and men, rabbis and nonprofessionals equal opportunities for influence and participation, many of them are located near college campuses where Hillel rabbis or faculty members help provide both continuity and emergency support when crises come. Yet these groups, too, have not been without problems. Despite their affirmed purpose, many members come for social reasons as much as religious ones—not only to meet other Jews (which, given the traditional interdictions against mixed marriage, has a religious dimension as well), but also because some members merely want to spend *Shabbat* in a pleasant "atmosphere," particularly if they are not ready fully to enter into studying or *davening*.

The social factor in the *minyan*'s purpose shows itself also in conflicts that take place not only around the form of service, but around questions of who has the right to exercise authority in the *minyan*. Have the rabbis any more rights than other members? Have vocal people more rights than shy ones? Do knowledgeable people in general, or members of longer standing? To what degree do old *minyan* traditions have to be observed now? Even a group with clearly defined purposes of praying or studying is forced, if it wants to keep its membership intact and active, to adopt as one of its functions the nurture of individual feelings and sensitivities as it struggles with questions of power and status.

Celebrations of time can be shared by most of these *minyanim* very effectively; the shared space, however, occasionally proves problematic. Most of the *minyanim* meet in borrowed quarters—Hillel foundations, unused parts of synagogues, etc. Many of them are very proud of that fact because they believe that it frees them from the "edifice complex" which has destroyed the spirit of so many synagogues. But there is a price to pay. While it is proper that Jews regard the Temple in Jerusalem as the only truly holy place, it is also true that a place which has been sanctified by the spiritual activities that people bring there can itself add to the spirituality of succeeding layers of experience. When the *minyan* members have no connection with the place in which they meet, when the institution views the *minyan* as merely another user of its space, it is almost as though an alien force, a profane force, were at work in the room undermining the holiness that the members and the texts bring to the *minyan.* The group with which I *daven,* the seven-year-old Westwood Free Minyan near UCLA, used to meet in the apartments of members until it grew too large to do so, after which it moved to the interreligious building it now uses. Somehow members' apartments were places much more capable of being infused with holiness than the lounge where we now meet. Each apartment belonged to someone, it was already infused with the personality of one or more members, and each new arrival at an apartment brought back specific experiences of other *minyan* meetings there. In Roy's house an important fight over the Torah discussion took place, in Shoshanna's a beautiful discussion about names once occurred—and each time the *minyan* returns to that place, the holy sparks of those seminal gatherings regather and sow new insights into that day's *davening.* Particularly in a *minyan* where most of the members are novices at *davening,* it is very easy for stray thoughts (*machsh'vot zarot*) to enter into one's prayer—not so much the sexual fantasies the Chasidim worried about, but concerns about home and work, or merely daydreaming. Such diversion of concentration is sensed by others, and gradually starts to lessen the well of spiritual holiness from which everyone must draw.

Ironically, if the *davening* is uniformly intense and the level of spirituality consistently high, another problem presents itself: do *minyan* members become dependent not on the Jewish people, which is universal and through the prayer book transportable, but on their particular *minyan,* which is not? Many members of alternative *minyans* find themselves able to pray only in a similar *minyan,* which can be found now only in a handful of larger cities. This is, indeed, a problem with Hillel foundations in general: the world of campus Jewry is often an intense, spontaneous, uplifting community whose nature derives from the peculiar time of life of college students and their interchange with faculty intellectuals. It is very hard to reproduce once one leaves the campus.

We cannot conclude this discussion of inhibitions of community intrinsic to Jewish life without making express mention, as has already been done in passing, of the problems that flow from the traditional limitations on the participation of women in Jewish life.

Both men and women in mixed groups have often been self-conscious about how much women "were allowed" to participate in worship, and even when the group is intentionally egalitarian, men often discover an instinctive resentment against women engaging in roles or wearing garments traditionally reserved for men. Many women are themselves surprised by how reticent they sometimes feel to do those things. In that way they are not too different from ordinary men and women who try to work themselves out of stereotyped sex roles and find that the conditioning they have already undergone throws up unsuspected obstacles to doing what their reason and even their conscious emotions tell them is right. We have been part of a community of our own gender most of our lives, and to join a new community which is tearing down those traditional sources of sex identity can for a time feel terribly threatening to our sense of who we are.

OBSTACLES FROM NON-JEWISH SOURCES

It would be unfair to mention all these inhibitions of community found among Jews without noting the origin of most of them in actions and prejudices from non-Jewish culture. In a sense, while it is Jews who divert themselves from community in the ways we have been describing, their diversions are usually inspired by attractions or detractions from the realities of living in a non-Jewish world.

It is first essential to note that the majority of Jews, whether members of synagogues or not, can hardly be called participants in a "community" at all. One very good reason for this is the historic Gentile suspicion of Jews as "clannish," a typical example of the majority pointing a finger at a condition caused by the majority's oppressiveness. Jews have tended to live in proximity to each other and prefer each other's company not only because it was easier to observe Jewish law by doing so, but also because non-Jews could not be relied upon to make them feel welcome or at ease. Nonetheless, Jews in the West, aware that they are considered clannish by non-Jews, have a tendency to become very self-conscious about Jewish groupings, as though merely for Jews to mingle together is to prove the truth of the stereotype. Why "clannishness" should be a bad thing is unclear; if it were called "cohesiveness" or "group self-selection," or other neutral or positive terms, it would be seen as an

ethnic benefit. Non-Jews interested in assisting Jews to fulfill themselves might try to become more aware of how often they are prone
to comment when they see Jews sitting together.

One of the beliefs that lies behind this attack on Jewish cohesiveness is the Western notion, cited above, that religion should be an
individual matter. Both this and the resultant attack on clannishness
force Jews into viewing any kind of overt identification with a Jewish group as a direct attack upon the individualistic views of the
non-Jewish majority. It is also an attack on the Western notion of
self-reliance: "Why do you have to rely on others for your religious
needs?" Strongly influenced by Western ideas of proper religion,
early Reform Jews retained the plural language of prayer but eliminated the requirement of Eastern orientation and the restriction that
certain prayers might be said only when a *minyan* was present. Moments of spontaneous silent prayer were encouraged, and the use of
organ music at such times encouraged the individuals to draw into
themselves and approach God individually. And if I am a person
who is "Jewish in my heart," I don't need a synagogue to commune
with my own being; and if overt association with the Jewish people
makes one liable to non-Jewish censure, then individual prayer is
really a solitary experience, for one is afraid even in one's own room
to acknowledge a need for the Jewish people in experiencing God.

Jewish sensitivity to the beliefs of the majority develops in some
Jews a belief that, since the majority is not Jewish, there may be
something intrinsically wrong with being Jewish. From this view
comes an ambivalence found in large numbers of American Jews.
On the one hand, "being Jewish is good because it is what I am"; on
the other hand, "being Jewish is bad because it is what others are
not." This ambivalence leads Jews to join synagogues, but change
their names or their noses; it leads them to support the United Jewish Appeal, but go to their offices on the Sabbath or holidays. It is
difficult to participate fully in a community if one's heart is divided;
it is especially difficult to let the community—*minyan,* synagogue,
chavurah—lead one into greater Jewish observance if the authority
of that community must always compete with the perceived opinion
of the non-Jewish majority. This ambivalence born of the dual authorities in the lives of Westernized Jews is probably the most persistent obstacle to a significant rise in the involvement level of
American Jews. And, of course, for those in college, living in the in-

secure world of the student where one's primary authorities are outside oneself, this ambivalence can assume staggering proportions. Everyone else's opinion is important at this stage, and being surrounded by so many Western models makes swinging fully over to the side of the Jewish models in one's life extremely difficult. It is even more difficult when the Jewish authorities manipulate the individual's guilt feelings: "What kind of Jew are you if you don't do what I do?" It is not only cultists and evangelical Christians who fight for the souls of Jewish students; a lot of Jews are fighting too.

Jews who manage to overcome their ambivalence sufficiently to join a Jewish living group, *minyan,* or Hillel organization, are then faced with another effect of living amid non-Jews that obstructs not so much the Jewish part of their lives, but the part that might wish to participate as a Jew in Western society. Part of the glue that keeps some Jewish community groups together is a shared memory of horrors which non-Jews have inflicted on Jews, which have been in great part responsible for the continued minority status of Jews down through history. Most communities try to deepen in-group solidarity by continual reminders of what members of the out-group have done (alternative Jewish communities also gain strength by comparing themselves with the failings of the "Jewish establishment"). But the horrors committed in living memory by such varied non-Jewish groups as the Nazis in Germany, PLO terrorists, oppressors of Soviet Jews, leaders of Ethiopia, et al., give this in-group/out-group conflict a morbid reality which cannot be ignored. Or, rather, ignored by Jews. It is too frequently ignored, we perceive, by non-Jews, who argue that Hitler was a long time ago, that we don't want to appear anti-Communist, that Israeli reprisals are worse than PLO terrorism, that the Ethiopian Jews are too small a group to worry about when there are so many others.

It takes a great deal of self-confidence for Jews to rise above these memories and say, "But in addition to cruel or indifferent non-Jews, there are also suffering non-Jews whom we need to work with to help bring messianic dreams about." Jews who feel empathetic about general human concerns already use their perception of Jewish skittishness about non-Jewish causes as one of the rationales for withdrawal from involvement in Jewish groups. And of course the fact that active, public Christian evangelicals are frequently on campus following Jews around, beating them over the head with

Bible quotations, playing on all their ambivalences and self-doubts, doesn't help any Jew feel more positively about relationships with Christians in general. The evangelical offensive tars even liberal Christians who themselves resent the evangelicals, because Jews tend to feel (unrealistically) that these Protestants could do more to restrain the evangelicals, and their refusal to do so seems to signify support of their position.

In addition to these conditions within non-Jewish society which inhibit Jewish involvement per se, there are some other kinds of non-Jewish behavior which in their own ways are inimical, particularly to the formation of Jewish communities of faith, because their existence makes Jews think that religious concerns must pale in the light of the political attacks on Jews. Among these "political" obstacles are anti-Semitism and anti-Zionism; insensitivity to Jewish distinctiveness and vulnerability; and the shattering memories of the Holocaust.

A Jew's first experience of anti-Semitism is a wounding experience—sharp, unexpected, weakening, hurtful. To realize suddenly that another human being regards you not as a co-creature of God, but as an exemplar of a tainted caste is a blow both to one's own sense of individuality and to the group which forms part of one's identity. When it is only the first of many such encounters, it stirs the will to retaliate. Its companion, anti-Zionism, produces a similar reaction in Jews for whom the state of Israel is not merely a nice place to visit one's relatives and language, but is a part of one's religious identity, and can be as much a part of one's relationship to God as the people of which one is a member. It is surely true that anti-Zionism should be seen as a separate phenomenon from anti-Semitism, and that there are Jews who are both anti-Semitic and anti-Zionist—but it is irrelevant. Both *antis* are wounds to the person of the involved Jew, and while it would benefit all of Israel's supporters to look at her with critical as well as loving eyes, it is vital that non-Jews who want to have a positive relationship with Jews should be sensitive to the vital role Israel plays in the self-image of increasing numbers of Jews.

Sensitivity is an important factor with us. Our history of suffering is also an important constituent of our identity, and when anyone tries to tell us it wasn't so bad, or that somebody else's is worse, that person treads thin ice. It is true that many Jews have their own biases against other minorities, and too seldom in the past decade have Jewish organizations supported black needs in an aggressive manner. But when we are lumped together with the white majority, which has oppressed us as it has blacks, Latinos, and most other groups in America, we often feel that the tables have been cruelly turned, and that we are being tarred with the brush that has tried to obliterate us. We are not in the majority; whatever wealth or security some Jews may have, we are still a very vulnerable minority in the world, and it is seldom that the morning newspaper does not remind us of that.

The attack of Hanafi Muslims on the B'nai B'rith building in Washington, D.C., the comments of an American army chief of staff or the brother of the president of the United States, the calumny uttered by the revolutionary leader of Iran, the newest terrorist attack on Israeli civilians—to read the newspaper with Jewish eyes is to fume when someone calls us part of the power structure, because to read the newspaper with Jewish eyes is to read about the Holocaust every day, even in stories which have nothing to do with Germany, Nazis, or even Jews. There are too many Jews in the world whose family tree has great stumps that can never grow again, who therefore feel that a part of themselves can never grow again—and because God allowed that to happen, because anti-Semites and anti-Zionists abound, because insensitivity to Jewish vulnerability abounds, it may be fatal to concern oneself overmuch with religious questions when Jewish survival is at stake. Join a *minyan,* a *chavurah, daven* every morning when Jewish lives are on the line every moment? Don't be an ostrich! Prayer won't keep Jews alive. Protest will, organizing will, politics will. Holy time? Holy purpose? The only time that matters is this time, today, when Jewish survival is constantly on the line, and ensuring that survival is our only purpose. You can't count on God or the Gentiles to help keep Jews alive.

And yet a lot of us do. We protest, we organize, we politick—but we also believe that God is keeping the promise to Abraham to ensure the survival of the Jewish people and the land of Israel. Indeed, given the existence today of a Jewish state and a significant rise in Jewish involvement and assertiveness, God is doing very well. But our part is not only to do politics, it is also to observe the *mitzvot,* in which are included prayer and study, as well as the *mitzvot* to rescue captives and to settle and protect Israel. Non-Jews have been helping preserve Jewish destiny recently too—sometimes consciously, sometimes not. In addition to the impetus in self-respect provided by the Six-Day War of 1967, Jews on campus particularly received a tremendous incentive from the preachings of black power that were so important in the formation of American life in the late 1960s. The message that everyone's identity was good, whether the majority agreed or not, was a powerful tonic for young Jews who had often felt as inferior about their heritage as blacks had about theirs. That black studies should be incorporated into university curricula jolted young Jews into the realization that some Jewish studies had been taught at their colleges for decades, but they had never taken them seriously—or even taken them—and, in any case, many more should be taught than were. Blacks taught Jews that the university should include Jews in its understanding of what culture and learning were, as well as Western whites. If blacks could demonstrate publicly for black studies, then Jews could—should—demonstrate for Jewish concerns, on campus and off, as well.

Even the evangelicals and the cultists, for all the problems they have caused, have taught us something. They have forced us to confront the importance of spiritual questions for young Jews, who have been willing to seek it in Christianity and Eastern sects when they thought it did not exist in Judaism. The proselytizers have sent us back to our own sources, as the black power advocates did a decade ago, but this time to unearth the roots of spiritual concerns, of encounters with God and the forces of holiness in the universe, that lay in rich splendor in the texts and observances of our tradition. Jews who have been quickest to recognize the challenge of the cults have been the Orthodox and the Chasidism, but the insensitivity of some of their leaders to the sensitivities and struggles of ambivalent Jews is gradually leading liberal Jews to explore other sources of spirituality in Jewish tradition, sources that can be tapped without the surrender of oneself to a way of life totally disjunctive from one's previous identity.

At the same time as Jews are rising up against evangelical proselytism, the willingness of some evangelicals to join in such interreligious endeavors as the National Institute for Campus Ministries has helped motivate Hillel directors, once extremely skeptical of the benefits of such activity, to seek out the spiritual values of encounter with serious Roman Catholics and Protestants. Efforts at cooperation in common action projects have been made for years in civil rights, the Vietnam protest, the farmworkers' struggle, hunger marches, etc., but the contribution of NICM has been to extend such mutual endeavors from outward, society-oriented protest to inward, religious searchings which, unlike the action projects, do not blur over religious differences but explore them, confront them, and realize that in embracing them is found a special kind of holiness. I have a feeling that in the 1980s a new kind of activism, inspired by respect for different convictions, will flow from the interreligious understanding NICM has inspired, an activism that may surprise us all.

COMMUNITIES THAT WORK

Given all these obstacles that confront Jewish faith communities, is it possible that any can succeed? The criteria for "success," of course, will be hard to agree upon; large numbers and longevity, the usual measures of achievement in the establishment world, are not necessarily definitive. How committed are the numbers? How vibrant are the years? Do the members have a high rate of participation in the group? Has the community persisted because it is meeting a need in people's lives and adding depth to the Jewish tradition, or is inertia keeping it going, like a bad marriage that is less traumatic to sustain than to dissolve? It can be argued, in any case, that numbers and longevity, like the promise to Abraham to multiply Israel over time, are in God's domain, and that the human imperative is to fill the numbers and the years with significance.

The criteria for significant Jewish communities suggested so far in this chapter are a sharing of holy time, holy space, and holy purpose. Holiness—*kedushah*—means setting limits or, more precisely, perceiving the limits that exist between holy and profane, spiritually full and materially empty.

Sharing the holiness of time, space, and purpose may also assist the members of the community to perceive the way in which they can touch the holiness of the Jewish people's encounter with God in a manner that can erase much of the ambivalence born of life in the West, as well as lessen the fear of non-Jewish perfidy that keeps them from opening their secure spirits to work with Gentiles in cooperative endeavors that can add a messianic dimension to an otherwise this-worldly life, no matter how spiritually satisfying communities of merely prayer and study may be.

A community covenanted to sharing a particular holy time goes out of existence when that time is over. Numerous Hillel foundations invite students to come together from Friday afternoon to Saturday night for a *Shabbaton,* an encounter with *Shabbat,* which begins with preparing body and spirit to receive the "extra soul" which, tradition has it, helps us sense the presence of *Shabbat,* and continues with the sharing of prayer, study, the special meals with their ties to the temple altar, songs sung only on this day, rest which attempts to imitate the rest of God, which enables one to sense one's soul more deeply. When darkness comes again on Saturday night, *Havdalah* is recited, commemorating through wine, spices, and light that the limits of the holy *Shabbat* have been reached and the moment has come to step over into ordinary time, enhanced by the experience, fortified against the ambivalence of the Western week. One ideal of the *Shabbaton* is to offer its participants ingredients they can build into their own *Shabbat* in the weeks to come, freeing them from dependence on a particular group (*Shabbatons* take place but a few times a year with different participants each time). The *Shabbaton* can be extended into a weekend retreat, adding a communal experience of an ordinary Sunday, suggesting ways for individuals to add Jewish dimensions to the weekday as an additional fortification against the ambivalence of the "outside world."

One of my favorite examples of shared space was Monson's Motel in St. Augustine, Florida, to which there flocked in June 1964 about a hundred members of Martin Luther King's Southern Christian Leadership Conference, SNCC, and seventeen rabbis from the Central Conference of American Rabbis. The motel was, for the blacks in that old city, a symbol of their exclusion from public facilities; but on the nights and days when it was integrated, the street before it became a grand praying place, where Christians knelt and Jews sat in prayer led by the holy voices of Dr. King, Hosea Williams, David Abernethy, C. T. Vivian, and the rest. How all our spirits filled that profane space those nights! How close seemed the stars, with their convenantal promise of the future destiny of the oppressed! The conviction and piety and humor of the black leaders, the courage and determination of their young followers, the earnestness of the rabbis thrown together in a jail cell, longing to play a role in the liberation of those so cruelly isolated in their own town—Monson's Motel seemed to have been built as a vessel for just that profound moment.

In Los Angeles, a less exalted use of space can be found every day in the Westwood Bayit, a space shared by some twenty-five young Jewish men and women, UCLA students, who have covenanted to live in the same ex-fraternity house, manage a kosher kitchen, observe *Shabbat* and the holidays, and conduct occasional study groups with rabbis from Hillel and the Lubavitch branch of Chasidism. The Bayit is a rather rundown place, but the signs in Hebrew and English, the pictures on the wall, the remarkable *succah* built each year for the Feast of Booths—all bear witness to a building that has been elevated from the mundane to a vessel for divine encounter. There is passion in the eyes of Bayit members, there is a conviction that Jewish destiny lies in their hands—but not (and this is what saves them) in their hands alone.

Shared purpose is both easier and harder to encounter because, while it does not demand a commitment to shared time and shared space, the limitations set by a circumscribed purpose can cause complications in relationships that break off when the purpose is fulfilled. Further, because the enforced intimacy of significant time and space is absent, the commitment to the purpose can sometimes become diffused. Despite the problems cited above regarding the Westwood Free Minyan, it is a community that fulfills the needs of significant numbers of its members for shared prayer and study on *Shabbat*. That we do not spend all of *Shabbat* together means that we are open to each other as vessels for our common prayer and study, and value each other for that, even though we all might not choose to spend all of *Shabbat* together all the time. It is revealing that when the *minyan* has done a *Shabbaton* together out of the city, the *davening* then and for a few weeks afterward has been more intense, but the growth of families has made the logistics of that experience difficult to arrange. *Minyan* members sometimes berate themselves for a lack of participation that leads to long minutes of standing around, wine glasses in hand, waiting for all the offices for the next week's service to be filled before *Kiddush,* the blessing of wine for *Shabbat* morning, can be said; nonetheless, we have managed to fill these offices every week for almost eight years, which suggests that the *minyan* is important enough for enough people to take the risks of volunteering to keep the group going. We agree in what we want: an elevating *davening* and study experience. If the *davening* is unspirited for a few weeks, some members will inevitably take the responsibility for doing something about it: one of the more effective *daveners* will volunteer to lead the service, a meeting or a workshop will be convened, inspiring English readings will be chosen, etc. The sharing of responsibility, with no designated leadership, is evidence that the purposes are shared and that a common understanding exists of what constitutes elevating *davening* and study.

What makes it elevating? As egalitarian a community as we are, we rely very much on whoever is the *chazzan,* the leader of the service for that particular day. We try, many of us, to lift ourselves out of the muck of daily secularity by thinking, as we come to the *minyan* about the week's Torah portion, about a particular passage in a prayer, about the beauty of the trees and sky about us, but despite our individual attempts we are very much dependent on the day's *chazzan* to pull us all together and, once together, upward. If I come well prepared for *davening* but I sense a lassitude about me, I become distracted very quickly. But even if I have not been particularly well prepared and the leader (let's say it is a woman) is very much into her *davening,* her intensity becomes infectious, spreading throughout the room as an undergirding for everyone's prayer. We feel carried along, encouraged to ruminate on each significant word, each phrase, closing our eyes as word pictures billow up before us, clearing the space between our metal folding chairs until it becomes the place wherein the angels raise their voices to the holiness of God, the place where Abraham offered Isaac up in the faith that somehow the covenant of progeny would yet be fulfilled in his act, the space wherein the rest which was created on the world's first *Shabbat* may breathe into the rest which we have helped each other find this day, and thus become divine.

We are not strangers. Our prayers have mingled often enough within these eight years that our cadences and timbres are familiar, one to the other; and when the person who volunteers to be our representative before the throne of God this week finds the power to stir us to the best we have inside, we are there, our pasts as a people and a *minyan* and as individuals are there, and we surge together to lift what we have brought before the throne which has been raised up between the metal chairs. *"Y'yasher co'ch'cha,"* we say to the *chazzan* when the service is over. "How powerful your strength, how you have empowered the strength of each of us!"

Is it possible these days to create a community which can share holy time, holy space, and holy purpose? Of course it is—but it is hard to find. That is why so much attention has been given in this essay to the obstacles which Jewish life in a non-Jewish society has thrown up to the existence of such communities—because to a great extent the struggle against the obstacles helps in itself to lay the groundwork for the communities of the future. One of the remarkable features about working with that particular segment of the Jewish people which finds itself in the university is the opportunity of confronting so many of these obstacles, and developing relationships and structures that one by one can overcome them. On campus we need not throw up our hands over the "cardiac Jews"—we can walk over to the dormitory, knock on some of their doors, and for a few moments, or for a sustained period over an academic year, assist people to relate to the *materia* of Jewish life which can help them give voice to their own silent Jewishness, be it enrollment in a class, involvement in a dormitory *Shabbat* meal, or a discussion on the floor in which other silent Jews discover for the first time their commonality, their concern about their Jewish competence, and their willingness to trust each other's mistakes and self-consciousness as they explore their own abilities to take charge of part of their Jewish lives.

In a campus setting, students used to the domination of rabbis, professional *chazzanim,* or influential synagogue leaders can gain the experience of leading services themselves, or coordinating a *Shabbat* meal or *Pesach* seder where the food is not the prime purpose but merely an element of a spiritual event whose significance they are now beginning to understand. The campus is the place where Jewish competence can be taught and strengthened, and the sense of "Jewish unworthiness," formed as we have seen by so many factors in Western Jewish society, can gradually be overcome.

Another grand advantage of communities that can be formed on campus, one that in the past decade too few of us have really plumbed to the fullest, is that Jewish students and faculty live out their academic lives amid all of the disciplines that make up Western culture and amid a goodly sampling of the individuals who make up Western society. A Hillel director aware of the insularity that can be bred in active Jews by a knowledge of the oppressions of non-Jewish powers has ready at hand members of the clergy, Christian students, Moslem and Arab students, faculty schooled in the history and nature of the oppressors and the oppressed—all of whom can assist in breaking through that Jewish insularity bred of fear or resentment and help to forge new campus coalitions of religiously sensitive people, or of people who have been the victims of one *anti* or another in their lives, determined that personal history or conviction should no longer stand in the way of cooperative effort toward a world where cruelty and injustice know no place. Most of us who have been involved in any part of that effort know that the air which has shared such intergroup discussions is charged with holiness, and like the space between a *minyan*'s metal chairs, so the room in which we have met will never be the same again. There is so much to do now, as there has always been—so many desperate people, so much agony in the shadow of so much comfort, so much danger from so many weapons ready at any moment to blow us all apart.

And when the students have left the campus, what remains of what we have done that they can take with them? I think our main contribution lies not in the structures we have formed—a Hillel student board, a Bayit, a *minyan*—but rather in the sense of Jewish competence those structures have helped develop in the individuals with whom we have worked. A student who has *davened* in a good campus *minyan* can enter into the life of a synagogue with the confidence that she can find her own holy space wherever she is, and that she has some knowledge with which she can help others find their way to celebrate the holiness of time. A student who has talked with uninvolved students in a dormitory can approach his synagogue or federation with the experience of some approaches to the unaffiliated which have borne results, just as a student who has shared the pain and sweat of interreligious activism knows where and how bridges out of insularity can be built, and can show others how to build them. To fight against the obstacles in a college community can give one confidence in the possibility of achieving holy purpose; it can teach a student how to help create a community in all the paths of life that lie ahead.

In a Jewish environment on campus, individual students, wherever they scatter, can learn how to carry the community of Israel inside themselves.

Let me close with an example of what I consider a holy community of individuals scattered in disparate places but united by a common purpose, which experiences itself each year at a fixed time. It is the annual conference of Hillel directors held every December in the borscht-belt resort hotel called Grossinger's. A debate has raged for years in Hillel as to whether we are a service agency or a movement, and the people to whom the directors' conference means most are those for whom Hillel is a movement, a committed community of rabbis, educators, and social workers whose purpose is to work toward the creation of environments in which the holiness of the Jewish people with God can be experienced in as many ways as students and faculty, enmeshed daily with the culture of the West, can evoke.

At Grossinger's we come together to inspirit each other, and in the process we form our own community during the limited time of four days, days whose existence is measured by our presence with each other in a place to which we are almost oblivious except that it houses our community. For us the rooms and corridors of that sprawling resort are settings layered with the connections we have kept alive despite our scatteredness around the continent for all the years we have come back there—so many confrontations of principle and personality, so many openings of lives and dreams, so much anger shared and so much love. We come to worship with each other early each morning, offering up our high moments and our despairing ones in the year since we have seen each other; we come to learn texts from each other with a respect for each other's learning, a realization of our own limitations, and a new realization of how much we value the sense of our own Jewish competence conferred by our collegiality with Jews more observant and less, more carefree in their learning and more intense. We shake each other's lapels over this cause and that, convinced from year to year that all of Jewish life will rise or fall if this issue is not joined, if this terrible problem is not rooted out, if this magnificent person or organization is not given a hearing on every single campus in the country. There is so much to do, we come away reminded; there are so many good people doing it; there is so much within each of us that has the power to transcend the obstacles to what our life should be.

For me at least, being with my colleagues every year helps me sense a little something of what it will be like when Jews scattered for centuries in the diaspora come back again under the Messiah's gentle hand to the ruins that are the Temple Mount, and from the rubble come as physically close to God as humans can—because we all will be there together. That is perhaps the great value of community: to know that we are in the struggle against the obstacles together, and that together we are on the road to building the ultimate community which God has promised will one day dawn in the world we have helped to shape.

How easy it will be then to be alone, for we shall never be alone again.

"... according to the grace given us"

Elaine M. Prevallet, S.L.

The thesis of this paper seems deceptively simple: that the primary responsibility of a community is the authentic development of the ministerial gifts of each of its members. I risk, of course, stating the individualist point of view at a time which clearly needs to address itself to the societal, the structural, the political impact of faith communities. It is my hope that others in this volume will voice that imperative with eloquence and cogency. But there has been evidence, in the tragic and bizarre mass suicide of nine hundred persons in Guyana in 1978, of how a faith community, under the impact of a charismatic leader, can turn into a deadly instrument of oppression, and how the power of faith can be turned to demonic ends. Collectivism is a perennial danger to genuine community, for it represents the easiest substitute for the responsibility of freedom. A crucial test of authentic faith community will always be the quality of faith and the quality of freedom it engenders. And so I have chosen to focus on the varieties of faith communities as themselves a ministry to the individuals who comprise them, for it is my conviction that the authenticity of such communities will be reflected in the degree to which individuals are challenged and empowered to find and to live their own proper ministries.

For purposes of discussion, we might say that faith communities may have two possible foci or emphases: the emphasis of interpersonal life, and the emphasis of ministry. I need to say strongly at the outset that these emphases can never be exclusive, and that a community will be healthy precisely to the extent that it can hold them in creative tension. Common sense tells us that interpersonal relationships become excessively dependent, inbred, and unhealthy if they do not at the same time cultivate personal autonomy and a broader societal concern. A group turns in on itself and becomes a collectivity rather than a community. Equally, ministry can never be engaged at the expense of individual freedom, and becomes impossible if there are not supportive interpersonal relationships. So we distinguish these emphases just for purposes of discussion, hoping that it will be understood that the ideal always, more or less, in some way or other, includes them both.

Of central importance theologically is the scriptural saying that "you together are Christ's body; but each of you is a different part of it" (1 Cor. 12:27); or "all of us, in union with Christ, form one body, and as parts of it we belong to each other. Our gifts differ according to the grace given us" (Rom. 12:5–6). This saying has always been taken seriously, and it has also been a source of tension; and that is surely not less the case now in post-Vatican II Roman Catholicism. Catholics might once have interpreted that statement as structural, applying primarily in terms of authority to the division between hierarchy and laity. Christ, and under him the pope, was the "head" of the body, and the "head" gave all the directions to the rest of the body. The "head" was represented more proximately by the bishop and the priest who told the laity what to believe and do. Of course that is overstated, but I suspect that the best interpretive image of the church, current before Vatican II, was that of the church as mother; the pope, bishops, and priests as fathers; and the congregations of laity as the children of God. The image is expressive of a highly collective mentality.

Perhaps that image can illustrate a serious difficulty to which we will be referring in other parts of this paper: that of finding the proper relationship between individual values, ideas, and styles, and collective ones. The values held or assumed by a society often reflect the profound wisdom accumulated by centuries of human social living. An individual needs to be formed in that kind of matrix. But collective values and ideas then begin to be taken for granted: "this is the way it is." Thus, they need to be challenged and changed if any real development is to take place in human beings; they need to be tested and either appropriated or appropriately modified by the individual. Society has a vested interest in the preservation and continuation of its present accepted values and status quo. Early education may well be its vehicle. But the quality of life for the future depends upon their modification by individuals who engage the ongoing search for the truth of human existence. To enable people to think and act in new ways, independent of collective pressure, is one of higher education's most essential functions, the one on which the future depends. But it is a function in which education fails most consistently, being for the most part only an instrument of social adaptation. To enable people to envision and to value from a ground and perspective different from that of the collective is one of religion's most essential functions, and one in which it also fails most consistently.

The Roman Catholic church, with its emphasis upon authority, orthodoxy, ritual, and rules, has been viewed as one of the greatest perpetrators of a collective mentality. As the aforementioned image suggests, Catholics were encouraged to obey and conform rather than risk thinking heretically or making a wrong decision. Religious orders had a very strong collective sense: everyone followed exactly the same regimen, dressed, ate, expressed their faith in the same ways, and were likely to think alike. For Catholics, there was safety and a sense of unity in the uniformity, and there was doubtless some value in that.

The strong collective identity was challenged as Vatican II changed the image to that of the "people of God," emphasizing that lay people are full participating members, each gifted by the Spirit for her or his own contribution to the body. But the working out of the relation between individual and group is still difficult. How and by whom are gifts to be discerned? What is the relation between a gift of leadership and, for instance, a hierarchical role? The identity of the one with the other has been assumed and, strangely, assumed to be given only to males. That is being challenged. Nor does the image make clear how conflicts are to be resolved when one person's gift seems to contradict that of another, or how different points of view, particularly in matters of dogma and morality, are to be dealt with. These are real problems in contemporary Roman Catholicism, not only in relation to persons in positions of authority, but perhaps even more as they affect people's responsibility to appropriate their own faith, to know their own gifts and find a way to make them available to the service of the body. An additional difficulty is that that cannot be done without a community which is smaller and more personal than the institutional structure of the church generally provides.

A BRIEF HISTORICAL PROSPECTUS

In Roman Catholic history the "variety of gifts" took a peculiar form that has some bearing on the question of faith community. Certainly, Christianity in its origins was intensely communal—a necessity, one might judge, for a newly formed, countercultural religious sect. The growth and expansion of the church led to the structuring of Christian community in the form of dioceses, local churches, parishes. The end of the third century saw the monastic impulse to a life apart, on the fringes of society, first in anchoritic (hermit) and later in cenobitic (communal) form. These were specific faith communities, formed, as some have said, not in order to escape the world, but to protest the world in the church after the peace of Constantine. There seems to have been a dual direction: a man (and we seem here to be dealing largely with males) would withdraw from society, but would live in proximity or companionship with others, learning ascetical practices, preferably with a seasoned ascetic, until such time as the inner combat with the demons within was seriously engaged. Then he would move into still greater seclusion. Finally, he would emerge, as did Anthony, the prototype of anchorites, as a sort of spiritual father, able to counsel, to heal both spiritual and physical ills, gifted with clairvoyance, able to exorcise. At this point he re-engaged the world to some extent, though still preferring his solitary life. It became commonplace that the solitary life was no life for novices, but was permissible only for those who had seriously engaged the active life within society (generally referring to serious attention to the development of virtues), and were practiced ascetics. It might be noted, incidentally, how much this resembles the Hindu framework in which a man is to live as a householder and businessman and only in later life becomes a mendicant and sannyasin.

By the fourth century, the tendency rose for solitaries to group together to form cenobia, leading then to the formation of monastic communities. In monastic communities, as distinguished from solitary ascetics, ministry to the others in the community was basic, coupled with a ministry of liturgy and prayer; and, where no ministry to the "outside world" was engaged, there was enjoined the ministry of hospitality. In any case, by the time of Gregory the Great in the fifth century, the forms of Christian life were distinguished as active (good works) and contemplative life (devoted to prayer).

Forms of Christian communal life evolved further in the Middle Ages. Monastic institutions continued, ideally characterized by distance from "the world," but now clearly related to the institutional church and, through it, to the prevailing culture. From time to time, there were reform movements, efforts such as Citeaux, to return to a genuinely countercultural, marginal form of faith community. As need and desire emerged, to be at the service of the church or society, groups of canons organized around cathedrals, living a communal life and engaged in pastoral works; there were groups such as Premontré, which wanted to be flexible enough to combine monastic structure with pastoral activity. For a time there was a movement for women who, sometimes singly and sometimes in groups, maintained a dedicated life of chastity, poverty, and prayer in the midst of ordinary social activity. Francis appeared, inspiring groups of men to a life combining poverty, fraternity, and itinerant preaching, while also allowing time apart for contemplation. It would appear that religious orders began to form a sort of vanguard or, less favorably viewed, elite, in the styles of Christian life: while the medieval layfolk seem to have been limited to a spiritual diet of morality combined with somewhat superstitious piety, the monastaries and religious orders drew people who wanted their Christianity to become a more conscious and complete way of life. Of course, generalizations like this cannot avoid falsification: there were always some in religious orders for very worldly motivations, whose piety was only a thin veneer for a worldly life; and there were layfolk distinguished in their commitment and their spiritual development. The Reformation rightly stressed the importance of faith for all Christians, and the value of living it out in mundane settings. Finally, after the Reformation, there emerged still more celibate orders for men and women, engaged now in various degrees and kinds of pastoral work, with a regular regime of life and prayer.

The point of this historical sketch is that, if one speaks of faith communities in a Roman Catholic context, one has to give both weight and proper balance to the presence of religious orders. The contemporary church has wanted to reemphasize the whole church as the people of God, each person or group with its special gift and task and spirituality the special province of no one particular path or group, but the responsibility of all. It remains true that Roman Catholicism, with its dubious genius for organization, continues to want to provide institutional framework, structure, and organization for faith communities, and allows limited latitude; but large numbers of new forms, not seeking institutional approbation, have, happily, sprung up.

Religious orders, traditionally requiring celibacy, continue to include groups of men or women designated monastic or contemplative, which have little or no active involvement in ministry in the world. Other orders provide their members with a regular alternation of action, liturgical observance, and prayer. Still others seem to understand themselves primarily as facilitating each member to follow her or his individual ministerial call, providing a supportive and nurturing framework in which that can be done. Some have a specific ministry in which everyone in the community is engaged—for instance, teaching, hospital work, work with the poor in particular locations. Some, such as the Little Brothers and the Little Sisters of Jesus, have as their primary ministry simply to live and work and pray among the poor.

In recent times, there is evidence of a desire among religious orders to find ways to extend their membership to nonvowed persons so that they can share their life and spiritual aspirations, can include and be enriched by other perspectives, can cooperate in ministry. Franciscans have long had such an extension in their "third order"; many more orders are now designing ways of affiliation or co-membership. The charismatic Benedictine group at Pecos, New Mexico, opens itself to affiliate members for temporary commitment. In this century, too, groups designed specifically for lay people, like The Grail (for women) and Madonna House, have emerged to provide a framework of support for a committed life of faith and individual or group ministry. In the variety of groups, charismatic Catholics such as the Word of God community at Ann Arbor, Michigan, should also be mentioned. Different, but equally important, is the presence of the Families of St. Benedict in Kentucky, a group which intends to provide a monastic life style for families or single persons, and The Grange in Connecticut, a monastic community of primarily lay persons.

There are groups which emphasize one or another facet of ministry, like the Catholic Worker houses in many cities, with their emphasis on poverty, pacifism, and hospitality for the poor. A number of groups have sprung up in or around Washington D.C.: the Community for Creative Non-Violence which engages in several forms of ministry, including a soup kitchen and a medical clinic for the poor; Emmaus House, the pacifist Jonah House, and Tabor House, where a ministry of hospitality is combined with ministry relating to Latin America. It can be seen that there is wide variety in theory, strategy, and style: some groups are primarily engaged in direct action for social change, while others aspire primarily to a ministry of identification with the poor and oppressed. Obviously, there is more than one "way."

These examples only scratch the surface of the myriad forms of faith community that have sprung up in recent times in response to felt needs for new ministries. Each would need to be described in detail, but they all witness to a new spirit and a very vital one. For many of these communities cut across traditional lines: many include members of religious orders, families, married and single persons; many include persons of various Christian denominations. This is itself an indication of a new sense of ministry to be engaged: the desire of persons living various life commitments to enrich and support one another's needs and thereby to facilitate each one's ministry is indeed a new form of community life in Roman Catholicism, and seems to suggest new breadth in the way the Spirit is at work in the world.

It may be well to say here, for it will emerge again later on, that a life of contemplation in a monastic setting or in any other form, even though it involves no active engagement with "the world," is generally recognized in Roman Catholic tradition as itself a ministry, making available (it may be thought) that love-energy or grace that contributes in an unseen manner to the welfare of humankind. The life is itself an affirmation of faith, insinuating as it does that that which is unseen and intangible is nevertheless real and active and as necessary to the process of redeeming the world as are those actions directly visible within the political and social structure. So, groups totally "withdrawn" from the world are viewed as having a ministry quite as important to the world as groups more visibly involved: all are mutually and *reciprocally* engaged in the work of redemption. It seems important that the "ministry of faith communities" be kept in this broad perspective.

The "many gifts but one Spirit" is a statement about ministry: each ministers by being true to her/his gift. It is Christian faith that gifts are given in adequate profusion for the ministry of the Body of Christ; everything depends upon each one's fidelity to his/her call.

If an individual has a special gift of prayer, of healing, of ministry to the poor, the redemption of the world depends upon the exercise of that gift.

Communities, therefore, can be organized which focus on one or another gift, that group together persons gifted in similar ways; or communities can simply focus on the persons, and facilitate the development and expression of each one's gift. Most of us, we may hypothesize, have some combination of gifts, and these gifts will take expression in a life style, celibate or married, living singly or living in groups. At some point in our lives, it may be important to give clear and full expression to a certain gift which seems, for that time at least, to take precedence over the others. For instance, there may be times in our lives when we are "gifted" for very intense and active direct engagement with social and political structures. There may be times when we need to withdraw from that, to engage the inner life more directly and undistractedly. To be able, at such times, to find one's way into relationship with a community which can facilitate the expression of that gift would indeed be a grace. And for a community to make itself available for the facilitation of that gift, whenever it emerges and for as long as it manifests itself, would indeed be a ministry. It is particularly important that young persons who are so often searching for community, should have awareness of and access to some such groups.

No community can be or do everything; each one must be realistic about its limitations, even deliberate about its limitations, and deliberate also in maintaining within itself the tensions imposed by its limitations.

It seems appropriate, before passing on, to say a word about the role of the Eucharist in Roman Catholic life. Traditionally, the celebration of the sacrament has been the communal expression of faith-bonding, in varying degrees of importance. Though its full power may be experienced only rarely, I think it must be conceded that there is at least some vestige of faith community in the variety of faces and hearts gathered around the altar, hearing over and over again, "This is my Body. . . . This is my Blood," and saying amen when the priest hands them a wafer or piece of bread and addresses them with the words "Body of Christ." The Catholic tradition has placed great stress upon sacrament as both expressive and formative of faith community: that the community which gathers to offer Eucharist is saying who it is and is becoming who it is in the gathering. We must not underestimate the depths at which this symbolic ritual action affects the persons who participate in it. Even if one does not believe the Roman Catholic dogma that sacraments give grace *ex opere operato* (simply by the placing of the action), or does not regard that dogma as magical, or at best cannot understand it, still it seems that repeated performance of that ritual, repeated exposure to that symbol, does almost inevitably have some effect. It forms a "faith community" at some level. For those whose presence and participation is perfunctory, the level may not be very deep or conscious; for those who know how to read the signs, the sacrament in a unique way collects, expresses, and effects the deepest meanings of their faith. They are gifted with nourishment in the life of God through Christ; they are formed into a community because they share that same life. And they individually and corporately ratify their identity as the Body of Christ broken and given for the life of the world; they express their commitment to heed his words, "Do this in remembrance of me," not just in ritual, but in their lives. The symbol becomes lived reality. At some level, then, shallow or deep (who can judge?), Catholics are formed by participation in the sacrament. The Eucharist is a powerful collective symbol.

CULTURAL AND SOCIAL FORCES INHIBITING FORMATION OF FAITH COMMUNITY

Having just spoken of the Eucharist, it may be well to move directly into discussion of some of the difficulties that beset the exercise of the sacrament in the contemporary church. For any faith community, the role of communal worship will be a critical question. For Roman Catholics, some specific problems come into focus because of the importance of the eucharistic form of worship in the tradition. Some of these problems are directly connected with the church as an institution. For instance, the Roman church's tenacious adherence to an exclusively celibate priesthood, and to an exclusively male priesthood, and the blatant use of sexist language in liturgical usage make it difficult, unconscionable for some, to participate. The opulence of some churches and the apparent complacency of church leaders and congregations leads many who are most dedicated to justice and sociopolitical reform to despair of finding support, let alone inspiration, for their involvement. If faith community is to be distinguished by its marginality from the dominant values of society, to celebrate liturgy in an opulent or complacent setting, without reference to obvious tragic injustices and inequalities, seems a travesty of worship. And finally, the celebration of mass in homes or small group settings has made real for many that the liturgy can be a genuine personal experience of forming and expressing faith community. Here the Word of God is addressed to people ready to ponder together its meaning, willing to respond to its challenge. Here the bread broken and shared, the cup passed, represent a real sense of sharing a life, of community. But, having had this experience, large impersonal Sunday gatherings come to seem irrelevant and sterile. And the problem becomes one of maintaining any meaningful relationship with the larger, more inclusive Body of Christ, or with the institutional church. The liturgy and the Eucharist present many problems for many people.

Perhaps the deepest problem however, is the fact that so many people seem to feel a kind of disjunction or discontinuity with the past. We tend to think we are new—our inventions, our style of life, even our problems, seem to us to have no historical precedent. It is obvious enough that the acceleration of changes that affect all areas of our lives has left us somewhat disoriented, unrooted; the organism has not had time to adapt itself to its changing environment, and the environment has not stopped changing. That that sort of disorientation would infect liturgical celebration is to be expected. Liturgy and ritual intend, by use of symbol, to put people in touch with that which is far older and deeper than their own historical existence, with what transcends the present by rooting it in the past and opening it to the future. Liturgy intends to give us grounding by relating us to the long and magnificently varied company of Christian people who have been our predecessors in living the faith; it intends to provide us with support and impetus to translate that faith into the future. And yet we find ourselves uneasy, dislocated.

We had taken the mass for granted as a collective expression of faith; we had assumed the meanings we were told. Perhaps the changes from Latin into the vernacular since Vatican II just brings the problem to a head. As scientific-minded Westerners of the twentieth century, we assumed we could relate to the liturgy in a totally rational way, that we could now *understand* what was going on. Indeed, the vernacular has helped. But we have forgotten that those symbols and rituals touch us in quite nonrational, evocative ways, and need to retain something of mystery and transcedence. Having absolutized rationality, we are uncomfortable with what eludes rational grasp, and tend to dismiss it as meaningless, or magic, or superstitious. We want to get it to "work right," which usually means we want to be in control of the meaning conveyed, and its effectiveness, just as we would be of a theatrical performance or a television ad. We keep trying new things. Certainly, adaptations need to be made, but the real difficulty is far deeper, in our psychic inability to respond to the symbolic. We are out of touch with our own symbols. A time of social change will obviously produce malaise in this area.

There are no easy solutions to these problems. The difficult relationship between individual and collective is apparent here. Many move along in a kind of of uneasy peace with a church that seems too cumbersome, unregenerate, ill-adapted to contemporary needs and aspirations; but yet they feel some deeper, instinctive loyalty to the church, and an unwillingness to simply separate themselves. And, indeed, the Roman Catholic celebration of the liturgical year continues to offer the rich spectrum of the seasons of the spirit, an orderly unfolding of the Christian message, and a sense of rooting in something older and deeper than one's own personal history. Here the collective can function in a valid, vital way. And many know, perhaps intuitively, that that is necesary for them. I believe the Roman Catholic church has a real gift in its symbolic heritage, a gift which it must struggle to maintain and represent. The sense of sacramentality and incarnation, so strong in Roman Catholic tradition, derives in large measure from this celebration, and becomes instilled in the communal identity: it is a sacramental community. The Eucharist has an important, if often subliminal, formational influence on many Roman Catholic spirits. The Eucharist continues to be a valuable and powerful collective symbol.

I have already referred to the difficulty involved in distinguishing what is valuable and what is reprehensible in both collectivism and individualism. Collective pressures are always a threat to genuine communal bonds. They are unmasked as collective rather than communal chiefly when one probes into the area of personal freedom and responsibility. While our age seems consciously afraid of rampant individualism, the problem seems to me to come from the other side: it is the overly strong collective mentality that issues in excesses of individualism. We need to be alert to this, for all the instruments of collective mentality are in gear: advertising, the radio and television, newspapers and magazines—they are constantly at work. We know how difficult it is to discover what is true—about foreign affairs, about political motivations and machinations, about the economy. This experience should alert us: it is impossible to live in this society and not be infected. As the power base begins to shift away from the United States, as the economic ground in this country grows more and more shaky, as affluent life styles are more imminently threatened, and as eschatological fears become more pervasive, as the sense of threat looms larger and touches all segments of society, unpredictable violence is likely to increase. We as a nation can become more and more prey to the sort of demonic power that took hold in Nazi Germany. In an age when there seems to be chaos in many areas, even or perhaps especially in the area of faith, people are prone to follow anyone who will speak with authority, tell them what to believe, decide what they should do, envision the future for them. People are prone to wanting to feel safe, to following a leader at the risk of no matter what loss of freedom. At such times, it is very difficult to *see:* to see the subtle effect the prevailing values of society have upon us, to see how to be marginal in ways that matter. It is difficult, in a word, to be a faith community; but it seems increasingly essential.

Still, it is a subtle difficulty for such a community to discriminate the way the collective mentality functions in the "faith" itself. A case in point is surely the current "question of women." How much of the exclusive dominance of the church by males is a matter of revelation, and how much simply a collective attitude, unjust and discriminatory, perpetuated by the theology and structures of the church? Surely this attitude has strong vehicles for its perpetuation: the patriarchy, assumed in the human background and context of the Scriptures, results in the absence of feminine attributions to God, male language throughout, and subsequently a long tradition of exclusively male priesthood and hierarchy. Those assumptions are bred into people who have never, from childhood, heard *God* referred to in feminine terms, but only the (lesser) human Mary, mother of Jesus; who have connected the Father-God with the father-priest-authority; who have never experienced a woman in a hierarchical or leadership role. It is difficult to stand outside that perspective to "see" what really is, especially when the issue is inseparable from complex sexual roles in society. The official channel of change would be the hierarchy, those most subtly invested in maintaining the status quo. How then distinguish what should be changed, and when, and by what means? Obviously the process will be slow and tense and fraught with problems.

This issue simply points up a tendency, perhaps especially strong within Roman Catholicism, to insist too strongly on telling people what to believe and how to say it, what behaviors are and are not permitted, without allowing or encouraging personal dialogue with the tradition, without insisting upon its personal appropriation. Obviously this process needs personal attention, and is best accomplished in a community in which the members engage in frequent and honest conversation relating to faith—a context not easily realized in large parish churches. The same is true for the development of each one's sense of ministerial gift: it too seems to presume a more personalized, nurturing community. There is clearly need within Roman Catholicism for smaller, more intimate groups, which can help people dialogue with the strong collective sense communicated through the tradition.

But that leads to another question, namely, how much diversity, or perhaps *what* diversity, can be permitted without compromising either fidelity or genuine unity. In our time, "celebration of diversity" is a kind of keyword. We are aware that credal statements alone cannot bind a community, that wide divergences of meaning can lurk behind innocently uniform creeds. We are aware that members of the same denomination may differ profoundly in the way they interpret their faith and values, while members of different denominations may feel themselves quite kindred. What are the criteria of faith for members of a faith community? What are the tests? When should a community bend in order to include; when is it legitimate not to bend but simply, in a firm but friendly way, to exclude? How can a group have its priorities clearly enough set, how can it be deeply enough grounded so that the unity is unassailably rooted and can admit diverse styles, expressions, modes, without breaking under pressure or without becoming mere compromise, homogenization, indifference?

Our times have necessitated that we be deliberate in dealing with this problem. We know enough history to be acquainted with the evils engendered by exclusivism; we are sophisticated enough to know how relative and limited our own definitions and conceptual or behavioral boundaries can be. More importantly, we know that to some extent the future of humanity depends on our being able to think and act inclusively rather than exclusively, in global rather than national terms, for instance; to think in terms of the good of humanity rather than this or that nation or group. Our consciousness has certainly been broadened, universalized, and we recognize the need to deal consciously with diversity as one of the principal ascetical disciplines of our age.

Is it possible, then, to allow that a group needs an identity over against others, and may make reasonable and justifiable delimitation of its membership? What is the relation between the ideal of universal community and particular communities? Can we be exclusive without being sinful? Can exclusion, particularity, be used in the service of universality?

It is not necessary here to detail the process of group socialization and selectivity: anyone acquainted with community processes knows well enough the pain of having to exclude. Some communities establish subgroups or affiliate groups for just such a purpose: you can't be one of us, but you can be in relation to us. The Church of the Savior in Washington, D. C., has required a faith commitment; if a person can't make that commitment, that person may still join in some of the projects or in the worship. Religious orders require vows, but, as previously mentioned, some orders have designed ways of extending association to include people who cannot or choose not to take vows. These represent, I believe, instances of sensitivity to the question, ways communities have found to maintain what they consider crucial to their essence or identity, while at the same time having enough concern to be creative about maintaining relationships with those who for one reason or another do not "fit." All involved in such a process gain by being able to share to some extent a perspective, a commitment, an aspiration which is similar enough to be kindred and supportive, but different enough to be enriching.

Probably every community will have members whose tendency is primarily to protect the identity of the group, and members whose tendency is to extend or expand that identity. It is a blessing if both can be accepted and valued, for the healthiest response will be to be conscious of the tension and to try to keep it in some kind of judicious balance.

REFLECTIONS FOR THE FUTURE

I have stated that faith communities minister to the people who comprise them by helping them develop their respective gifts. At certain times in one's life, one may want/need to focus energy in one area or another: interpersonal growth, or ministry by way of attention to inner life, or ministry in the world; I also suggested that each of these must in some way include the others, at least as a healthy tension in its own life. All would be well served if a community knew what it did and did it well, and could take in a person who needed that particular facet for as long as it was needful. I want now to describe briefly the ways such communities might serve.

For communities which I have designated as emphasizing interpersonal life, the commitment to share their lives might mean a communal effort to nurture the life of each one in such a way as to allow each to live her or his calling as fully and truly as possible and to challenge what does not seem congruent. It would thus involve a continual dialogue between individuals and group. These groups may or may not live in proximity to one another, but they are bound together by common aspirations, a common commitment of faith and by a networking of personal ties. Such groups can "model" many things: they can facilitate individual freedom by insisting that each be responsible to her or his own calling; they can model non-authoritarian modes of government, simply because they do stress individual freedom within the group; they can model adult relationships of caring and nurturing which are not conditioned by sexual roles and expectations; they can model simple life styles, sharing of goods and resources.

Many religious orders for women have, since Vatican II, begun to identify themselves along these lines. Much struggle and pain have been integral to their process, since it represents a radical shift from a strong collective mentality to an emphasis upon the responsible freedom of each individual. The common vows of poverty (or simplicity of life), celibacy, and obedience (to one's calling, within the group, rather than to a superior) form the basis of a commitment of life to God and to one another. They may live or work together, but some live or work singly, or with other groups. The group networking provides challenge, resources, support. Since group emphasis is upon responsibility of the individual, there is little need for heavy-handed authority or excessive structure, and authority is viewed rather in terms of facilitation. Communal decision-making processes are becoming more widespread. Communication within the group allows exchange of points of view from various ministries and perspectives, and affiliation of lay people within the community allows yet another facet of breadth, so that a fairly broad horizon of consciousness becomes possible. The non-hierarchical position of women within the Roman Catholic church is in this case an advantage, for it allows sisters to develop new modes of operating and governing, relatively free from institutional pressure.

These are relatively stable groups, having historical roots and tradition. But the same kind of community is possible for a group of families, or married and single persons. With varying degrees of investment or involvement or structure, people can form units of support for one another, to help each other find the most congruent way to live the gospel, to challenge one another to live it more deeply. Often it is a question of recognizing the need; but then it becomes a question of taking the time and energy to find the like-minded people, to figure out what minimal/maximal structure, meetings, worship, investments of time and energy are necessary for the group. The church in this country could learn a great deal from the Latin American *communidades de base,* but following their example would mean reordering priorities of time and energy. In any case, one needs to know that community does take time. It is often easier to go it alone, to ratify the status quo. But one misses the challenge, the support, the unexpected and unpredictable grace that community is.

Turning now to forms of ministry, inner and outer, it is *au courant* in our society at this time to speak of (and have experience of) other levels of consciousness, heightened awareness, peak or ecstatic experiences. Where before such experiences were apparently the domain of an elite, the mystics or contemplatives, they are now being *sold* to any number of enthusiastic trainees by any number of enterprising groups. That such enterprises are the big businesses they are testifies to the longing of the human spirit for MORE that it instinctively knows is its birthright; but, sadly, it also testifies to the harnessing of that longing to ego desires for health, wealth, and success. It is an ambiguous sign of progress for the human spirit.

And yet, if other levels of awareness are available to human beings, and if certain techniques can be learned that conduce to such experiences, have humans the responsibility to pursue them? At what cost? It is well known that attention to the inner life requires time and concentration of energy—and is it elitist to turn attention inward when our sisters and brothers who share the planet are oppressed, starving, dying? Is it a temptation of the spirit to be resisted? Or is it a ministry to be engaged, since it looks forward to the development of new levels of consciousness that belong by definition to the future of human being?

In this case, a "faith community" would make a difference, for it would be a community whose goal is not ego aggrandizement or worldly success, but worship, union of love with God; not simply narcissistic self-development, but the following of an inner call which enables, in fact demands, that those persons quietly and often obscurely allow God access to the deepest reaches of their spirit, make themselves available to be totally penetrated inwardly by God, in order to release for others the love-energy which redeems the world.

It does appear that the reaching out of humankind in this century—out into space, out into the rest of the planet by way of communications, out into nature by way of technology—is being balanced by a turning inward of equal intensity. There may be operative a sort of cosmic ecosystem, something like inhaling and exhaling, that now pushes some individuals more deeply inward, simply to balance what has seemed the dominant thrust of this century, the push outward. It seems axiomatic that as the task of the outer world becomes more and more demanding of discipline, of knowledge and specialization, and of self-constraint leading to freedom, the task of the inner world becomes equally more demanding.

This movement need not be thought narcissistic or judged unfavorably as a response only by timid souls who "can't cope" with the turmoil and chaos of the world, and so desire to escape inward. Some may well seek escape in this direction, as others seek escape in other "good" avenues—work, service, pleasures or distractions of any kind. But no one who seriously engages the inner life does so in hope of escape—at least not for long. The confrontation of demonic power in the outward world must be dealt with in an inward way as well, at least by some. As long ago as the earliest hermits, the move to the solitude of the desert in its best impulse was not a move to escape but to confront: to confront the inner demons and wage warfare on that ground until one's spirit was purified. It would seem that that is not less necessary or possible in our day. And, indeed, the crowded, fast-moving cities seem to be leading some persons to seek places of solitude, not out of antisocial feelings, but precisely in order to be able to relate more personally, deliberately, and freely to people and society. The popularity of Eastern meditation practices is doubtless open to the charge of faddism, but at a deeper level it signals that human beings know inner areas of themselves that are being at worst violated, at best neglected, in the muddle of contemporary life. Psychology now, especially Jungian psychology and its offshoots, offers valuable theories and techniques for dealing with the unconscious levels of the human psyche. Techniques are only techniques, and cannot be absolutized into ends, or idolized; but they can be very useful means for probing the human spirit, for releasing the love-energy that redeems, for lifting the spirit in worship to God.

It is important, in this connection, that access to experienced guides be available when it is needed. Communities that have a tradition of experience in contemplation, communities that have a commitment to exploration of the inner life for the sake of worship, can offer competent guidance and share their experience with persons seriously seeking to attend to the inner life. It is imperative that these communities be broad-minded: aware of the relationships between Eastern and Western traditions of mysticism, alert to the ways that depth psychology can enhance the pursuit of the inner life. And it is at least equally important that these communities be sensitive to critical issues of justice, sensitive to global needs and problems, willing to relate from a very broad perspective to the universal development of humankind. They must be people who care very deeply about the future of humanity—who care so deeply that they are willing to give their lives for that future, and do it by following their call to solitude and contemplation.

There are modest signs of such development: monks from East and West have begun exchange, of ideas and views at first, and more recently of visits. Contemplative communities struggle to find ways to make their life accessible to earnest seekers, while at the same time remaining faithful to the integrity of their call to solitude. Some communities allow guests to share their life and work for periods of time. They might also open themselves to the nurturing of different communal forms of life—for laity, for social change—allowing them to benefit from monastic experience and stability. Such movements, indicative of new openness, will be immensely valuable, and are an essential ministry for our time.

If some communities focus on the inner life, others will focus on society and social change. And if, as I suggested, communities dedicated to the inner life need to be characterized by breadth of perspective and social concern, communities dedicated to social change have equally to be concerned that their modes of operation, their analyses, their strategies, proceed from a deeply grounded faith in a transcendent love. Only that will prevent them from growing callous, or cynical, or violent. Only that will allow them always to respect the freedom and integrity of every other human being, on whatever side of an issue he or she might be.

So much needs to be done. The needs of the poor, the sick, the elderly, must always be met. Some groups, as mentioned earlier, will choose a life of simple identification with the poor, as a life of compassion, suffering-with. But new modes of ministry are also evident. Consistent effort must be made to raise public consciousness on many issues, such as the madness of the arms race and the dangers connected with nuclear power. Environmental issues must be addressed. Steady work on issues of justice in this country and abroad—rights of migrants, coal miners, women, racial and ethnic minorities, economic exploitation here and abroad. The reciprocal relationship between society and individuals is important to remember. Structural evils need to be confronted structually—through law and politics and stockholders' meetings; society's structures must change so that people's minds can change. But they must also be confronted where they finally reside, in the men and women who hold the pieces of power that together make the structure what it is. These people are not "the enemy," they are not "evil." They are everyday citizens who, sometimes unknowingly, make decisions in terms of dollars rather than people. These people can be appealed to personally, individually, quietly and peaceably. Such one-to-one approaches can often be the most effective because they come closer to changing a person's mind and heart—conversion—than is the case when power is simply met with power and vested interests on all sides feel themselves threatened. It appears striking to me that, in Christian tradition, redemption is won through weakness, the folly of the cross, and not through power. That points, in my opinion, to a need to consider much more seriously a radically nonviolent approach to social action.

If communities are organized around issues or causes, it is important that they not get caught in their own kind of power trip, using power to fight power. Such involvement demands the most rigorous self-discipline and monitoring of ego-investment. If such a group strategizes, it must stay clear of idolizing, or even owning, its strategies; strategies themselves must be submitted to the most rigorous examination for traces of self-righteousness, group elitism, desire for success or winning. Consistent care must be taken not to hold oneself/the group superior to the "enemy," and to keep in realistic touch with common humanity, the tendency to evil in *us*. One may never be in a position of perfect purity on these questions, but one *must* be rigorously honest. Such communities must, then, develop ways of searching the truth of their own hearts, of submitting their strategies to the deeper will of God, of holding their actions under the scrutiny of the Word of God in the gospel, heard and interpreted within the community.

This kind of ministry will then demand a high degree of interior discipline, and communities must foster such discipline: fasting, communal prayer and reflection, time for searching, alone and together, the proper motives and the proper strategies. It is at this level that a community can minister to the freedom of its individual members: to free them from the pressure of societal values in order to be able to see what is evil and oppressive, to go against dominant social trends when necessary; but also to be free from the need to be right, to succeed, to win—in other words, free each one to act out of a deeply rooted liberty of Spirit. And, through mutual support, the community frees them to continue to hope.

It will readily be seen how necessary a community is for such involvement; it is also obvious that such a community cannot do without honest and supportive personal relationships and attention to inner life. It is a large order, immensely demanding. A group dedicated in such a way will surely need to extend itself to others who can support and share the ministry, though not engaged in it full time.

It is not difficult to imagine the Eucharist as the unifying symbol of all this. The meaning is there: the people of God come together to be nourished with the life of God in Jesus Christ, to nourish one another by their faith, their presence, their participation, with that same life. The Word of God in Scripture, sacrament, and in the community challenges each to find the way to express in her/his own life Jesus' pattern of self-donation: whoever will lose her life will find it. Not only challenged, but fed: each receives the bread and wine for him/herself; each says "Amen" to being/becoming the Body of Christ, bread for the world. All are nourished by the same life of Christ. Each will translate that life in his/her own setting and style; no two will be exactly alike. But all express and ratify their sense of sharing and interdependence, united as they are in the Body and Blood, the Life, of Jesus Christ.

While it is easy to say that the meaning is there, the difficulty remains: it must be perceived and appropriated by the community. We can hope, I think, for a renewed sense of the importance of symbols that unify us, given that we are beginning to recognize our need. We can hope that communities will work to find the settings and forms in which the sacrament can once again nourish them. Perhaps we can hope for openness, in the Roman Catholic hierarchy, to wider participation in sacramental ministry, especially for women. And always we can pray that some day we will realize in our lives the commitment we make when we gather for Eucharist.

CONCLUSION

A few remarks can be made in conclusion. The first is obvious: life is not so tidy as these neat groupings of like-minded spirits I have described. Our own gifts most often seem much more ambiguous than "a gift for this or that"; our own gifts are often not clear to us. It might be that that is so precisely because we lack communities that are deliberate about evoking, discerning, and encouraging them. In any case, while the models will probably never exist in pure form (except perhaps for a moment, prior to evolving into new complexity), it may be helpful to imagine them clearly, so that we can distinguish differences and have some notions of the factors involved.

A second comment pertains to a debate perhaps peculiar to Roman Catholicism about the relation of action and contemplation. Much depends upon how terms are defined. I have not attempted to engage the debate, but speak of each as a form of life having its own integrity. Each is a ministry of love; one need not be minimized or threatened by the other. The disciplines practiced in each are differently contextualized, but each must have ways to monitor ego-investment, and each must love as broadly and deeply as possible. Many persons will combine them, in alternating seasons of the spirit, in different ways and in varying degrees. Mystical experience can lead to deep social concern and insight; social/political engagement can be a way to "lose oneself" in love, and issue in deep union with God. Persons will be whole, integral, if they are doing what they are called to do wholeheartedly, with the deepest engagement of their being. Each one is a service. "Our gifts differ, according to the grace that is given us." We need to trust the gracious design that each of us is, and that all of us together are making.

And, finally, what of campus ministry? I suggested early in this essay that one of the most essential tasks of higher education is to enable people to think and act in new ways, independent of collective pressure. And I suggested that one of religion's most essential tasks is to enable people to envision and value from a ground and perspective different from that of the collective. Campus ministry is situated right at the hub of those two enormous tasks.

Places and contexts have to exist where persons who are engaged in the educational process can "come to themselves," sort out their own values, and find their life directions. In education, they are involved with an immense, massive system that is more than a little coopted by the principalities and powers that grip this troubled nation. It is a system which, in sometimes hidden and sometimes blatant ways, perpetuates the collective mentality of this society and which solicits many a compromise of values.

All I have said in this essay about the necessity of community in helping each one discover and live her/his own gift is applicable in a fundamental way to campus ministry. Here persons are at the beginning of adult commitments and life directions. They need to have a context in which they feel known and loved enough to explore their individual capacities and gifts. They need a place where they can come to grips with their own—or their parents'—tradition, in order to appreciate them. They need both challenge and support for the experiments they engage in in developing their own life style and values. They need a context in which they can test their ideas about their own future and humanity's future, and have those ideas challenged from the ground and perspective of a transcendent faith. They need a context in which they can question their own accommodation to the values and assumptions of the society in which they live, as these are perpetuated through the educational institution. A classroom may be a forum for such exploration, but ordinary class size and the untruth of a "value free" environment often make that unlikely. A campus faith community is the place where that can best be done.

And what I have said about the necessity of experiencing and validating modes of knowing other than the rational is clearly highlighted in an educational setting. "Academic" by and large means intellectual rationality, and education has surely focused on the development of that single human capacity. It may well be that society's loss of the sense of symbol is directly related to the assumptions propounded by the educational system to which all its members have been subjected. In any case, a community where another kind of knowing (i.e., faith) is valid, and where there is exposure to symbol and ritual, will be especially important while one is under the influence of the educational system. A campus community can provide small group settings for both individual exploration and liturgical experience.

Maybe it isn't as impossible as it sounds. I had occasion to visit a student community at the University of Wisconsin, chaplained by Edwin Beers who is one of the writers of this book. That setting is surely a prime example of the massive system in question. But on an unimposing street somewhere in the huge complex, a changing group of students lives in a large but unpretentious house. The group includes men and women, married and single, various nationalities, graduate and undergraduate, various denominational affiliations—an ecumenical microcosm. The group celebrated a Eucharist, preceded by psalms and songs selected by the student planners. We had a delightful meal cooked by a young man from

Mexico. There was some discussion of house responsibilities and the week's agenda setting at the end of the meal. Then we adjourned for a discussion in which some of them shared, spontaneously and soberly, some of the questions they face in the university. Can one prepare to follow a career in which one is gifted and to which one feels drawn, but which in actual practice seems to demand a life style and values that one cannot, in conscience, accept? How to deal with the money-related career expectations of parents when one feels drawn to a simple life style? How to deal with a strong sense of compromise of individual integrity that seems endemic to both the testing process and the writing of theses and dissertations within a certain department? We talked of the meaning of Christian commitment, of the role of the cross . . .

It was a quiet, probably fairly typical Sunday evening. A certain ease and gracious spirit about it. Nothing much went on. Low key, nothing fancy, nothing special. A community that probably has its troubles.

But it was all there.

That experience reminded me of something about grace and something about trust. It is, after all, a matter of grace, a gracious God sharing life with humankind, in a grace-filled process for their union with one another in God. Community lies at the deepest level of each of our beings, where God is; and in proportion as we live deeply, we discover the treasure—ourselves, one another and God, in community, inextricably bound. That always comes as a gift. We need to seek one another out, to do what we can to build community; but we need to go at it gracefully, in quiet trust. The gift is already given; our task is to let it be.

Religion itself will be greatly tested, in the decades facing us, whether it can serve as more than a palliative for frightened spirits; whether it can inspire people to firm and steady life patterns of simplicity, caring, reconciliation, of free, graceful presence. We will be tested on the depth and quality of our trust; whether our trust in God is equivalent to trust in our fellow human beings—for that is the difficult and decisive mark of faith in an Incarnate God. The need for community can scarcely be overstated. The campuses of educational institutions can—*must*—provide some beginning ground. We must move quickly to experiment, and learn quickly, now while there is still time.

WHAT IS FAITH COMMUNITY IN THE BLACK EVANGELICAL TRADITION?

Eric Payne

WHO EVANGELICALS ARE

Structures for Serving the Faith Community in Higher Education

Evangelicals acknowledge and affirm a more or less common theological commitment. As a result, evangelicalism borders on having a quasi-denominational status. The ecclesiastical structure of evangelicalism is represented by an abundance of independent churches which are nondenominational or interdenominational. Most of these churches participate in the National Association of Evangelicals. Equally represented in evangelicalism are the many individual denominations which align themselves with the evangelical perspectives.

The evangelical presuppositions have been consolidated into doctrinal precepts which have become the basis of theologically distinct seminaries. However, the mainline Protestant denominations have not surrendered exclusive use of the term *evangelical;* witness Garrett Evangelical Theological Seminary, which is United Methodist and considered to be liberal by most evangelicals.

Evangelicals have erected, besides the graduate schools of theology, a number of undergraduate colleges in their tradition. Wheaton College, Wheaton, Illinois, is the most prominent of the dozen or so of these undergraduate institutions. The more prestigious of these evangelical undergraduate colleges belong to the Christian College Consortium.

In distinction from these ecclesiastical and educational structures are a number of paraecclesiastical and educational organizations. Evangelistic outreach is the primary concern of most of these organizations operating alongside the church, but only a half-dozen or so have national ministries which focus upon higher education. The organizations having particular significance are: Inter-Varsity

Christian Fellowship (IVCF), the Navigators, Campus Crusade for Christ, and Young Life. Other related ministries are Youth for Christ, Teen Haven, Teen Challenge, the Seekers, and the Surveyors, but these are usually found in several specific large cities. Though they concentrate on the youth culture, they are not generally directed at higher education.

These parachurch evangelical organizations operate largely on secular campuses. Each of them often represents a differing type of staff person and of student constituent. Inter-Varsity has a very low key approach to evangelism. For them the ministry task is often intellectually motivated, resulting in a sort of informed "fellowship evangelism." As a result IVCF tends to attract a less evangelically aggressive student. The Campus Crusade for Christ employs a more confrontational approach to the ministry task, where the prospective convert is "pressed" to make a "decision for Christ." This not so subtle form of "coercion evangelism" attracts a more active, dominant, and extroverted student. The Navigators, whose emphasis is upon "evangelistic *discipleship,*" have tended to attract a more disciplined and ascetic student, able to forego immediate gratification in order to achieve a long-range goal. This is one reason why the Navigators have had a greater success within the military, where the movement originated. The staff personnel and student constituents for the Navigators are often former or reserve military men utilizing their G.I. bill benefits for higher education.

Young Life's clientele is primarily drawn from students in secondary secular public schools. Although this is not ministry in higher education, it is a key area of student ministry and affects ministry in higher education because it tends to push students toward higher education as part of an upward mobility effort. Conversion to Jesus Christ is often implicitly conversion to a white, American, middle-class life style as well. Thus, in accomplishing the ministry task, student radicalism and rebellion are effectively preempted too. Young Life thus receives a warm and open welcome from middle Americans seeking to reinforce their values in their children and who are seeking to prepare their children to go through college with minimal mishap and without dropping out.

Group Identity and Orthodoxy
There are a number of variant ideologies which are representative of evangelical theology/doctrine. Richard Quebedeaux[1] has sum-

marized the major distinctions in four categories: (1) separatist fundamentalism; (2) open fundamentalism; (3) establishment evangelicalism; and (4) the new evangelicalism.

The "fundamentals of the faith" have been commonly summarized as: the verbal inspiration of the Scriptures; the virgin birth; Christ's substitutionary atonement; Christ's bodily resurrection; and the Second Coming of Christ. Stated in caricatured metaphor, the "separatist fundies" are ultra right wing, conservative, isolationist. The "open fundies" are slightly to the left of the separatists, less vocal, and less isolationist. Both groups tend to be dispensational in their view of biblical history, and have been stigmatized as being anti-intellectual.

"Establishment evangelicals" are the "orthodox scholars." They also adhere to the "fundamentals of the faith," but not without a genuine, albeit limited, critical review in the academic arenas. Their laity still follow a dispensational theology, but there has been a strong influx and overlap with reformed and covenant theologies. Probably the greatest agreement among the "establishment evangelicals" and both of the "fundy" groups is open and unequivocal rejection of social conscience.

Quebedeaux recognizes a major divide between these groups and "new evangelicalism." The new evangelicals have made significant criticism of strict literalist interpretations of the Bible. They have made radical engagements with social action. There has been an informal break with dispensationalism. And the new evangelicals have participated in ecumenical dialogue and even co-ministry. In short, the new evangelicals have "touched the lepers" and thus become contaminated themselves.

My own correlation of these categories with the contemporary popular ministries in higher education from the evangelical tradition is: Campus Crusade for Christ would correspond to the "separatist fundamentalism"; the Navigators would correspond to an "open fundamentalism"; Inter-Varsity Christian Fellowship and Young Life would correspond to "establishment evangelicalism"; and the National Black Christian Student Conference and Tom Skinner Associates/Campus Ministry would correspond to the "new evangelicalism," or more properly the "new *black* evangelicalism."[2]

Quebedeaux also makes mention of the "Charismatic Renewal" which in many instances has a close association with evangelicalism. For specific concerns and expressions of "ministries of the Spirit" in the academy, one must look to the classical Pentecostal and Holiness traditions, and not to the more contemporary charismatic renewal movement. When researched, the astonishing facts are revealed that the contemporary Charismatic-Pentecostal movements are clearly traceable to black origins. The movement was founded by William J. Seymore, with the establishment of the Azusa Mission in Los Angeles, California, in 1906.[3]

THE BLACK COMMUNITY AND EVANGELICALISM

Black Evangelicals and the Institutional Church

The Negro/black church has been inherently evangelical, and this is true of its initial conception as well as of its development upon American soil, first under the auspices of institutional slavery and then under the auspices of the segregated society. Some historians date the origins of the Negro/black church to the beginning of the "middle passage," when the slavers would baptize the "heathen natives" before chaining them in the hull of the ship for the duration of the voyage.[4] This was done by the slavers presumably to appease their own consciences because of the foul injustices perpetrated upon their "human cargo." However, it is suggested that this terrifying and often confusing ritual invoked a divine "watchcare" upon the captives, enabling many to survive and flourish in a new world, when an estimated twenty-five million perished in that middle passage.

The more recent strains of black evangelicalism have their roots in the formation and proliferation of the African Methodist Episcopal Church (AME), founded by the Reverend Richard Allen and of the Free Baptist traditions, exemplified by a minister like the Reverend John Jasper. The African Methodist Episcopal Church is significant because it marks the first structural autonomy of a free black church. Likewise, Jasper, a fine primitive Baptist preacher, from Richmond, Virginia, is not rare as an example of the depth and breadth of the oral tradition characteristic of Negro/black worship experience. These factors of structural autonomy and the strengths of the oral tradition have both been fundamental in sustaining and nurturing the formation of the black faith community on the American soil.

Two crucial factors bear mentioning here. First, the evangelistic imperative did not emerge as the only important aspect of the Negro/black church because of the larger role the church was made to play as the *only* viable and independent institution in the black community. Everything which was pertinent to life for black people in one way or another was included in the Negro/black church. Charitable societies of all sorts operated through the church; burial societies, fraternal orders, and even higher education for black Americans can trace their origins in some way to the Negro/black church. Second, personal conversion was a more vital issue early on because of the psychic status it conferred on the slave. Salvation was equated with wholeness pertaining to one's humanity and personhood, and it meant *freedom.*[5] That freedom might only be rendered in "spiritual" terms was incidental because of the comfort and hope that freedom in any form offered to the slave. After the emancipation, the church directed its energy to the social development of the free Negro.

As Ralph Ellison has so aptly said, "Any people who could undergo such dismemberment, resuscitate itself and endure until they could take the initiative in achieving their own freedom are obviously more than the sum of their brutalization."

Black Evangelicals and Institutions of Higher Education

Unlike their white counterparts, black evangelicals can lay no claim to any particular institutions of higher education—theological seminaries, undergraduate colleges, or the popular bible schools—although there does and will continue to exist a small number of *minority* students (not necessarily black Americans) enrolled at any of these exclusive institutions. However, there do exist numbers of black colleges, seminaries, and bible schools which rather exclusively service the black faith community. The Interdenominational Theological Center in Atlanta, Georgia, and Howard University School of Religion are among the most prominent of the seminaries. There is a strange irony about black evangelicals and their quest for institutional realization. Of the 110 (give or take a few) Negro colleges in America, upwards of eighty-five have their origin in the Christian experience of the Negro/black church. Black colleges and universities thus historically founded might be expected to reflect a very high view of ministry in higher education. However, the overwhelming need for blacks to have a broadly based liberal arts education as a post-emancipation rite of passage and means of upward mobility led to the demise of the religious presuppositions upon which black colleges were founded. In view of the secularization of these black institutions and their campus environments, black evangelicals do not find them to be places where a wholesome, meaningful, and religiously integrated education can be obtained.

Black Evangelicals and Paraecclesiastical Organizations

In each of the major (white) parachurch organizations conducting ministries in higher education, respectable and responsible black individuals will be found. (We should understand respectable and responsible as indices for "how well blacks follow whites," not as a term for Uncle Tomism.) Where these major (white) evangelical organizations have articulated concerns for ministering to minorities (i.e., black Americans, American Indians, Spanish Americans, and Asian Americans), they have attracted a conglomerate of black and nonwhite individuals, and these individuals have formed into caucuses of that particular constituency. As minority caucuses, they are the prime recipients of *special* services, a reflection of an older separate-but-equal philosophy. This is the same separate-but-equal philosophy publicly and overtly abandoned by the secular institutions some years ago.

When a concern for ministering to black Americans becomes an important reality of the ministry, two things happen immediately. First, the concern is broadened to include more minority groups. Second, the focus becomes international. We may understand, then, that the *special* services are never intended to focus upon or address real issues confronting black Americans. They are merely a way of establishing the super-exoticness of a minority group and thus to serve as justification for its noninclusion into the mainstream of the religious life and tradition.

Black individuals participating in major (white) evangelical organizations, either in the leadership roles or as recipients of its ministry, have played two roles: first, as the frustrated second-class citizen and, second, as the refugee-exile isolated from his/her people. Aspirations for *total* reconciliation are not realized.

There are those individuals who have sought to build, as alternatives, evangelical parachurch organizations for and to blacks. The viability of these organizations has been determined and measured by: (1) autonomy; (2) financial independence; and (3) the ability to surface and/or define pertinent issues and concerns of the black community and to provide a meaningful response to those issues. One of the greatest assets of these organizations has been their ability to develop competence among indigenous leadership (as opposed to leadership supplied by whites). Although black evangelicals participate in this mode of leadership development, it is not a new process for blacks in higher education where the less than mediocre have been quickly and efficiently brought to a level of sufficient achievement. Many of these people have subsequently become leader-servants of the black community. One of the earliest black evangelical associations was the Harlem Evangelistic Association. From this group Tom Skinner emerged and formed Tom Skinner Associates, which conducts a multifaceted ministry to the black evangelical faith community in prisons, among street youth, in campus higher education, and in church services. The National Black Evangelical Association also supports a ministry to higher education through the National Black Christian Student Conference. The Voice of Calvary Ministry in Jackson, Mississippi, although largely community focused with an outreach to Jackson State College, has recently opened up an international study center. Among these groups only the Tom Skinner Associates/Campus Ministry and the National Black Christian Student Conference have national outreach and ministry to blacks in higher education from the evangelical tradition.

There are real differences in the ministries to black people in higher education provided by white and black parachurch organizations. The former have only slight concerns for change, hoping that the large-scale conversion of blacks will preserve domestic tranquility and thus maintain the status quo. The latter are governed by the heartfelt and real needs of their constituents. Their actions are primarily focused upon and directed toward black students in particular and the black community in general.

Black Evangelicals in Ecumenical Organizations

Black evangelicals have also found warm reception in some parachurch campus ministry organizations. Among these has been United Ministry in Higher Education (UMHE); National Institute for Campus Ministry (NICM); and, most importantly, Ministry to Blacks in Higher Education (MBHE). It is within MBHE, where ministries to blacks has been a primary focus and doctrinal issues secondary, that black evangelicals have been warmly accepted. One soon discovers, as I did, that my white evangelical brothers were selling a bill of goods about the liberals. In fact, it was often the liberals who where most earnest about *doing* the will of God when it came to actual ministries to black people within the academy. Black evangelicals have found an acceptance and meaningful participation, even to the board level of leadership, while acceptance and meaningful participation are, for the most part, only token in the white evangelical organizations.

FORCES INHIBITING THE FORMATION OF FAITH COMMUNITIES IN BLACK EVANGELICAL TRADITION

There are many forces which inhibit the formation of the black evangelical faith community in higher education. Some inhibitions are inherent in the theological perspective and/or the style of ministry. Others are imposed by the psychosocial forces of the culture.

One of the primary theological inhibitors is that it is only through *individual* faith in Jesus Christ (as Savior and Lord) that one can have a personal relationship with the one living God. "And there is salvation in no one else, for there is no other name under heaven given among men by which we must be saved" (Acts 4:12, RSV). Contemporary evangelicalism has no provision for *corporate* salvation except for an eschatological consummation which has no applicability to the here and now; it is otherworldly.

Also, where this absolutist attitude has touched higher education, there has often been an intolerance on the part of evangelicals toward other expressions of faith; particularly, those religions outside the Judaic-Christian tradition are considered to be apostate and idolatrous. Because of this sort of thinking within the arena of the academy, one can expect to find an immediate evangelical confrontation with other beliefs. However, evangelicals have often been the lesser in number and more ignorant concerning other religious experiences, so their natural reaction has been to withdraw or separate.

Evangelicals and the Anti-intellectual Stereotype

This same idea of absolute exclusivity is carried over to the evangelical view of the Scriptures as the inerrant, infallible revelation of God, a view better known as "plenary verbal inspiration." The Bible is a "faith document," i.e., the "Word of God." As such, it is the authority in all matters of faith and is to be accepted without criticism or question. This stance often led to the charge that evangelicals were anti-intellectual.

The requirements of both the absolute conversion experience and the absolute authority of Scripture have resulted in a tenacious and abrasive proclamation of the gospel. This kind of proclamation is more often than not considered proselytizing by those outside evangelicalism, and provokes a reciprocal reaction of intolerance.

Crisis in Christianity: Evangelicals in Conflict with Catholics, Protestants, and the Social Gospel

Within the boundaries of Christendom, evangelicals have conflicted with Catholics over: (1) papal authority; (2) the role of the priest as minister-servant; and (3) the extent of the canon. With Protestants, the conflicting issues have been over: (1) conversion; and (2) the nature and authority of Scripture. On the Protestant side, it was the fundamentalist/modernist controversy which led to the "great divorce."

The great Protestant schism was to come to a head with the upsurge of the "social gospel." The social gospel seemed to say that the ushering in of the earthly kingdom of God was fulfilled by addressing social needs of people, e.g., feeding the hungry, clothing the naked, providing shelter to the homeless. For evangelicals, the ushering in of the kingdom of God is predicated on the redemption of *individuals* who will be gathered together during the earthly rule of Jesus Christ commencing with his Second Coming. It is enough to say here that obviously the two groups, the liberal and the conservative, or the neoorthodox and the evangelicals, did not see eye to eye. The ensuing polarization of the two groups led to the liberal indictment that evangelicals have no social ethics, that their faith, without works, is dead. There is more than a twitch of truth in this accusation against evangelicals. Until very recently, evangelicals have only given lip service to a theology of social action, and most of that was derogatory. But more recently, "the young evangelicals" have embraced social action as a biblical imperative of the regenerated person. One example is the creation of Evangelicals for Social Action, an organization attempting to involve evangelicals in contemporary ethical issues.

Out of that religious conflict has developed an ethical double standard. I recently attended a college symposium on religion in American culture. A noted evangelical speaker was quick to state that the tragedy of Jonestown is an example of demonic influences operating in our world today. The same person was asked whether the tragedies of former President Nixon and Watergate were also examples of demonic influences in our world today? He replied, "Oh no! Nixon was only misguided!" It is also important to note that the majority of evangelicals who do involve themselves in these discussions on ethical issues falter and balk when the question of white racism is raised. Equally avoided are questions of sexism and capitalism.

Race, the Great Divide: White Racism, the Great Sin of Western Civilization

I must confess, it is with reluctance that I bring indictment against not only evangelicalism but all forms of contemporary Christendom since the Reformation, be they Catholic or Protestant. I am convinced that all of contemporary Christendom is infested with white racism. My reluctance is not because I think the charge lacks veracity or validity. Rather, as the only minority person of color associated with this project, I suspect that my associate writers and the readers will anticipate this indictment. Whites victimized by their own racism usually allow only two ways of hearing the issue. One is as a form of "systemic ventilation," as if the black victims of white racism had need for catharsis, and the other is as a means "to move to pity" the conscience of white folk by the display of black suffering. Both of these racist perspectives mean that black people— men, women, and children—literally bleed in the streets without response by white America. Both these perspectives have merely stimulated the voyeurism of Western civilization, the Christian church included. The majority of all race relations literature and race relations programs incorporate these two perspectives as primary for the examination of the "race problem" in Western civilization so that racial conflict is seen solely in terms of its symptoms; the root causes are not exposed. The results of such an examination ultimately conclude in *Blaming the Victim*, as William Ryan has aptly said in his book. The admonitions of Dr. Martin Luther King, Jr. ought to ring with a greater clarity and comprehension; as he wrote from the Birmingham jailhouse, "I am sure that none of you would want to rest content with the superficial kind of social analysis that deals merely with effects and does not grapple with underlying *causes.*"

We must in fact, seek to alter our vantage point so as to be strong enough, as well as free enough, to accomplish both significant, and relatively permanent, change. It is a process which must begin with and be applied to ourselves initially and, then, to our respective faith communities. It is in this hope of altering the typical vantage point by which race relation problems are viewed that I list the following axioms:[6]

1. "White racism" discriminates solely on the basis of race/color. The use of race/color as a means of achieving identity necessitated truncating of normal processes of personality development. The racist person is not allowed to develop to psychological maturity so as rationally to encounter and accept both the positive and negative aspects of oneself. Rather, one is socialized to project one's own negative qualities onto others through paired association. In the construction of white racism, peoples from nonwhite race/colors become a corporate negative other, a focus of a *continuing self-hatred* for whites. It would, thus, be correct to understand white racism as a *countertransference* and projection of a negative self-image upon others.

2. White racism is part of the primordial matrix of modern *Western civilization.* White racism was conceived and instituted to give northern European Caucasians unmerited status during the European imperialist expansion. White Europeans found it necessary to institute a visceral form of group identity and solidarity because of the apparent threat they perceived in the fact that the larger portion of the global community is nonwhite.

3. Social order has both overt and covert functions. The institutional components of a social order both anticipate and reinforce these functions. In relation to race, the institutional components of Western civilization have become surrogate parents. They are designed to anticipate and reinforce an individual's fixation upon race/color as means of establishing identity. Thus, there is a perpetual state of infantilism in the person's development.

4. Whites are the *primary* victims and the *most* victimized by their own racism because it interrupts the normal and natural maturation of human personality. Nonwhites are only the secondary victims.

5. White racism has created an incapacity of persons (white and black) from the same cultural context to relate rationally across social-cultural boundaries.

As higher education is merely a component institution of our particular social order, I see no need to give examples of independent application of these axioms. However, something should be noted concerning their applicability to the formation of faith community among black evangelicals.

Black Evangelicals: Displaced Persons

The *reactions* to white racism in the black community have caused identity diffusion, confusion, and often identity losses. This phenomenon occurs among black people in religious, as well as secular, terms.

For this reason black evangelicals today can be considered displaced persons. The theological composition of evangelicalism often causes emnity between one's childhood religious upbringing and the newfound experience of faith through evangelical conversion. Within black evangelicalism there is, thus, a dichotomy between "conversion" and one's indigenous religious upbringing. In application to black people, the inherent traditions of the Negro/black church are often junked or discarded in the experience of evangelical conversion. The evangelicalism inherent in the Christian religious traditions of the Negro/black church are, thus, overlooked. Black evangelicals have understood their evangelical commitments as a form of birthright, since it was through this particular proclamation of the gospel that they have come to be spiritually born or, rather, born again.

The new black Christian convert to the white evangelical community often finds that one of the community's demands, as evidence of *genuine* conversion, is that black persons part with their ethnicity. Besides the obvious physical impossibility of this demand, the black evangelical could not comply since ethnicity is, in another dimension, an imposed identity. There is no single twenty-four-hour period when black people are not imposed upon with a negative identity characterization. Thus, white evangelicals systematically deny their black counterparts' inclusion and access to the institutional structure of evangelicalism. White evangelicals have sought to use the conversion experience as a means of perpetuating the individual and community schizophrenia that has historically plagued the black and white religious community. This imposition is constantly reinforced, consciously and unconsciously. Thus, the sense of redemptive wholeness which black evangelicals had hoped to find in their rebirth is truncated by the white racism in their new community.

The tides began to change when black evangelicals understood that their real identity is derived from and exists in the One Living God. It is not rooted in the exclusivities of race or color. Black evangelicals have increasingly resisted and refused to bow to the Baal-god of race/color schizophrenia, not when Jesus Christ *has found us* and reconciled us to God, self, and neighbor—including our white neighbor, who is ofttimes "my friend the enemy."[7] Black evangelicals have now come to understand that *God* has made no racial demands. *God,* rather, prefers to use the obvious in the promotion of the kingdom, not discard it. "Blackness"[8] has become an affirmation of the faith and *an* integral part of the ministry task. God has not come to take sides; He has come to take over, as He did in Joshua 5:14. For this reason, the second and third generations of black evangelicals are emerging with a greater group definitiveness and inclusive solidarity. However, the *random* conversion and rebirth of blacks in the white evangelical tradition is still going on.

We have considered a number of factors which deter and inhibit the formation of faith community among black evangelicals. Among the deterrents I have listed: absolutism, anti-intellectualism, and white racism, which is the most significant. There is one final consideration. Varieties of evangelicals share things in common, but we must be wary before designating them as a *community.* Beyond the common "fundamentals of the faith," the practical outworkings of evangelicalism more aptly reflect an American civil religion, rather than a true faith community. There is a real lack of depth in interpersonal relationship(s) in evangelical fellowship. In part to blame is the "rugged individualism" implicit in the conversion experience as well as an upward mobility based upon the Protestant ethic. This lack of depth in interpersonal relationship is masked by vibrant "fellowship" and devotional bible study. As Bonhoeffer suggests, faith communities are often designed to collapse at their very conception because individuals bring contrived ideals or models of how the "community" ought to be.[9] But the deeper reality of a suprarugged individualism is made manifest in the group ostracism of the lonely, or angry, or divorced, or sexual offenders (hetero or homo), or of anyone who is not a dress-up look alike of the "establishment evangelicals." The rejection of those who dare express their discontent and/or remorse over a continual "sinful" brokenness bears witness to this collapse of a "meaningful" and "holistic" community experience.

Now, I would not argue that evangelicalism is completely devoid of community. But its real and functional fellowship has been deflected from the common circle of an indicative faith community. A "remnant" of such rejected evangelicals, while not condoning sin, have covenanted together on the basis of an unconditional acceptance and love for one another, founded upon the redemptive works and words of the Person of Jesus Christ, and have engaged in a mutual commitment to walk together in the pilgrimage of Christian brother/sisterhood. Such covenant groups are small and seem to be the exception, rather than the norm, in the formation of faith communities within either the black or white evangelical tradition.

THE SURVIVAL, MAINTENENCE, AND GROWTH OF FAITH COMMUNITIES IN THE BLACK EVANGELICAL TRADITION

The civil rights movement of the 1960s and 1970s accomplished tremendous gains in consolidating and advancing the common cause of black people. It was a movement spearheaded and sustained by a deeply religious people both in its clergy and laity. It was not just a socialist movement, nor did it rise up spontaneously. Rather, the movement was only a visible surface of the many processes of a divine national discipleship of black people in America.[10] Within this process of divine national discipleship, God was raising up men and women as concrete models for the general masses. These men and women also served as mouthpieces of the divine moral consciousness similar to that expressed in Exodus 2:24–5, where God heard the groaning of His people in bondage, saw their condition, and moved to alleviate their suffering. Thus, the process of "divine watchcare" of oppressed peoples continued to be acted out in human history. The future eschatological realities of the kingdom of God once again broke into and intruded upon the present. The hope of a thousand Negro spirituals, a hope of overcoming in the sweet by and by, was again made manifest in the nasty here and now. This divine intrusion on the behalf of the black people benefited the entire community, including the black evangelicals.

Cell-Group Structure

There had long existed a religious structure and a God consciousness in the black community, even before more formal church or parachurch structures serviced the faith need of the people. It is this informal small group structure which is being utilized and given new emphasis by black evangelicals today.

The contemporary term for these small groups is "cell groups." They operate on a variety of levels and serve to achieve many functions. Some of their versatility is demonstrated by their use for social fellowship, Bible study, prayer, evangelism, etc. It has primarily been at this level that black evangelicals have transcended the superficial facade of community formation within evangelicalism in general. It is in cell groups where a few black brothers and sisters have formed community by simply existing together. That is, they share the common experience of being in Christ Jesus and, as a consequence, through him they know and serve one another. Thus, in the cell group, the rugged individualism of superior Christian achievement is secondary to walking together with one another in the drudgery of the mundane. The frills of evangelicalism and the "goodies" of divine blessing via the Protestant ethic are insignificant to knowing one another in Christ and helping one another through Christ.

The Unifying Factors

Both the spirit of ecumenism and the cultural affirmation of blackness have been important forces for uniting black evangelicals in community. The days of the lone-ranger evangelist have long since passed. Other forces have emerged which have dispensed with the untenable position of authoritarian absolutism which was commonly associated with earlier forms of evangelicalism. As these changes evolved in the life experience of black people, they did so irrespective of secular and religious distinctions within the community. Thus, black evangelicals became co-belligerents with nonreligious groups in the common struggle against racism. But it soon became apparent that some distinctions were needed between those who saw—as ends in themselves—some particular, economic, social, or political goals and those who saw the establishment of the kingdom of God as the ultimate goal. So it was that black people out of a variety of Christian traditions began banding together as a people of faith. But the cell-group structure was not sufficient, in itself, to sustain the lasting relationships which were now possible through black ecumenism. Nor was the cell-group structure a strong enough base from which to wield the newfound power of black ecumenism. Both the black Christian students and those ministers who served them sought a more substantial means of identifying with a particular group within the faith community and at the same time uniting with the broader coalition of the faith community. Such a means was to be found in the "caucus" model.

Caucuses

By moving from the cell-group structure to organizing the faith community into a black evangelical caucus, a fresh sense of identity, strength, and autonomy began to emerge. Black evangelicals could harmonize their joint concerns for furthering evangelical beliefs with the egalitarian cause of black people. Black evangelicals moved freely in both evangelical and secular black circles. Black evangelicals as a caucus possessed the power of veto in various organizations, religious and secular. Also, black evangelicals could pick and choose who they let serve and represent them. In the area of higher education, often black evangelicals would align themselves with two or more of the larger evangelical denominations or organizations. So the caucus structure has become a more viable means of empowering the black evangelical cause.

The Black Christian Student Caucuses

The black Christian student became a double minority, in terms both of race and of religious commitment. Discrimination on the basis of creed became very significant with the increase of pro-Moslem student groups. Many a naive freshman from the Baptist tradition was surprised that someone had switched terms when he showed up for a BSA meeting—thinking Baptist Student Union—and found instead a *black* student union. Nevertheless, black Christian students hung in there, participating in the "new"

BSA and utilizing its structure to organize their own faith community around the Christian experience. Thus, a number of black Christian fellowships were organized on college and university campuses around the country, emerging as groups such as M:Tai M:Euse (Black Advocates) Christian Fellowship of Fisk University (1968), the Alpha Eta Omega (AHΩ) Christian Fellowship of Hampton Institute (1965), the Igbimo OTito (True Community) Christian Fellowship of Howard University (1970). Groups such as these which rose up from the evangelical tradition would often form alliances or coalitions with black Christian student groups out of other traditions, such as the Absalom Jones Society-Episcopal, the Richard Allen Society-African Methodist Episcopal, the St. Martin Club-Roman Catholic, the William J. Seymour Fellowship-Pentecostal.

The Black Ministerial Caucus Within Higher Education

As black Christian students began organizing themselves, there arose a clamor by students for more indigenous leadership, for more blacks among the ministers who serviced them. For black evangelicals this option was almost nonexistent, except for a handful of black staff persons working for the major white parachurch organizations. The emergence of black parachurch organizations to service the Christian community in higher education was a momentus event indeed. There are, as I said earlier, two black evangelical organizations which are conducting ministries with national focus to the black evangelical student: Tom Skinner Associates/Campus Ministry and the National Black Christian Student Conference. A third organization, Ministries to Blacks in Higher Education, is a classic example of the black ecumenism mentioned above.

Tom Skinner Associates/Campus Ministry began in 1969 when Carl F. Ellis, a graduate of Hampton Institute, joined the staff of Tom Skinner Associates. Carl Ellis had been a member and president of the Alpha Eta Omega Christian Fellowship while a student at Hampton Institute. During his tenure as a student at Hampton, Alpha Eta Omega Christian Fellowship was mostly serviced by the Inter-Varsity Christian Fellowship, with an occasional visit by various black evangelical leaders. Tom Skinner and William Pannel were two black evangelicals who visited campuses as guest speakers for an evangelistic outreach program conducted by Alpha Eta Omega. Skinner had founded the Tom Skinner Crusade which later became Tom Skinner Associates (TSA). The vision for TSA was that it should be a base of operation from which young black evangelical men and women could utilize their gift in ministries other than the church pastorate, and who could intentionally direct their ministry toward the black community. It was at Hampton Institute that this vision was sparked to life, and the Campus Division of Tom Skinner Associates became a reality.

The Urbana Missions Conferences, sponsored by IVCF, provided a primary context in which many black evangelical student caucuses met. In 1970 there was a tremendous lobbying effort on the part of these black Christian student caucuses to raise the interest, consciousness and efforts of IVCF services to the black Christian student. The conference is held every three years and, between the 1970 and 1973 conference, the concern and efforts of IVCF to address and service the real needs of its black constituency seemed to take a step backward. Disillusioned about the apparent insincerity of white evangelicals and their efforts to provide real and meaningful ministerial services to the black Christian student community, black students formed a new parachurch organization, the National Black Christian Student Conference (NBCSC). Among the original founders were Drs. William and Ruth Bentley, Wynn Wright, Ron Potter, and Walter McCray. NBCSC soon became the student component of the National Black Evangelical Association. Again its vision is to provide a deliberate and intentional ministry to the black Christian student community, particularly those black Christian students attempting to survive and flourish at predominantly white colleges and universities. NBCSC conducted its first annual conference in 1974. It services only black and/or nonwhite students, and it raises its support solely from these nonwhite sectors. Currently, it has expanded to sponsoring regional conferences in the Northeast and Midwest and is addressing issues pertinent to the daily life of the community, especially male/female relationships.

Black evangelicals were not the only ones founding parachurch organizations to service the black Christian faith communities in higher education. When, in 1970, Harold Lloyd Bell and a group of black campus ministers from various ecclesiastical traditions founded the Ministries to Black in Higher Education (MBHE) at a Convocation at Bennett College in Greensboro, North Carolina, a meeting became a movement. Based in Atlanta, Georgia, MBHE's black ecumenical appeal was akin to that of a white counterpart,

United Ministries in Higher Education (UMHE). MBHE's viability was realized in its ability to service the majority of black campus ministers who were in some way, shape, or form involved in ministering to the black Christian faith communities in higher education. The magnetic powers of this black ecumenism was very forceful indeed, in most instances mixing and crossing all prior individual party lines. Black evangelicals have joined in this black ecumenical effort. Besides holding an annual convocation, MBHE publishes a directory and a journal, *Towards Wholeness.*

Having looked at the progressive formation of faith communities in the black evangelical tradition, both from the perspective of the black Christian student and the black campus minister, and having seen a progression of structural organization from the cell group to the caucus to the establishment of autonomous organizations, let us take a look at an example of the black Christian faith community in higher education.

United Ministries at Howard University: A Prototype

United Ministries at Howard University (UMHU) in Washington, D.C., has the best of all worlds. UMHU is composed of campus ministers representing church denominations and parachurch organizations. It is staffed by both blacks and whites, males and females. I was a staff member. Unified under the banner of the Christian faith, we were not identified with other non-Christian expressions of faith. We could also unapologetically be very watchful in monitoring extreme nonorthodox cultic forms of religion which employ Christianity as a cover, e.g., the Moonies. Being assigned to the Howard University campus afforded us official recognition within the institution, individually and collectively. As the institution itself maintained and staffed a dean of chapel, whose responsibility it was to *administer* the religious life at the university, we were free to concentrate on the ministry task itself. The United Ministries shared a common goal, namely Christian ministry to both individual students and the institution itself. Aside from our particular responsibilities to our student constituents, who also worked harmoniously together, we shared a common pool of resources and were able to service with confidence and integrity the *unchurched* student population attending the individual schools within the university institution. The affection I have for the United Ministries' model of team ministry is not merely based on my personal involvement. My involvement with a number of major national campus ministries suggests that we would be hard pressed to find a more progressive model, although other models may be more appropriate given a different set of circumstances.

ISSUES AND ANSWERS

The organization of black evangelicals, both students and campus ministers, gave this faith community a new sense of strength and power with which it has been able to combat the forces of inhibition. The striving for academic excellence addresses the accusations of anti-intellectualism. The act of formation of community dispensed with the rugged individualism of solo conversion. The black ecumenism addressed both authoritative absolutisms and white racism. But something even more profound came out of this experience of community among black evangelicals, namely, a more definite calling to community within the context of one's enemies. Bill Pannel speaks extensively on this issue in his book, *My Friend the Enemy.* Bonhoeffer also touched upon it in his book, *Life Together,* saying,

Jesus Christ lived in the midst of his enemies.
At the end all his disciples deserted him. On the cross he was utterly alone, surrounded by evildoers and mockers. For this cause he had come, to bring peace to the enemies of God. So the Christian, too, belongs not in the seclusion of a cloistered life, but in the thick of foes. There is his commission, his work. "The Kingdom is to be in the midst of your enemies!"[11]

Thus, black evangelicals found not only a new wholeness in the formation of faith community, but also therein a new sense of mission and calling to ministry as ambassadors of the reconciliation of the world to God in Christ within a context of hostility.

Sustaining Factors

Although it might seem obvious, intercessory prayer and the devotional study of the Word of God are the basic sustaining factors for black evangelicals in higher education. But these disciplines are largely individual. The corporate faith community experience in the black evangelical tradition is fed very heartily by two other factors, i.e., black worship experience and the soul force of black spiritual music. Both the worship experience and the music are as varied as we are as a people. It was the Reverend Adam Clayton Powell who is reported to have said, "Black people in America come in colors from chalk to charcoal." In many instances the music is itself the worship experience. It is not unusual to find in even the secular black social club, a glee club or singing group which always includes in its repertoire a piece of gospel harmony.

The Negro spiritual represents a history of the suffering and brokenness which we as people have undergone. It equally represents the power of faith in God to enable us as a people to overcome the evils of the world.[12] I think the late Donny Hathaway spoke of the power of the Negro/black spiritual when he sang, "I believe in music, I believe in love. I can sing the music all day long, when I'm singing the music I can't do no one no wrong, maybe someday I'll come up with a song that'll make people stop fussin' and fightin', long enough to sing along." There was a scene in the first part of *Roots* when Kunta Kinte was a grown man and had escaped and made it to the nearby farm to see the African women who had been captured. During the recall of the brokenness of their experience which would not allow them to be together, he exclaimed, "The white man don't even leave us, us!" As a response to the experience of this depth of despair, one could sing, "What a friend we have in Jesus," or any number of Negro spirituals. While the music is certainly not a panacea, it pointed to the "substance of things hoped for and the evidence of things not seen" when everything around us was full of the bitterness and gall. The spiritual was the balm which eased the pain and has come to aid in the healing of brokenness. Along with Donny Hathaway and millions of others who traveled similar pilgrimages of suffering, I can also sing, "I believe in music, I believe in love," but to avoid the association with popular syncretism, as a black evangelical, I must be quick to add "... in Jesus Christ."

NOTES

1. Richard Quebedeaux, *The Young Evangelicals* (New York: Harper and Row, 1974), pp. 18-40.
2. Ronald C. Potter, "The New Black Evangelicals," in *Black Theology: A Documentary History, 1966-1979*, ed. Gayraud S. Wilmore and James H. Cone (Maryknoll, New York: Orbis Books, 1979), pp. 302-309.

3. James S. Tinney, "Black Origins of the Pentecostal Movement," in *Christianity Today* XVI, 1 (October 8, 1971): pp. 4–5.

4. Daniel P. Mannix and Malcolm Cowley, *Black Cargo: A History of the Atlantic Slave Trade 1518–1865* (New York: Viking Press, 1965), pp. xiii, 8, 105.

5. Clifton H. Johnson and Paul Radin, eds., *God Struck Me Dead* (Philadelphia: Pilgrim Press, 1969). See Introduction by Charles S. Johnson and Foreword by Paul Radin.

6. James Tillman and Mary Tillman, *Why America Needs Racism and Poverty* (Atlanta: Four Winds Press, 1973), pp. 3–66.

7. William E. Pannell, *My Friend The Enemy* (Waco, Texas: Word Books, 1968), pp. 61–78.

8. Carl F. Ellis, from unpublished speech given at the Inter-Varsity Christian Fellowship-Leadership Conference (Reidsville, North Carolina, 1969).
   Enlightened Definitions of Blackness:

   (a) Blackness is the self view of a non-white person of African extraction, in terms of values favorable to those aspects of his or her physical characteristics that are non-white and defined as black, which repudiate existing cultural values hostile to his or her non-whiteness and secures for him or her a better chance of survival as a unified being.
   (b) Blackness is the affirmation of a culturally negated humanity.

9. Dietrich Bonhoeffer, *Life Together* (New York: Harper and Row, 1954), pp. 26–30.

10. Carl F. Ellis, "Black Testament," in *His,* Vol. 35, No. 7 (April 1975): p. 1.

11. Bonhoeffer, *Life Together,* p. 17.

12. LeRoi Jones, *Blues People* (New York: William Morrow and Company, 1963), pp. 32–49.

A MAINLINE PARISH-BASED PROTESTANT MINISTRY WITH STUDENTS

Joseph C. Williamson

In the 1960s, the prevailing assumption for ministry with students was that the "action" was the critical ingredient, the means of grace, the evidence of God's redemptive work. The action was most frequently identified as some kind of "movement," such as the civil rights movement or the anti-war movement. Ministry with students meant taking their concerns and preoccupations seriously. It meant being freed from the demands of organizational maintenance and institutional self-justification. It meant that ministers spent more time going to meetings than attending to the celebration of the sacraments in their traditional forms.

The theological justification for this particular expression of ministry was drawn from a wide range of sources. But the basic factor was the rediscovery of the theology of the Old Testament. The importance of the category of history was critical. History meant movement. History meant secularization. History meant the God who Acts and the people who act. Greek modes of life and thought were in disfavor. The Hebrew emphasis was on the verb, the deed, rather than the noun or concept. Bonhoeffer called all of us to radical obedience, to participation in the sufferings of God at the very center of life. It was, indeed, a very heady time to be alive.

Invariably, the traditional forms of parish life seemed dull in contrast. The more stable and inevitably more conservative parishioners were less mobile, less active, less able to "sell all that they had" and join the marching movement. So parish ministers and parish churches of the "mainline" type more or less abandoned a ministry with students. However, as the decade drew to a close, shifts began to take place within both the theology and the politics of the movement people themselves. By the early 1970s, it was becoming apparent that the advantages of an activist style of religious life also contained disadvantages. There was a need for discipline as well as for freedom. There was a need for solidarity as well as for "doing your own thing." There was a need for roots, for commitment, and for a place to be.

It was about the time that this transition or shift began to appear that three campus ministers associated with the Boston-Cambridge Ministries in Higher Education were contracted by the Church of the Covenant in Boston to serve as an interim ministry team in that place. The campus ministers were Jack Hornfeldt, Larry Hill, and myself. The Church of the Covenant was a federated congregation of Presbyterian and United Church of Christ affiliation. The congregation had been trying unsuccessfully for over a year to call a minister. It had a small membership of around two hundred people. Most of them were over fifty years of age.

In one sense the Church of the Covenant represented the antithesis of the work with students being done by the three campus ministers during the rest of the week. Covenant is situated in one of the prestigious areas of the city of Boston. It is shadowed by Brooks Brothers and the New England Mutual Life Insurance Company. The people of the congregation at that time were not at all "political" in the jargon of the day. It is clear in retrospect, however, that it was time to explore again the possibility of doing ministry with students from a mainline Protestant parish base. Jack, Larry, and I agreed to become the interim ministry team. The rest of the staff collective at the Boston-Cambridge Ministry in Higher Education reluctantly agreed.

The experiment is now, almost a decade later, no longer an experiment. It has been sustained over a period of more than eight years. During that time there have been many changes. Many of the older congregation have died or else moved on. What has happened since 1970 is the creation of a congregation which does maintain an active ministry with students, both undergraduate and graduate. Moreover, many of the people who have affiliated with the congregation regard the student movement of the 1960s as a formidable and formative experience in the shaping of their lives. They see their participation in the life of Covenant as a way to extend and sustain the commitments which they made during those days. They clearly regard their participation in the life of this congregation as a way to affirm both their religious and their political convictions.

SPIRITUAL AND THEOLOGICAL BASES OF THE COVENANT FAITH COMMUNITY

From the beginning of our ministry at Covenant, we have been intrigued by the theological issues that are suggested to us in the designation of ourselves as the "Covenant" people. The original choice of that name was probably made for pragmatic rather than theological reasons. The pragmatics were that the Central Congregational Church had a rather formidable building of Gothic style but no sizable constituency, and the First Presbyterian Church of Boston had a healthy congregation but no adequate building. So a marriage of convenience was arranged, and a "covenant" was ratified. That happened in 1932. However, names are never merely arbitrary or pragmatic. The naming of the new arrangement as a covenant did tap the resources of a particular theological tradition.

Covenantal theology was brought to the colonial American scene from England by the Puritans. Its development historically had been shaped by those Dutch Calvinists who were opposed to the rationalizing tendencies of seventeenth-century Protestant scholasticism. Behind this lay the immense wealth of biblical material which sustains that theme. So the choice of "Covenant" as name and as theological motif was not merely fortuitous. The merged congregation did represent the larger tradition of Reformed theology in both its English Congregational and its Scottish Presbyterian roots.

In order to make apparent the implications of that particular basis, I want to contrast the covenantal understanding of faith community with two other prevailing models which coexist with us. The dominant Protestant model for faith community in the United States is not so much covenantal as conversionist. The latter model has its roots in the revivalist tradition which has always been particularly amenable to the New World promise of new beginnings. My observation is that most of the Protestant religious groups in America are deeply informed by conversionist sensibilities. Grace is found and love is experienced in the dramatic and intensely experiential focus of "new birth." It is through the conversion experience that one enters the faith community which is called into being by all those who share that experience.

The second model for faith community is more objective than it is subjective in character. Its objectivity is set primarily by the sacraments as a means of grace. Obviously this model for defining faith community is informed by the Roman Catholic and Episcopalian understandings of ecclesiology. The sacraments exist in their power and mystery apart from human intellection, volition, and affection. As such, this tradition stands as a corrective to the excesses of subjectivism which appear under the revivalist tendency. God's grace is efficacious apart from our feeling states, whatever they may be.

The covenantal definition of faith community is neither revivalist nor sacramentalist. The covenant model insists that it is the covenanted people in their corporate reality who are indeed the means of grace. Grace is mediated precisely by those persons who are bonded together in covenant with each other and with their God. So salvation is appropriated through the life of the congregation. God's love is experienced and expressed through the love of the faith community. Participation in the life of the people is necessary to participation in the life of the Spirit. In a strange way, this radically "low church" conviction is analogous to the traditional Roman Catholic claim that there is "no salvation outside the church." The community of faith is necessary to the invigoration and the nourishment of the faithful. There is no such thing as a solitary disciple of Jesus Christ.

The biblical basis for this central theological conviction is of prime importance. For both the Old and the New Testaments there is an absolute insistence upon the corporate character of the people of God. To be corporate means to be indissolubly interconnected with those other persons who make up the covenanting community. This means that the category of the "personal" is necessarily a "social" category. There is no such thing as an individual being "personal" in a solitary state. The individual is really "subpersonal" or "waiting to be personal" in and through the mediatorial activity of the community. To be corporate also means, however, to understand the thoroughgoing "material" reality of the community. The people of God do not understand their bonding in some esoterically spiritual way. To employ the New Testament image of the faith community as the Body of Christ, we must understand that there is a necessary coherence between the material and the spiritual unity of that community. Such unity is more like solidarity in common struggle than any other definition will allow. The hand without the body cannot function as a hand. The foot without the body gets one nowhere. The body cannot be the body apart from the interconnection of its members.

To claim the biblical warrant for this definition of ecclesiology is to raise the ultimate question for mainline Protestant people, that is to say, the question of authority. That issue cannot be evaded at the Church of the Covenant, nor can it be evaded in the context of this ecumenical discussion. The question is not, of course, the special province of the evangelical members of this dialogue. That is no more the case than is the concern of justice for women the province of feminists. I am not able to give a systematic response to the issue of biblical authority, but I do want to indicate some of the critical factors in the consideration of such a response. When I first began to preach at the Church of the Covenant in the fall of 1970, I asked the people what they expected of me. The answer was that they wanted to hear biblical sermons. I agreed to accept that requirement, and began after several years of silence to preach again. Two things happened. The first was a sense of my coming alive at the level of my own theological imagination. Something turned over for me. As I began to do my work with the texts I found that the texts were beginning to do their work with me. I had paid some attention during my years of graduate studies to the development of the discipline of hermeneutics. Now, as I began to rediscover the importance of the Bible for preaching, it became clearer to me what the issue of the authority of the Bible was all about. I became convinced of the importance of the Calvinist understanding of the necessary interrelation between the Word and the Spirit. The Word by itself was not enough. It was too objective, too external, too archaic. The Spirit by itself was not enough. It was too subjective, too internal, too ephemeral. What was required for a biblical hermeneutic of the imagination was both the reality of the Word and the reality of the Spirit in penetrating interplay. It was out of such an interplay that the dynamics of biblical authority began to assert fresh power in the life of the congregation.

The second thing that happened was the creation of a series of study-action seminars which addressed the relationship between the biblical message and the needs of the contemporary world. It was apparent that Covenant could not survive as a parish unless it found ways to do the evangelistic work of both inreach and outreach. In response to the missional imperatives which were opened up for us by the study of Scripture, we began to see a fresh flow of energy in a variety of directions. It seemed as if we had found a way to mediate the dynamic relationship between the mystical and the political. The congregation was the mediatorial agent, and the biblical authority was the generating power behind both the mystical experience and the political expression. Since those early experiences, I have come to find that much of this same rediscovery was also taking place concurrently in the various theologies of liberation. They, too, made their fundamental appeal to the biblical witness. They, too, were committed to a corporate understanding of the life of the people of God. They, too, understood that religion and theology are necessarily political in the broad range of their significance and impact.

It was clear from the beginning of the Covenant venture that we could justify our existence as another dominantly white, dominantly middle-class urban congregation only if we were able to carry out an effective missional commitment which extended our work beyond the sanctuary place. There are, after all, seven other Protestant churches "just like us" within a four-block radius of our location. On ecological grounds, or on tax revenue grounds, or on theological grounds, we were in a defensive posture. We needed a very good offense. Although chastened by the inadequacies of the student movement, we nevertheless were committed to both the theology and the politics of liberation and empowerment. Time and again we found ourselves returning to the fourth chapter of Luke's Gospel as the paradigm by which our own ministry should be both judged and shaped. If we were about that work of liberating and empowering, then we believed that our existence was justified.

I shall say more in the final section of this chapter about the various strategies which we developed to carry out our theological convictions. However, the challenge of mission always needs to be set in its proper dialectical relationship with the realities of the world. Time and again we have been forced to consider how, if at all, we might serve as an agent for empowering nonwhite and non-middle-class persons in the urban context. Can the "haves" minister to the "have-nots"? Can we avoid the almost inevitable patterns of paternalism and maternalism? In what sense are we willing to give up our own pretensions in order that those who have no pretense might be able to affirm the dignity which is already theirs? Can we in some small fashion be anything to any person other than ourselves, much less all things to all persons for the sake of the gospel? These are enduring questions for us. I return with no small measure of discomfort to the warnings of Reinhold Niebuhr against the religious delusions of those who are in power.

Despite all of the contradictions, the people of this particular covenanting congregation have chosen to live out their religious and political commitments by staying where they are. The decision to do so is complicated by the deterioration of the more than one hundred year old building which houses us. At a congregational meeting some years ago the people voted to spend one dollar for mission for every dollar which we spent to maintain the roof and spire. We may not keep that vote to the letter of the law, but it is expressive of the spirit of the people. The mandate is given in the New Testament claim that if we seek our life we shall lose it; only if we lose our life can we expect to find it. That mandate is usually interpreted with reference to an individual. We have tried to ask what that might mean for an institution also. What is implied in the losing of the life of the Church of the Covenant? The theological demand is not easy for us to tolerate. We claim little other than to say that so far this engagement has been more than worth our while.

There is one final theological conundrum with which we have tried to come to terms. The issue is that of the discipline which is accepted by the members of the faith community. The assumption is that there must be some way of differentiating the members of any given faith community from those who stand outside. The biblical understanding of covenant requires a standard or a stipulation by which the terms of the covenant are set. There must be some norm by which to discern who is obedient and who is not. Witness the importance of the scriptural designation of the "remnant" people as that faith community which bears the promises of God despite the faithlessness and idolatry of the larger culture all around. The covenanting nucleus of those who are the remnant is therefore called out as nonconformists to the present age. The Puritan covenanters understood this to be definitive of their religious and political identity. So Michael Walzer describes what they were about as "the revolution of the saints." To take this legacy seriously means to address the theological issue of sanctification. By what standards are people held accountable? Who is included and who is excluded from the life of the covenanting people?

Each September as the student population returns to Boston we are forced to consider this issue. Of course "everyone is welcome" at our worship services. But we want people to affiliate with us who share our basic vision. Minimally, that means caring about the city and the people of the city. Beyond that it means a willingness to live in that tension between religion and politics which is never easy to sustain. I have sometimes said that the sociological category which I would like to devise for the Church of the Covenant is that it must be a "nonsectarian sect." That may not be quite right, but we are in some sense trying to be both inclusive and exclusive at the same time. Our theological commitments do require that of us. Whether or not we are able to be faithful to those commitments remains to be seen. The proof of our faithfulness will be discernible only to those who come after us. They will have the right to judge whether our mission is in any sense accomplished.

THE SOCIAL FORCES WHICH INHIBIT THE FORMATION OF FAITH COMMUNITY

No faith community is easily come by. There are always disaffections going on. There are always movements out as well as movements in. This phenomenon is particularly the case for a parish-based ministry with students which is situated in an urban context. I cannot calculate exactly the average tenure of membership at the Church of the Covenant, but I would estimate on any given Sunday that one third of the worshiping congregation is affiliated as members, one third is made up of friends, and the remaining third is composed of strangers. We are always trying to remember the names and faces of those persons who are in the process of becoming integrated into the life of our community.

One of the problems which this high level of transiency creates is the difficulty of maintaining a sense of our tradition. As a result, we are frequently much too improvisational. We are always devising new liturgical expressions and new programmatic schemes. This preoccupation with novelty and change is part of the Covenant genius, but it is also part of the difficulty which we experience in the formation of community. So we find it necessary to work constantly on the creation of a sense of tradition. We tell our story over and over again. We observe each November an annual service of Covenant Renewal. The ritual of that service is intended to remind the gathered people of the history of pilgrimage which brings them to the present time and place.

No element in our constituency is more susceptible to the threats to the formation of faith community than are the students. They are the most transient persons in the parish. They are the ones most likely to experience a sense of being marginal. They are frequently anonymous, never really confident that they are at home. In his study of *Ideology and Utopia*, Karl Mannheim employs the typology of horizontal and vertical mobility to define the breakup of religious cohesion and security. Students are by definition on both mobility tracks. They are horizontally mobile. They have left home with their back packs to explore a new culture of strange languages and mores. They are also on a vertical mobility track. To go to college or to university is by definition to be on the way up. In American society, class variables are determined more by socialization processes than by income. The student is on the way to certification by the university and that is the basic element for gaining social status.

Mannheim sustains his argument by claiming that the person who is horizontally and vertically mobile is the one who cannot live according to the myths and rituals of a unitary religious world view. The result of mobility is the recognition of cultural and religious relativism. The old truth claims are no longer exclusively defined. The very nature of religion is called into question. Therefore the faith community is also under threat.

This analysis provides us with one perspective for understanding the difficulty of ministry with students in any urban setting. Part of the difficulty is the sheer disruptiveness of being mobile. Community is difficult to create at any time, but when most of the potential members of that community are on the move it becomes more difficult to achieve. The theological issue is even more decisive. The faith simply cannot be assumed. Its formulations can never be taken for granted. The received vocabulary of the cult has no self-evident meaning. Everything is up for grabs. So, in one sense, it is always necessary to begin at the beginning. Certainly, there is no such thing as faith exclusive of doubt. Perhaps we are also learning that doubt is likewise necessarily inclusive of faith.

The patterns of mobility, with their concomitant recognition of both pluralism and relativism, are located geographically in the city. They are located institutionally in the university. So the urban university is the institutional reality which by definition threatens the formation of faith community. In many ways the city of Boston, with its plethora of colleges, represents the quintessential expression of this problem. The other side of the issue is that the students who are engaged in this double pattern of mobility do not experience it as a problem, but as an adventure. One of the psychosocial differences between undergraduate and graduate students is that the former are enticed by the freedom which their mobility offers. They are not constrained by the old social bonds of family and religion. They are free to explore, to go it alone, to play out the expressions of individuality and eccentricity. The latter are beginning to come to the end of the exploration cycle. They are in search for a place to put down roots, to build the larger and more stable configurations which offer the conserving patterns of meaning for their lives. It is for this reason that Covenant has developed a much larger student constituency among persons in graduate degree programs, both professional and academic. In some real sense they have been mobile long enough, have traveled far enough, and now are seeking some sense of being in community again.

Of course there are many other forces in American culture which inhibit the development of faith community. Above all there is the endemic "pursuit of loneliness," as Philip Slater chose to call it, which threatens all forms of collectivity in our society. The underlying mythologies are rooted in the libertarian and individualist impulses which shaped the development of this nation and its primary institutional structures. Robert Bellah has identified the pervasive "taboo against socialism" as expressive of the American commitment to competitive rather than cooperative economic patterns in both the national and the multinational arenas.

It is not necessary to elaborate further the cultural dynamics which make the development of faith community problematic. It is my conviction, however, that human nature is by definition unfulfilled apart from some corporate expression of interdependence and meaning. Surely that is why the heterodox Christian sects are all around us, why many conservative churches are growing. We do live in a culture which is both pluralistic and relativistic. That is all the more reason to identify ourselves with some community of "believing" persons who do confess their sins and who do long for deliverance from the several bondages of their lives. For us at the Church of the Covenant the message of God's kingdom stands over against the multifarious messages of an individualistic culture which is now disintegrating. That message calls us into solidarity with all whose lives are disempowered by the forces of alienation. It is precisely in that solidarity that we discover what it means to be sustained and nourished by our fellow humans as they mediate to us the grace of God.

STRATEGIES FOR THE DEVELOPMENT OF FAITH COMMUNITY:
MINISTRY PATTERNS AT THE CHURCH OF THE COVENANT

The interim ministry team at the Church of the Covenant served from the fall of 1970 until the fall of 1972. For two years, we explored with the existing congregation the possibility of developing the model into an ongoing pattern. In the late spring of 1972, the pastoral search committee made the decision to call me as part-time pastor with the proviso that the congregation also hire other part-time persons who would constitute a permanent team ministry. All of us would work both inside and outside the congregation. None of us would be, therefore, exclusively dependent financially on one source of income. All of us would be able to express our vocational commitment in secular as well as religious institutions.

The gamble seemed to be worth it. Fortunately, the older members of the congregation had developed enough confidence in us as ministers so that they were willing to support the new design of a multiple but part-time staff. We were able to claim the venture's advantages on both pragmatic and theological grounds. Pragmatically, the congregation would have a seven-person ministry staff for approximately one and a half salaries. There would be more energy, more imagination, and more time available to the congregation than the more familiar one pastor pattern could possibly allow.

The theological issues were also significant in our defense of this proposal. It seemed that a collective staff committed to developing collaborative styles of ministry could help to break the dominantly individualist models which were more commonly practiced. Part of what we had learned from doing ministry with students during the 1960s was the ineffectuality of the "lone-ranger" style. Rescue operations might be dramatic, but they were not adequate for the long haul over the long term. Of course there was still to be an officially called pastor at the Church of the Covenant, and there was still a certain deference to him among some of the congregation, but the redefinition of the pattern began to make a difference on both the symbolic and the operational levels. Power was being redistributed, and the move toward a collaborative effort was on the way.

A second theological issue was clearly in our common minds. The interim team had all been men. The congregation was approximately two-thirds women. We had experienced a sufficient raising of our consciousness to know that no ministry with students could be done unless there was a strong feminine presence and voice on the staff. The multiple and part-time combination allowed that to happen. At first there were two women of the seven staff persons. Currently, there are three. More than any other single factor, this has made a difference in the development of the ministry and in the attraction of new persons to the life of the congregation.

The third theological issue had to do with the interrelationship of the sacred and the secular in the life of the clergy as well as in the life of the congregation. We were committed to being "in the world" as the place where human need was most acutely felt and also as the place where that need was being most significantly met. Since the structures of alienation were also secular structures, it was important for us to be willing to participate in them as well as in the institutions of religion. I realize the fragility of this linguistic distinction. American society and culture is always and everywhere both secular and religious. Nevertheless, we did not want to spend our entire ministry in ecclesiastical institutions. We wanted to share in the more urbane and the more profane issues which the nonecclesiastical institutions provided to us. A concomitant issue which impinged upon the sacred-secular issue was our commitment to reinforce those patterns which gave primary emphasis upon the ministry of the laity rather than on the ministry of the clergy. As I liked to put it, we wanted to laicize the clergy and clericize the laity in order to make effective the total ministry of the whole congregation. Of course the unpersuaded could and did argue that a ministry staff of seven persons would do just the opposite. The fear was that the organization would become clergy heavy and that the laity would languish under the weight of that heaviness. The counter argument was that diffusing the clergy power would in fact open up the structure so that there would not be such a weight of investment in one clergy person. The debate still goes on. But the evidence which is accumulating is that the ministry of the congregation has been enhanced and invigorated under the present staffing arrangement.

A word about the assignments of the staff is needed. As the called pastor, I have been responsible for approximately two-thirds of the preaching and the coordination of the mechanics of organization. Alice Hageman, now a practicing lawyer in the city, has served as liturgist and staff liaison with the worship committee. Elizabeth Rice and James Fraser have had primary responsibility for the educational program in cooperation with the education committee of the congregation. Elizabeth is also serving as organizer and fund raiser for a shelter for battered women and children. James is on the faculty of the Boston University School of Theology. Donna Day-Lower has primary responsibility for coordinating the ministry of the Board of Deacons which supports the missional life of the congregation. In addition, she is working with a small, white, working-class church in East Boston. Larry Hill is on leave of absence at the time of this writing. In his place, Martin Mullvain is directing the choir and sharing the development of the arts program with David Schermer, organist, and the creative arts committee. Martin has been a staff member along with Larry at the Boston-Cambridge Ministry in Higher Education. David is a teacher of piano and organ. These primary areas of responsibility do not define the total concerns of these persons. Each of the ordained staff members also preaches, administers the sacraments, and assumes pastoral responsibilities within the life of the congregation.

From the very beginning, we who were part of the Covenant venture were committed to exploring ways in which we could define ourselves as doing ministry in the larger urban community as well as in the life of the congregation. Each staff person had a previous history of involvement in some nonparochial ministry. Our intention was to do work both inside and outside the congregation. We saw Covenant as a base, a place from which we could move, and a place to which we could return.

The people who made up the staff all understood that their commitment to the life of the congregation implicated them in a commitment to the life of the city. The strategic issue was how that commitment could be executed. Fortunately, we had friends within the ecclesiastical bureacracy. They encouraged us to apply for national missions money from the two denominations. We hoped that such funding would enable us to begin an outreach program which would help define the dynamics of our life as a congregation. After some deliberation, we decided to identify three target constituencies to which we would relate our programmatic efforts. The first constituency was the elderly who lived in the brownstone apartments and rooming houses in the adjacent neighborhood of Boston's Back Bay. The second was the large number of artists, mostly unemployed, who were looking for ways to express their artistic sensibilities. The third constituency which we identified as a primary focus for our ministry was the large number of women in the area who were victims of a wide variety of sexist patterns of discrimination. Our intention was to develop programs which moved from the Covenant base out into the community. We hoped to develop what I called "overlap" organizations which would tap the resources of the congregation, but which would be flexible enough to develop their own style of leadership and programmatic expression. We were able to secure a "seed grant" from the United Presbyterian Church, and some supporting money from the United Church of Christ. We were convinced that we had a chance to initiate and sustain an outreach program which would effectively address the needs of the persons with whom we were engaged in common struggle.

It is impossible to detail the full narrative of our work with those constituencies. Suffice it to say that today there are three organizations which were generated out of the life of the Covenant congregation which serve the needs of those target groups. The first which was established was the Back Bay Aging Concerns Committee. That organization still is housed at the Church of the Covenant, but its program of outreach and advocacy extends into the neighborhood at large. The second major effort involved us in a sustained commitment to explore the relationship between religion and the arts. The number of unemployed artists in the city of Boston is staggering. Soon after we began our ministry at Covenant we were approached by the Theatre Company of Boston to explore the possibility of using Covenant as a place in which to produce Shakespeare's *Richard III*. The lead actor had already agreed to play the role of Richard. That actor was Al Pacino.

It seemed to me to be a perfect break. I advocated allowing the Theatre Company of Boston to use our sanctuary as a performance space. The Covenant Council agreed. We received excellent local and national publicity. For the first time in the memory of most of the congregation Covenant had been identified as a congregation which was vigorously committed to supporting the arts. From that initial venture, the Pocket Mime Theatre negotiated with us the establishing of Covenant as its permanent home. Subsequently, we were able to support the opening of an art gallery in the church, the Newbury Associated Guild of Artists. Meanwhile, Larry Hill began to do some exploratory work concerning the creation of a choral group which would utilize the Covenant facilities for rehearsal and performance space. Under his organizing and conducting skills, the Back Bay Chorale was established. His latest venture is the creation of the Pro Arte Chamber Orchestra, which is a collective of established musicians which performs a full concert series of classical music in the Covenant sanctuary. We have also been supportive of a range of artistic programs which have a citywide base. The most significant of these is the Jazz-Arts ministry created by the Reverend Mark Harvey, a United Methodist minister. The All Night Jazz Festival, which is sponsored by this ministry, is held annually at the Church of the Covenant. Over one thousand persons attend this major jazz festival each year.

The third constituency which we identified as being particularly important for our wider ministry is women, particularly those women who are disadvantaged because of marginal social and economic status. This commitment has been expressed in a variety of different forms and programs. Our primary support has been given to a shelter for battered women in Boston's South End, Casa Myrna Vazquez. The house is a multiracial organization that offers sanctuary and support for women who are homeless and without adequate financial and emotional resources. A significant number of Covenant women have served in a variety of volunteer capacities in the Casa Myrna program.

There is a fourth venture in which the life of Covenant has been engaged. That is the development of a yoked support ministry with the Presbyterian Church of East Boston. One of our ongoing concerns relates to the fact that Covenant is a predominantly upwardly mobile middle-class congregation. We have no significant ministry with working-class persons. Because of that it seemed important to us to explore ways in which we might develop a relationship with a working-class constituency. When the pulpit of the East Boston congregation became vacant, two of our staff persons were assigned to that church as interim ministers. It is too early to say what the outcome of that venture will be. But again we have been able to develop a strategy which has stayed the patterns of attrition and decay. Our hope is that this congregation will be linked with others in that section of the city so as to develop a larger network of religious and politically progressive persons who will be able to act effectively among the people whom they represent.

Thus far in my description I have written chiefly of the ways in which we defined our ministry at the Church of the Covenant in terms of mission to the city. There is another side to our existence as a congregation. It is the sense that we have of ourselves as a faith community at worship. One of the inadequacies of campus ministry during the decade of the 1960s was that we did not pay sufficient attention to the needs for cultic worship, for celebration, and for ritual. We defined ourselves in terms of being committed to a cause. We did not see clearly our need for nurture within a community enriched by the gifts of tradition and sacramental attestation to the means of grace.

The last thing that I thought would happen to us at the Church of the Covenant was the creation of a vital sense of ourselves as a worshiping community. Very early on, I came to see how wrong my assumption had been. All of us began to experience a renewed awareness of the importance of liturgy, of music, and of the drama of the sacramental acts. The designation of a specific staff person, Alice Hageman, as liturgist was a key factor in this development. Alice had received her training in liturgics while participating in the life of the East Harlem Protestant Parish in New York City. With an invigorated worship committee, she began to push us toward an appreciation of the richness of the liturgy and symbols of our faith. In addition, we established a committee on the creative arts which began to develop a variety of artistic expressions to nourish what Jonathan Edwards called "the gracious affections."

The major problem which we faced liturgically was the sexually exclusive language which dominated the metaphors and symbols of our tradition. Our response to that is still unfinished. But we began to modify the "father-brother-man" language so as to make it inclusive of all persons. The most threatening question, of course, was the modification of that language as it pertains to deity. How is it possible to renovate the masculine ascriptions to God as they appear in prayers, in hymns, and in the sacred Scriptures themselves? We have tackled that issue head on. We have not begun to resolve either the theological or the aesthetic dilemmas that we face. But at least we have not ignored the problem. We do edit the language of the hymns and of Scripture. We do sing the trinitarian ascriptions to God the Creator rather than to God the Father.

The hard questions remain. How does this particular attempt to reinvigorate the life of a downtown Protestant parish enable us to do ministry with students? What do we "offer" the student population from the one dozen colleges within walking distance of the Church of the Covenant? What do those students "offer" us? Although the answers to these questions are elusive, I am certain that I shall never forget that morning when our first student, a young Massachusetts Institute of Technology junior, entered the sanctuary. He was literally inundated with greetings from us all. Within a week he was ushering in the services. That scene has changed. Now students come and go anonymously. We still search for ways to know them and the issues of their lives.

At the risk of being simplistic, I want to generalize about the two major factors in the life of our congregation which attract students to join with us. The first is the mission commitment of the congregation. When we began to create projects which extended beyond the life of our small institution, students became interested. Approximately one-half of the members of the Back Bay Chorale are students. The volunteer staff of both Casa Myrna Vazquez and the Back Bay Aging Concerns Committee have significant numbers of students working with them. These persons do seek to break through the patterns of "the culture of narcissism." They are looking for ways to express their commitment to the struggle for peace and justice in our time.

The second aspect of our life as a congregation which has attracted students is the way in which we worship together. If students have experienced the loss of a symbolic center, if the moral and religious cohesions of their adolescent life have been eroded, then what are they to do? Whom are they to believe? The people who affiliate with us are usually postmodern, postscientific. Their sense of life is that it is much too dense, too complicated, too mysterious, to be defined by either theological or scientific rationalism. So they seek some transcendent center, often as yet unnamed, and there are those times when the Church of the Covenant can help them speak the name.

Some of this may sound glib. I have focused on what we have been able to do rather than on what we have not done. The problems are omnipresent. We may not be able to stay in the rapidly deteriorating building, and clearly our location is a key factor in our being accessible to students. Part of the complexity is that students do not generally stabilize the life of the congregation. They are not a source of financial support. They are not able to provide sustained leadership. Before long, they will be on their way.

Perhaps the major inadequacy in our ministry with students is that we have found no way to influence directly the educational institutions in which they spend the major portion of their time. More explicitly, campus-oriented ministries have access to the centers of power and administration. Of course we do not. We are not close enough to the issues of life and death that are being engaged in the classrooms and in the dormitories. We must admit candidly that the life of our congregation is tangential to the rest of what preoccupies the student's time. Perhaps it is true that we function partly as "refuge" or as "hiding place" for the students who associate with us. Those images seem problematic, but still we know that in the stress storms of our culture there is need for that religious mooring also.

The Covenant venture is still in process. As of this writing no one can predict its long-term viability. What is clear is that there is no instant achievement of the purposes of ministry. That is true of students just as much as it is true of ministry with any other group. We have no illusions about that. One of the saints who has given inspiration to us over the years has been the Chilean poet Pablo Neruda. He has enabled us to see and hear what is for us the necessary relationship between poetry and politics. In 1971, Neruda received the Nobel Prize for Literature. At the conclusion of his acceptance speech he said, "Only with a burning patience can we conquer the splendid city which will give light, justice, and dignity to all humankind. In this way and this way alone will the song not have been sung in vain." The necessary ingredient for urban ministry, or for any ministry, is the quality of "burning patience." If that can be sustained, then I am convinced that what we are about shall be worthwhile.

V

Reflections ROBERT RANKIN

I wish to end this work with some reflections about changes in my thoughts, feelings, and convictions during the course of the study. This personal afterword also records impressions, and some hunches about the present conditions and future prospects of ministries in higher education. While these reflections are informed by the wisdom and criticism of my editorial colleagues and members of the Danforth Foundation staff, they are mine. Those persons should not be blamed for any flaws which appear, yet they are to be credited for many of the most stimulating and enduring alterations in my mind and spirit.

I hasten to add that these changes did not occur only within two encapsulated years, 1978–80. The introductory chapter correctly reports that old baggage was hauled into the task from the past. And no doubt the job has been finished with many of those parcels intact and unopened, containing old wine in old wine skins. Yet not all are old. The process of editing this book has been stimulating and life changing.

I

During the early stages of the project, I feared that the design we had developed—which sought the cooperation of Jews, Catholics, and two wings of Protestantism—was a product of liberal Protestant bias. The project ended with that fear both confirmed and challenged. On the one hand, there is no doubt that a Jewish or Catholic or evangelical editor might well have gone about the task differently. On the other hand, the design seemed to have furnished sufficient space for all four groups. For example, Rabbi James Diamond noted:

While it is possible to say that the tripartite schema (spirit, action, community) is a conceptualization derived from liberal Protestantism and imposed on the . . . [plan], this may not be true. Each of the three categories has available referents in the Jewish tradition. It is possible that the third element, community, may be the central one . . . [but] the other two certainly are there. In fact a case might even be made that action is the core of the Jewish way (as opposed, for example, to creed). But the schema can work for the Jewish context, as long as differences are provided for.[1]

At the same time, Rabbi Diamond said that Jewish campus ministry, largely expressed in the B'nai B'rith Hillel Foundation's movement, "is inherently pluralistic. The three papers, excellent as they are, reflect only a narrow part of the spectrum which Hillel people cover . . ."

It must be added that, while we appointed writers with fierce loyalties to their faiths, we chose persons with whom we could work and laugh. There were disagreements by the score among them, but none was ugly, of the kind easily available on the American religious landscape.

As it turned out, our largest flaw, in my opinion, was an offense against liberalism, namely, the low number of writers and consultants among minority clergy, Protestant liberal women clergy, and Roman Catholic clergy.

II

Work on this book began with the assumption that three elements of faith and ministry are important to ministries in higher education and all ministries: spirit, action, and community. It ended with a passionate conviction that those three are not only important but indispensable, and that without them the work of campus ministers is radically hampered. Without them the vocation can be impressive here and attractive there, but in the long run will not and cannot endure. It will only lure people and programs into gimmickry and, worse, imbalance. At the beginning of the project, I assumed that these three dimensions of ministry were separate. The study has ended with a strong conviction that they are inseparable, that they are the warp and woof of a whole interwoven cloth. The need and the hope for ministries in the universities are determined, I am convinced, by this inseparability. They call for fidelity to wholeness in the *spiritual* response of the human being to God, in *contemplation and action* requiring the doing of justice, through *communities of faith* which sustain and nourish us and determine our communal strategies.

The project led not only to an increased degree of commitment to a tripartite ministry, but to changes in kind as well. For example, as a result of our work with Roman Catholics, my eyes were opened to a different and startling view of the connection, the lifeline, between spirituality and justice. They are two views of a single reality. The doing of justice depends upon personal and corporate actions which are rooted in spirituality and which issue in disciplined contemplation. There is such an intimate interconnection between contemplation and action; they are parts of a unifying flowing phenomenon of the Spirit. Contemplation ignited by spirituality is a necessary precondition to action. Contemplation without action hangs there, unfinished, incomplete. Contemplation fused with action is a prerequisite to the doing of justice. Love *is* action, as Thomas Merton said.

Remember the way that David Hubbard put it: "The three sections of this book are of–a–piece: community, contemplation–action, and spirituality. Each is inextricably interwoven with the other. Pull out the strands of any, and the pattern of the other two will unravel."

III

Ministries will unravel if one of the three indispensable parts is neglected; but are the faith communities inseparable? The three dimensions of ministry are interwoven, but I am convinced that the communities of faith are not. I found that, while I longed for catholicity in our relationships, the realities, the needs, and the hopes for campus ministry now and in the immediate future, and recovery of Spirit through them, lie in the mystery and power of the differences among the four faith groups. They *are* linked by their highest common denominators and by cooperative interconfessional work. But, given the power and richness of our present differences, the only way that they could be interwoven would lead toward a tepid pantheism. This would rob us of our stimulating particularities and would debilitate our energies by defusing power through settlement on the lowest common denominators and tempt us into dreary error.

It was exciting, however, to imagine, as Richard Levy suggested, that a new activism may be emerging, arising from efforts to enrich one another through our differences in religious commitment. The Reverend Faith Ferré, a consultant to the project, concurred. In a comment about the work of the National Institute for Campus Ministries, whose mission is inspired by respect for different faiths, she noted that "groups around the country are ready for such communication" and agreed with Rabbi Levy that something new "is in the wind."[2]

The vitality of a new activism depends as much upon recognition of the legitimacy and value of our differences as it does on the knowledge and commitments we hold in common. David Hubbard noted that, while each writer in his section testified to the spiritual enrichment drawn from "the collegiality of others in whom the Spirit is lurking," he also noted that "all the authors write from fierce loyalties to their own traditions."

As I see it, and this is an opinion strengthened by several writers and consultants, the differences among the four faith traditions bring about a "creative tension." As that tension is held and maintained, I dare say that we become vulnerable to one another's highest aspirations and more open to the work of the Spirit.

It is intriguing to reflect how often during the two-year inquiry I heard friendly warnings aimed by liberal Protestants at evangelical Protestants about the possible dangers of evangelical shifts onto liberal trajectories. The former are actually waving stop signs! They know at first hand not only the perils of the liberal track, but the ecumenical damage which would be suffered if the stimulation and challenge of the evangelical difference were exhausted and lost. A witness from another quarter, a university rabbi, made a comparable comment, saying that "the evangelicals are just what the doctor ordered." Their disturbing questions, he said, rout apathetic Jews out of their lethargy and send them running to Hillel for answers.

Something of the same impulse has registered in my mind about the two-way discoveries among Roman Catholics and Protestants. It is from the Catholic difference that liberal Protestants often draw spiritual power, as Edwin Beers testified. It is from the liberal Protestant difference, particularly from its concern for social justice, that some Roman Catholics and some Protestants evangelicals draw inspiration, as Mary Luke Tobin and Ronald Sider have reported.

It is the Christian difference that Max Ticktin found so profoundly influential in his rabbinical growth.

And it is from the sharp and often painful differences between evangelical and liberal Protestants that we so-called mainline people are reminded of the vacuum in campus religious leadership for which we, together with rampant secularist ideologies, are in large part responsible, a vacuum which is being increasingly filled by evangelicals. Surely the time is at hand for liberals to overcome defensiveness about evangelicals, to listen to them and to take them seriously. It is time for us to own up to our own deficiencies, without abandoning for one moment the critically important prophetic functions of challenging social irresponsibility and political reaction wherever we find it whether within or outside evangelical circles. I believe that we are called not to arrest the work of others but to get on with our own work, and to deepen our resources. It is time for us to expend energies not in dreary recitals of unproductive war stories about the admittedly questionable conduct of some other ministries, but in the proclamation of the Gospel story. If we seize the moment to listen to evangelicals carefully, I believe that we will learn largely and some of them will listen to us.

Since I am an ecumenically minded liberal Protestant, it surprised me to recognize the importance and usefulness of differences occurring within the Protestant mainline churches. I began to discern that the recent rise of denominationalism, which had disturbed me, was a useful development. This movement toward renewed denominational identity, which to some critics comes across as a minor scandal, now appears to me to disclose the presence of another kind of creative tension.

One cause of the new denominationalism comes from disenchantment in some churches with an apparently exhausted ecumenism in liberal Protestant campus ministry. This situation has not been resolved by attempts to solve our problems of depleted energies and budgets by organizing and reorganizing and widening the scope of our work. As one who has observed these goings on for thirty-five years, I am tired of them. There is no salvation in organization or reorganization. Power is not generated by talking and writing about power. As a bureaucrat of twenty-two years standing in the ranks of philanthropoids, I know those games from the inside out. I know how aimless it is to play those roles, particularly when the parts are played by bureaucrats who think alike, as if each person in the cast consists of interchangeable parts.

There is no possible way for the church to contend with the ferocity of the narrow mind, the tragedy of Jonestown, the rise of commercial and emotional aggrandizement in religious practice, the mind-boggling ideologies spawned by intellectual secularism—let alone drug abuse, sexual irresponsibility and, underneath it all, systemic greed, racism, and violence—by resorting to organizational charts. The power that is needed to contend with demonic forces comes from the Spirit, a power which requires moral action and generates community, the power of God whose wonderful justice and terrible love broods over us all, a power which I believe is embodied in Jesus Christ.

IV

One of the basic problems of ministries in higher education—perhaps most visible among Protestants, but found among Catholics and Jews as well—is created by the separation of those ministries from the religious communities from which they sprang. Campus ministry has always involved a tricky balance with one foot in the church and one foot in the academy, an awkward straddling position. In many instances, campus ministers have identified themselves more comfortably with the university than with the church and have been infected by academic disdain for institutional religion. This action is caused not simply by apprehensions about the separation of church and state but, more powerfully, I believe, by academic snobbery about the church and the synagogue. I must say that it was far easier, and indeed often a relief, for me to identify with Oberlin College, the Claremont Colleges, the Rockefeller Brothers Fund, or the Danforth Foundation, than with my denomination.

The embarrassment in academic circles over ecclesiastical connections has led to a thinning of relationships between the campus minister and the source of his or her power. Moreover, the campus minister's identification with the academy has provided little spiritual support. What does shore us up and give us the needed connection and depth to channel spiritual power into the academic community? It is not one's identity with the university, but with one's religious community. In that tricky balance, with one foot in the academy and the other in the church, the foot leaning into the church must now carry far more weight than before. Campus ministries are in, but not of, the academy. They can draw strength from intellectual work and from critical minds and scholarship, but not their direction, not their purpose, not their passion. These are generated through the synagogue and the church.

As I have reflected on twenty-two years of experience as an administrator of the Danforth Foundation's programs in campus ministry, a disturbing question has arisen. The Foundation, through its projects and grants and most particularly through its fellowship programs and the conferences conducted for recipients of fellowships, created a fellowship of its own. A community of campus ministers, including a large number of advisors and consultants, took hold and grew. I have come to ask myself whether or not these associations and conferences created something akin to a parachurch—a disquieting thought. The Foundation provided the identity as well as the support, and its officers, including me, served as high priests. Unwittingly the Foundation may have become the locus of a substitute for church, a diversion from church identity.

V

In pondering the three dimensions of faith and the separation of some campus ministries from the churches, I have come to see anew that a dangerous political vacuum exists in campus ministry. I reported it years ago in an article published by *Danforth News and Notes* on the economic reversals suffered by campus ministries. I noted that "the financial problem is by no means caused exclusively by economic recession or a lack of perception and appreciation by educators and churchmen about the realities of campus ministry. The problem is created in large part by campus ministers themselves, particularly by the limited interests among some of them in the churches and their lack of talent in interpreting and developing their mission to the churches." I then quoted a study about campus ministries conducted by Parker Palmer, who had written that "the axe is being wielded by congregations and officials . . . who are thoroughly alienated from the dominant images of what campus ministry is all about. . . . We must put prime culpability in the laps of campus ministers who have proclaimed themselves independent of the parishes. . . . In political terms, campus ministers have simply not cultivated their prime constituency."[3] Since that time little has happened to solve the political problem. This study has convinced me that campus ministers and judicatory officers of the denominations must find a solution.

It may require identification of campus ministry with local parishes and local church organizations. The illustration which Joseph Williamson has contributed to this book about a parish at work with students and faculty is undoubtedly a precursor of things to come. We are seeing in many cases a shift in responsibility for campus ministry from national to local groups. This is happening across the board among Jews, Roman Catholics, and Protestants. One national officer of a mainline Protestant denomination told me in a personal conversation that this is precisely what should happen and that this calls for a "deprofessionalization of campus ministry." I understood him to mean that a greater identification of campus ministry with local parishes is very much to be desired. But are the resources available in the parishes to do the job wisely and well? Could this shift only indicate an invention necessitated by an unfortunate accomplished fact, namely the depletion of energy, commitment, and funds among campus clergy and the denominations? In any event, successful fulfillment of this mission through parishes will not take place by assuming that it will happen. It will come about only through careful, long-range planning and sacrificial investment of leadership and money.

On the other hand, some denominations, unsatisfied with present ecumenical ministries in higher education, are moving on their own to develop new strength in the profession of campus ministry within their own confessional groups. This is not necessarily bad news for ecumenism. I repeat, it may well be that a new denominationalism, in which mainline Protestant churches re-own campus ministry, is required to recover ecumenical strength.

This has led me to reflect again on the research of Kenneth Underwood. It will be remembered that he insisted upon a fourth modality of ministry, the kingly role, the responsibility for governing. (I prefer the word *political* since the interpretation of *kingly*, biblical though it is, has proved to be troublesome.) He correctly perceived that campus ministries are especially flawed in the prophetic and governance responsibilities—a regrettable fact about the 1960s which unfortunately remains true in the 1980s. Those frailties should challenge the church and the university to join forces in the pursuit of "policy research," Underwood's secular term for prophetic inquiry, which, as noted in the introductory chapter on the project's beginnings, could release humanizing energies in both institutions.

A consultant to this study, the Reverend Patricia E. Farris, a United Methodist minister, has added this strong challenge: "If we liberal Protestants have erred on the side of institutional change in the past at the expense of nurturing souls, let us not seek to atone for our sins now by ignoring the governance and prophetic modes of ministry named in the earlier Underwood study. God forbid that our campus ministries become primarily havens within the university where people are healed and protected with little critical regard for the society and institutions which keep us less than whole."[4]

In planning the present volume, I assumed that political responsibility of ministry was contained, in part in the second dimension through prophetic action emerging from contemplative life, and in part in the third, through the governing of religious communities. It is. Yet, as I have reconsidered our original assessment of the essential function of campus ministry, I have concluded that our plan is incomplete. Something basic is missing. Quite apart from the larger purpose of Underwood's work—to assess the church, the university and social policy which, as reported earlier is not within the purview of this book—urgently important political needs within its smaller compass are not addressed. These range from questions repeatedly raised by church officials about the linkage between campus ministries and the denominations, through those raised by academic administrators about the involvement of ministry in the formation of university policy.

To be sure, many of the book's authors, notably but not exclusively in the section on contemplation and action, have worked directly with questions pertaining to the social requirements of the tradition and the gospel. Yet, had we, at the beginning of our work, added the political function to the three upon which we settled, valuable information to the church and the university might have been gleaned. It would have been productive, for example, to have explored fully within the four faith groups the claim made in a report to the Danforth Foundation by Robert McAfee Brown, who said that "campus ministers will not themselves change university policy," but they may be the ones to enable others to come together to "create a healing rather than a destructive environment."[5]

VI

The questions we face are not about the life or death of campus ministries. Rather, they deal with *how* these ministries will live. Will they serve the churches and synagogues responsibly, intelligently, and faithfully? Will they generate strong and well-balanced ministries which honor the missions of the universities and the men and women who live and work within them?

My colleague Warren Bryan Martin, in a staff paper on future trends in higher education, commented about the continuing needs for ministries in higher education. He declared that:

> The values question . . . is fundamental to all else now. The answers to that question . . . will determine how . . . technology is used; how people respond to the ideational challenges of irrationalism; . . . how education is defined.
> All planners must go beyond the "how to" questions to the "why" and "so what" questions. And to move in that direction is very soon to get into the domains of philosophy and religion. There is no escaping hard work in these arenas if we are serious about finding meaning in our daily lives and assigning meaning to our collective future. And for this essential work we need the help of those persons most skilled in it, those for whom those domains are their turf, those persons called theologians and philosophers. . . . And we need their allies, those persons who stand in the border situations between education and religion, between the theory and practice, between college and church—the campus ministers.[6]

Robert McAfee Brown also addressed the values question:

> The minute we begin to press [the values question] we discover . . . that there are different answers; there are competing values and value-systems [which] compete for their survival on the campuses. . . . As we deal with competing value-systems we discover that many of the values by means of which the university and the culture operate are covert rather than overt. Many within the university and the culture have made a value choice that is implicit in their decisions although often not explicitly stated. . . . This suggests that one of the most crucial things for the health of the university and the culture is to get value-assumptions out in the open where they can be examined, tested and when necessary challenged.

Brown then asked, "Who is doing this job in higher education?" In his search for the answer to that question, he found few persons dedicated to that task. He concluded that:

All of this points to a significant and indeed essential role for campus ministry. Whatever else campus ministers do, they have an obligation to raise questions about the values assumption of the community they serve, particularly when others are failing to do so. . . . Their professional training is precisely in [this] area. . . . They are the inheritors and articulators of tradition that have placed central premium on identifying and embodying the values by which we live and die. . . . At a time when the value-assumptions of many within the university are covert, the value assumptions of campus minsters are overt, or should be, and this enables them to insist that others be equally forthright about where they stand.[7]

Reflections on the values question have led me to review the work of the Danforth Foundation in this field, namely support for research in the developmental stages of moral growth. At first, I questioned the validity of the research because it seemed to ignore the religious faiths from which values derive. However, it became increasingly clear that the separation of values eduation from explicit religious commitments was caused primarily by a legitimate concern about the intrusion of religious doctrines into public education. Moreover, the results of the research proved to be immensely useful to campus ministers. Beginning with a consultation with the leading investigator in the field, Lawrence Kohlberg of Harvard University, the Foundation initiated a series of seminars led by Robert Spivey, now president of Randolph Macon Woman's College. Those meetings demonstrated clearly that the techniques of values education can be useful tools for ministries in higher education.

The pioneering work of James Fowler of Emory University, who applied Kohlberg's research to faith development, is equally significant. Fowler, in collaboration with Gary Chamberlain of Seattle University and Sharon Parks of the Harvard Divinity School, served as consultants to our investigation and prepared working papers which persuasively articulate the usefulness of this new interdisciplinary field—faith development—to ministries in higher education.

Growth in stages is as old as humankind, as old as families and schools and spiritual nurture. Some critics find a theological problem in the idea of faith "development" because faith, they contend, is given in grace and not cranked up by human effort; yet the discipline of faith development addresses directly a widely recognized problem. The problem is caused by the unfortunate separation of religious growth from intellectual growth which often occurs in the teaching-learning process. When a student, or a teacher, remains fixed or retarded in his or her religious perceptions, while moving rapidly into new and sophisticated perceptions in other areas, faith inevitably becomes anachronistic. Growth in both must be congruent, equally well informed, for the person to achieve autonomy, responsibility and balance. On that ground alone, the investigations of Chamberlain, Fowler, and Parks are worthy of attention by persons concerned about the recovery of spirit in higher education.

VII

For its own health, the university needs competing epistemologies and spiritual disciplines to help clarify the values which undergird its life. In his interpretative commentary for this book's essays on community, Myron Bloy reminds us that communal problems created in academic life are serious ones indeed: "Higher education today is not merely empty of its formerly communal purpose and character, but it also serves as one of the great socializing instrumentalities for the atomistic individualism which has deeply undermined all of our traditional forms of community and even our primary cultural and spiritual capacities for knowing as communal beings."

This dangerous communal void can be filled, at least in part, through the cultivation by campus ministers not only of spiritual perception but competing epistemologies. It is in response to such need that David Maitland, chaplain and professor of religion at Carleton College, noted in a commentary for this book that campus ministers and religiously committed professors are called to a lover's quarrel with the university. Parker Palmer also reminds us of it in his comment about the "difference of assumption behind contemplation in spiritual tradition and contemplation in the university. The intellectual eye looks around and sees smug self-serving notions . . . and looks for the scalpel to dissect them with. The spiritual eye [sees] . . . brokenness and fragmentation and alienation and proceeds to seek a source of healing and wholeness." Palmer argues that religious traditions "see beyond the facade of unity and beyond the inner brokenness into that loving source which sets all life in motion and yearns to restore us to our original wholeness . . ."

VIII

Another observation with which I began this work remains fixed: the needs we confront for religious leadership are so large and variegated that it is impossible and wasteful to leave the solution of these problems only in the hands of professional campus ministers. Robert L. Johnson, president of the National Institute for Campus Ministries, estimates that as many as twelve thousand people are "giving primary attention between religion and higher education."[8] Yet, considering the extent of the need, the variety of skills required, and the immensity of the academic population, that reservoir of talent is not nearly sufficient to solve the problems we confront. Solutions must often start with professional people, but they are the first to insist that the ministry of the laity and the collaboration of faithful persons in all academic disciplines are fundamental to the task of ministry.

Nothing has happened during the course of the two years of investigation to change that opinion. I have in mind not only the financial and advisory assistance that members of faculties and administrative staffs supply to campus ministry programs, but, far more important, their contributions to religious vitality through their primary vocations as professors and administrators. A striking personal experience has dramatized this conviction and has furnished abundant evidence that there is, among American academic people, a large reservoir of men and women whose work makes a critical difference in the spiritual and moral quality of academic life. It furnishes ground for hope that the need for leadership can be met.

The evidence has been supplied by more than three decades of experience I have had with faculty members, especially during the last twenty-two years, with persons appointed to the Danforth Graduate Fellowship Program and the Danforth Associate Program. The Associate Program, which I directed for seventeen years, has appointed thousands of carefully selected college teachers and their wives and husbands to seek to improve the quality of teaching and of student-faculty relations. In the early years of the Foundation's work, these men and women were chosen in part because of their explicit commitment to religious faith, as well as their concern for humane values in academic life and their scholarly talents. In later years, less explicit emphasis was placed on religion, yet the commitment to humane values and professional excellence have been maintained.

These are academic people who combine competence and compassion; they possess a keen personal concern for students and for the quality of life on campus. Those seventeen years of work in the selection of Danforth Associates and in directing national conferences for new appointees and annual regional conferences for all Danforth Associates, convinced me that, throughout our academic institutions, there are many teacher-scholars whose values and intentions are similar to, and often identical with, those of campus ministers. It is, as Myron Bloy claimed earlier in this volume, "the presence of faithful Jews and Christians ... which can bring a steady, healing challenge" to academic life. For one, I do not hesitate to say that they comprise a latent church.

IX

We are witnessing an exciting development in the leadership of the American religious community which holds large promise, I believe, for the recovery of spirit in higher education. It is rooted in the women's movement, cultivated by recent dramatic increases in the enrollment of women in theological schools, and refined in the persistence of women to become ordained and to achieve full recognition in the church and the synagogue. Strikingly different religious leaders are appearing who are beginning to make a profound, and I dare say urgently needed, impact on ministries in higher education. Their contribution only begins with their insistence on equality.

Where is the Spirit moving? In reply to that question, the Reverend Patricia Farris wrote, "One answer I would give is in the souls and lives of women coming to a new consciousness and action. .... I know the joy of awakening in women faculty, staff and students, new senses of themselves, their potential, their spirituality and their power to make decisions about their lives."[9] And the strength begun in this new awareness enriches the whole community. "One of the beauties of the women's movement in the church," the Reverend Faith Ferré wrote, "is that it includes all people in the revisions it would make ... not just women."[10]

Of course, women have served with distinction from the beginning: notably among nuns of the Roman Catholic church and Protestant women serving in such organizations as the Young Women's Christian Association. These were, and are, precursors of the new wave of strength and renewal created by women and felt in all sectors of American religious life. It is significant that the final class of Underwood fellows appointed by the Danforth Foundation for the academic year 1976–77 contained more women appointees than men. This was the first time that had happened during the twenty years Danforth campus ministry fellowships were offered. It is also significant that that class included women from the Jewish, Roman Catholic, and Protestant communities. This kindling of women's leadership promises to be one of the most crucial and beneficial changes in American religious life, because it brings not only new energy, but new vision and hope for ministries to reach women— and men. Yet the fulfillment of that promise will turn on the vocational opportunities opened to women in religious professions whose appointment policies and practices remain dominated by men.

X

My reflections about this book prior to our deadline for the first drafts from the twelve authors coincided with a curious and revelatory circumstance of sequential readings and happenings. By that time, I had become addicted to the writings of Lewis Thomas and had read his celebrated *The Lives of the Cell.* Early in that work, Thomas quoted a scientist (Ziman) who had noted that "the invention of a mechanism for the systematic publication of *fragments* of scientific work may well have been the key event in the history of modern science." Thomas then added, "This technique, of soliciting many modest contributions to the store of human knowledge ... achieves a corporate, collective power that is far greater than one individual can exert."

Lewis Thomas then examined the word *explore.* It has, he wrote, "its origins in the sounds we make while engaged in it. We like to think of exploring in science as a lonely, meditative business, and so it is in the first stages, but always, sooner or later before the enterprise reaches completion, as we explore, we call to each other, communicate, publish, send letters to the editor, present papers, cry out on finding."[11]

This book consists of fragments which, I believe, call to one another, build on each other, and together make a corporate sound which we believe needs hearing. We disagree about many things and I go off in quite different directions, yet the sounds we make are not babble but clear calls. We need each other.

It was at about the same time that I found myself preoccupied with problems caused by the fierceness and the blandness of religious beliefs, by the frightening power generated by tight doctrinal and behavioral constrictions of some religious communities and the flatness of some others which are so wide open as to require nothing at all.

Both invite trouble. Width can lead to such openness among some intellectuals that, as a college president once said, "one can hear the wind howling through their open minds." On the other hand, the narrow mind can come close to, or move well into, irrationality and gross irresponsibility. It can create self-righteousness on a colossal scale, escalating into a wretched idolatry in which we confuse our minds with the mind of God. It can create Jonestown. It is particularly dangerous during times of crisis and fear, precisely the mood which is mounting in our land.

I found myself struggling over these questions as the deadline for these drafts was approaching. For reasons beyond my ken, I began to think about these phenomena in symbols related to water. The ferocity of the narrow mind reminded me of the immense power created by a mountain stream pouring down a canyon, plunging and spraying as it descends from great heights through the narrows of confining rock, its power generated by huge quantities of water forced through a narrow passage, like the nozzle of a hose. On the other hand, the lassitude of the wide-open mind reminded me of the water at the bottom of the mountain, moving out into shallow streams, into the flat lands, there to spread out until its power is dissipated in the swamps or evaporated in wide-open spaces.

These water symbols were still swimming around in my mind when Mrs. Rankin and I celebrated our wedding anniversary in September of 1979 and, a week later, my birthday. These occasions are of no moment save for two insights they generated. On our wedding anniversary, we chose to have dinner on the *Belle Angeline,* a Mississippi riverboat. As we boarded, I was struck by the powerful movement of the water flowing hard and fast downstream under the boarding ramp; as we sat near a riverside window, I was fascinated by the wide sweep as well as the swift and vast current of the great river. How to understand it?

At the birthday party a week later, a friend brought the gift of a paperback book he admired. The next day, a bright and sunny Saturday, I casually picked it up as I went outside for some relaxing poolside reading. The water symbols persisted, not only in the setting of a swimming pool, but also in the book. The opening paragraph of Mark Twain's *Life on the Mississippi* hit me with the force of revelation:

The Mississippi is well worth reading about. It is not a commonplace river . . . instead of widening towards its mouth, it grows narrower . . . and deeper. From the junction of the Ohio to a point half-way down to the sea, the width averages a mile in high water; thence to the sea the width steadily diminishes, until at "The Passes," above the mouth, it is but little over half a mile. At the junction of the Ohio the Mississippi's depth is 87 feet; the depth increases, gradually reaching 129 feet just above the mouth.[12]

There it was: the combination of the river's width, depth, and embankment which creates a steady flow of force. The width means openness and perspective. Shoring of the width brings greater depth. The embankment contains and disciplines the flow, preventing dispersion and division. Here are some ingredients for healthy balance: the depth of religious experience and the width of the intellect; the width of religious faiths and the depth of the intellect. In combinations of intelligence and grace, of width and embankment producing force and depth, the needed perspectives and power of campus ministry can be nurtured.

Are these easy to achieve—this balance of width and depth, this joining of mind and spirit, this linkage of Athens and Jerusalem? Emphatically no. They require hard work and sacrificial labor to achieve and grace to receive. We help one another by the sounds we make as we test the depth and the width of the river and the shores of commitments. Here is challenging space for the vocation of campus ministry, for the rabbis, priests, nuns and ministers who invest their lives in colleges and universities.

XI

The study began with an assumption on my part that campus ministries are here to stay, and that assumption has become a conviction. Good or bad, weak or strong, balanced or unbalanced, whether or not committed to the mission of the university as well as the church, whether in established residential universities or in community colleges, ministries in higher education are a permanent feature on the American landscape. Various forms of the vocation vanish, often deservedly, but not its function or its people. They cannot be stamped out by the ferocity of opposition, nor withered by yawning indifference. The vocation has been on the American scene from the beginning of the colonial colleges with their president-clergymen, to the variegated ministries at work in the large secular multiuniversities of our time, and they will continue. Religious faith is indelibly imprinted in the soul of America and it will be expressed wherever people are gathered together, especially in visible and vulnerable places such as our colleges and universities. The forms and functions and the means of support change, and their qualities vary from the ghastly to the magnificent, but its presence is inevitable. Although the two years of investigation found many flaws in the vocation, nothing has been discovered to challenge the assumption that these ministries are in place permanently.

XII

In the introductory essay, I questioned the significance of such trivial events as those which occurred in a little California parish thirty-eight years ago. I have come to see that they were not all that trivial. They revealed the urgent need for balanced ministries and were related to the challenge of world issues.

Thus, at the end of this book, I dare to declare that small and almost invisible actions can make all the difference in the world. Concerned campus ministers, teachers, and administrators, through their attitudes and intentions, can remove the chill from an academic world which sometimes seems impersonal and purposeless. Their passionate concern for the recovery of Spirit in higher education and their genuine interest in persons can convert the climate of an academic institution from the fetid atmosphere of a suffocating imprisonment to the open and fresh air of intellectual and spiritual freedom.

Their passion derives from a loving power at work in our midst, sometimes seen fleetingly as through a mirror darkly, sometimes felt in the process of daily work, through a power which haunts, excites, and beckons us, despite our uncertainties. It is not that our eyes see outwardly toward God, but that God sees inwardly into us. We are being watched by one who cares for us with an overwhelming passion—one who knows us and our history with an intimate knowledge beyond the telling and with an unquenchable desire for justice. Here is the highest common denominator.

NOTES

1. James Diamond, memorandum to editor, January 1980.
2. Faith Ferré, United Campus Ministries, Drake University, letter to editor, 1979.
3. Robert Rankin, "Campus Ministry—Dead or Alive?" *Danforth News and Notes* 7, no. 2 (February 1972): p. 1.
4. Patricia E. Farris, United Campus Ministries, University of Delaware, letter to editor, September 1979.
5. Robert McAfee Brown, "A Review of Danforth Campus Ministry Grants, 1973," in *Church Society for College Work Report* 33, no. 1 (January 1974): p. 4.
6. Warren Bryan Martin, Danforth Foundation staff statement, May 1979.
7. Brown, "A Review. . . ."
8. Robert L. Johnson, "What *Is* Campus Ministry," in *The NICM Journal* 4, no. 2 (Spring 1979): p. 6.
9. Farris, letter to editor.
10. Ferré, letter to editor.
11. Lewis Thomas, *The Lives of a Cell* (New York: Viking Press, 1974), pp. 15, 16.
12. Mark Twain, *Life on the Mississippi* (New York: Bantam Books, 1979), p. 1.

Appendices

APPENDIX I

Formation of Religious Communities
Lucien Roy

Anxiety and concentration on the how and why of community is a phenomenon of an age which has lost it. As Rosemary Ruether points out, "When communities are working well they don't ask themselves what makes a community work, people just assume that this is the normal way to be."[1] For many people today, however, the sense of belonging that extends beyond our family and intimate friends is destroyed or diminished. With the growth of bureaucracy, the individual has come to feel progressively isolated amid a bewildering array of social systems. Many people are suspicious of others' motives and even of their own. This alienation results in a social demoralization and powerlessness that permeates the lives of those in higher education as deeply as anywhere else in our society. On campuses, as elsewhere, people are looking to religion for assistance in resisting the debilitating effects of this isolation.

Turning to campus ministers and rabbis in this crisis is not without reason. Both Hebrew and Christian Scriptures are filled with images of community as willed by God, as essential to humankind, as the dream and paradigm of salvation. Centuries of teachings and theologies speak of the special character of the "people of God." Yet there is an ever-present temptation for religious groups to be lulled by our language and blinded to the erosion of our actual community life. Some religious groupings experience difficulties unique to themselves, but common to all the faith traditions are these recurring obstacles to genuine community: the mobility and transiency of

EDITOR'S NOTE: This article was prepared originally for an address given to a conference sponsored by the Indiana Newman Foundation and the Danforth Foundation, the first of a series of consultations conducted in 1979–80 to explore the initial findings of the Danforth study. While the perspective of Dr. Roy's paper differs from the points of view of the other chapters of the book, I know that readers concerned for the health and endurance of religious communities in academic institutions will find it useful and stimulating.

student members; the history of American self-reliance and the current "pursuit of loneliness"; the issue of inclusion and exclusion—of who belongs and who does not; the tension between local community and universality; the issue of diversity and unity; and, in all of them, the role of women.

It is with conviction of the need for authentic communities of faith in the present and concern for their survival in the future that we wish to turn for the moment from religious reflection to sociological analysis. Our search is for the working knowledge and skills that can help us contribute to the establishment of faith communities that will last into the future. Our dream is of such communities of faithful Jews and Christians situated in and responding to the world of American higher education in the decades ahead.

We propose first to examine community as a sociological form and then to reflect on specific qualities which characterize a healthy faith community. In light of these considerations we hope to identify certain skills required of any of us who wish to collaborate in building those future faith communities.

COMMUNITY

In speaking of community, we are not only talking of a feeling or an experience. The term *community* has the connotation of certain feelings for all of us—warmth, belonging, neighborliness, connectedness. To have participated in Pope John Paul II's mass in Chicago was an excellent example of that feeling. To have held hands with the million gathered there and softly to have joined in singing "Amazing Grace" was such an experience of community. But that is not what we are talking about here.

Nor are we concerned with the use of *community* as a term to mask or disguise harsh bureaucratic realities, as when one refers to the "intelligence community" rather than to the CIA.

Nor again are we interested here in the use of the term to express our dreams for the whole church or the entire world as one community. Such language can deny our experience of disjointedness.

Rather, we want to speak of local faith communities, the groups of believers with which we are involved on our campuses. We are to think small, to identify a particular group of people and to focus on them as we examine the concept of community as descriptive of a particular pattern of interactions.

Evelyn Whitehead has constructed a convenient chart which identifies six stable elements characterizing any grouping of persons (see below). She identifies, in a vertical listing, the following six dimensions of group interactions:
1. the major focus of the group
2. the extent of involvement of the members
3. the appropriate level of emotional sharing
4. the ways in which behavior is regulated
5. the nature of the members' obligations
6. the basis for evaluation.

Each of these six elements is situated along a horizontal continuum on which one can plot the manner in which each of these interactions is carried out in a particular group. For purposes of illustration, we will sketch the characteristic patterns of interaction for the two extremes on the continuum. No group exists in such a pure form. Rather, these extremes are models for our understanding. At one extreme is the primary group, the clearest example of which is the family. At the other end of the continuum is the associational group, exemplified by the factory or corporation.

In the primary group, the major focus of the group members is on themselves. The extent of involvement is total, that is, the whole person is engaged and not some limited aspect. The appropriate level of sharing is complete in range and depth. Behavior is regulated by implicit norms that are taken for granted and rarely need to

DIMENSIONS OF GROUP LIFE[2]

A. primary focus of group	*internal* (group itself)	4	3	2	1	2	3	4	*external* (task)
B. "how much" of the individual is involved	*total* (many aspects of self shared)	4	3	2	1	2	3	4	*partial* (role)
C. degree of emotional involvement	*emotional* depth	4	3	2	1	2	3	4	*emotional neutrality*
D. basis of regulation	*custom/ social pressure*	4	3	2	1	2	3	4	*law/contract procedures*
E. scope of obligation	*diffuse* (whatever is needed; loyalty)	4	3	2	1	2	3	4	*specific* (limited by contract)
F. basis for evaluation	*ascription* ('one of us,' belonging to group)	4	3	2	1	2	3	4	*achievement* (fulfills tasks: performance)

be made explicit. The obligations of the members are extensive and diffuse. The basis for evaluation of the group members is that of ascription, the feeling that a given member is "one of us."

In the pure model of associational grouping, the major focus of the group is the performance of a task or the production of some product. The members are expected to be involved partially, only in terms of the roles they play in relation to accomplishing the group task. Very little is expected or tolerated in terms of emotional sharing; the preference is for neutrality or superficiality. Behavior is regulated by detailed and articulated norms. Obligations are specifically limited and clearly stated. The basis of evaluation for each member is solely in relation to production and achievement.

In order to be able actively to take a role in community formation, it is crucial to realize that community is neither primary group nor associational group, neither family nor factory. Rather, the model of community is located between the extremes of the continuum. As a pattern of social interaction, community has some features of the family and some of the factory, but none in an extreme form.

Like the formal association, a community is characterized by a major focus that reaches beyond the group members. There is concern for a task to be achieved. Like the family, there is a community expectation that more than isolated aspects of the members' lives will be involved. In the community, there is a higher expectation than in the association for in-depth sharing of emotions. But the community shifts toward the associational end of the continuum with its more explicit ways of regulating behavior. The obligations and rights of the community members are rather well spelled out. Depending on the particular community, a rather high priority may be given to the accomplishment of the task as a criterion of evaluation.

In the same way that no family or association exists in a pure form, no one community will exactly resemble another. Communities will differ from one another in the stress put on one or more of the variables on the grid. We can think, for example, of the differences between a small team of ministers and the larger congregation that gathers for Sunday worship.

In summary, then, as Evelyn Whitehead points out in her article, "Clarifying the Meaning of Community," the community fulfills a number of important functions for its members. It provides a social setting beyond the family where members experience themselves and can be experienced by others in a more complete and authentic manner than their social roles often permit. The community allows the members to express both emotional and intellectual aspects of themselves. The community provides a vehicle for greater public involvement; it serves also as a buffer between the individual and the public world. Community points to the possibility of a shared vision that can move persons to purposeful action in a public sphere, undertaken in a context of mutual concern.[3]

CHARACTERISTICS OF COMMUNITY

This clarification of the idea of community can help us to focus on our role in developing future faith communities. Having located community as a social form between primary group and association, we will now study five elements or characteristics present in any community. These elements are:
1. a common orientation toward some significant aspect of life
2. some agreement about values
3. a commitment to common goals
4. opportunities for personal exchange
5. agreed-upon definitions of what is expected of membership in this group.[4]

Any community that lasts will be marked by these five qualities. Our interest, however, is not just in community in general, but in the particular characteristics of a faith community. We will examine each of the five elements listed above in the particular context of a faith community. We will then indicate the knowledge and the skills that seem to be needed by anyone who would take an active role in the formation of such faith communities.

COMMON ORIENTATION

The first quality of the successful community is that of "common orientation toward some significant aspect of life." For the faith community, this will clearly be a religious concern. For the Jewish community, this may be expressed as concern for "the fulfillment of the covenant between God and Israel." In the Christian context, the concern of the group could be expressed as faith that Jesus the Christ is risen and lives today and the community gathers in his Spirit in worship of the Father and service of their sisters and brothers. Unless this concern is of vital personal signifiance to the members, the community will be short lived and superficial. In addition, it is clear that in the context of the university, such a community must include faculty and administrators as well as students if there is to be continuity. Likewise, unless the community concerns actually address real university issues, it will not be a faith community in the university context.

The skills required of those who wish to form such community are rather clear. There is a genuine need for the ability truly to make accurate assessment of real needs. Such assessment of actual situations must be made in the light of one's religious tradition. Secondly, there is the need for vital communal worship as an extrarational statement of the group's common orientation. This entails true celebration of the communal commitment to this religious concern. Thirdly, the members of the community need continually to monitor the changes in their situation and gauge impact on both individuals and the systems in which they are involved.

There must be some congruence among community members about the basic values of their religious experience. The values—standards accepted with commitment and carried out in action—are those formed in the faith tradition, tested in one's experience, and applied to the present situation. There need not be an absolute conformity on the part of the members. What is needed is tolerance and the ability to share to some degree without divisiveness. The challenge of endurance is to accept these differences and to harmonize these in ways that contribute to the group's functioning.

Care must be paid both to accomplishment of the community task and to the maintenance of the individual members. In this striving toward congruence in values, the community must be vigilant in resisting reductionism and one-dimensional simplicity. A faith community that can last with tolerance is already exhibiting a prophetic stance against the current trends toward repression and conformity.

In addition to that staunch resistance to reductionism, the group must have the ability successfully to mediate conflict. The ability productively to work through the tensions of conflicting values toward a working compromise that incorporates genuine conviction is essential to the life of the faith community. It may be appropriate at this point to remind ourselves of the need to cherish ecumenism and interfaith endeavors as genuine values and not as expediencies where lack of budget and personnel necessitate collaboration.

COMMON GOALS

Community, as has been noted, exists not only for the members, but for action outside the group. In theological language, those actions are described as the fulfillment of the covenant or the building of the kingdom. One portion of that action is, however, directed toward the members in helping to prepare, develop and train them for action. For the faith community, this clearly includes contemplation and prayer as well as skill development. The action orientation of the faith community is not an optional aspect. As a matter of fact, in the case of many faith communities, the outreach program or mission has been one of the most attractive features for new members. Beyond the element of attractiveness, it should be remembered that a community is not likely to endure without some common action.

In terms of the qualities required in the community to assure this commitment to and pursuit of goals, there is need for assessment and planning skills, adeptness at problem solving, and, in particular, the need to call the community to concreteness. One area where faith communities often fail is in their ability to move their overarching goals into operational behaviors. Faith communities also need continually to examine whether or not they are taking a systemic approach to problems.

OPPORTUNITIES FOR PERSONAL EXCHANGE

The fifth requisite characteristic of communities that survive is the presence of opportunities for personal exchange. The form and the forum for such exchange will vary from community to community. But regardless of the type selected, those opportunities must enhance the development of mutuality in interpersonal relationships between members. These dimensions of mutuality are especially important in the overall context of the faith community's goals of striving to achieve religious values. Egan and Cowan outline three levels of interpersonal relationships, each of which builds upon the preceding one.[5] The first level is that of *support*. In this dimension, the members—at the least—regard one another and relate to one another with basic decency. The members feel that they need not be "on guard." Rather, there is a confidence that they will be heard and understood. The second level is that of *responsible challenge*. Members can expect that, within the atmosphere of understanding and trust, they will be positively challenged to consider their behavior from frames of reference other than their own. This type of positive challenge results not in defensiveness, but in the exploration of one's behavior to consider alternatives. The third level is that of *immediacy*, which is described by Egan and Cowan as "the ability of persons to talk directly about the current state of their relationship as it pertains to the common mission."[6] For example, a priest in the community may be invited to explore the impact of his recent ordination on a female colleague. Again, this confrontation is done in such a way as to invite me to explore my actual present behavior and to change in a way that enables growth.

The skills required of group members to provide and take advantage of such opportunities for personal exchange are as follows. At the first level, the skills needed are those of self-disclosure and accurate empathy, the ability to communicate to another that I understand that person in his or her own frame of reference.

The level of responsible challenge supposes that members are capable of not attacking another member's weaknesses, but, in an atmosphere of trust, of inviting the member to reflect on his or her behavior from another's point of view. A member can also be challenged to examine his or her undeveloped potential. Without these skills, the feedback and acquisition of new information needed by the group will not be possible. Only in this way can the faith community avoid stagnation and remain in touch with the real changing environment. This dimension of responsible challenge is also the way in which faith communities can avoid taking advantage of persons who might at first gravitate to the group because they are hungry for relationship and seek security. This guarantee of responsible challenge can alleviate any fear of unfairly attracting unsuspecting people to the group at a vulnerable period in their lives.

The skills appropriate at the level of immediacy include the ability to confront a real present issue between the individual and another group member that is preventing or limiting growth. It should be remembered that this type of challenge is appropriate only with reference to behaviors involved in the achievement of the community's task.

In this fifth dimension of the life of the faith community, we touch upon those elements which are most apt to be the downfall of the community. Faith communities are often designed from the beginning to fail because the members bring rigid notions of how the community ought to be and function. It is in this context that the use of the grid conceived by Evelyn Whitehead can be used to clarify the precise expectations of the group members. This ministry of clarification is a necessary step in providing for the continued life and development of the faith community. It is in this area that some form of consensus needs to be reached concerning roles and responsibilities as well as about details such as frequency of meetings or the place to gather.

In light of the needs of the members, and as a response to some of the obstacles described earlier, there are four qualities which in my judgment should be present in a sound faith community.

First, we must recognize that the gift of the individual is for the community. Therefore, the healthy community will recognize and support the gifts present in each of its members regardless of that person's sex or office. The group that is blind to the presence of those gifts or refuses to benefit from their exercise can never expect to flourish. In this regard, it must be remembered that leadership is not necessarily linked to office.

Secondly, the healthy faith community must move away from dependence on the clerical model of the designated minister. Instead, as Egan and Cowan suggest, we should move toward the model of the ministering community in which the believers minister to one another.[7] Only then can we move away from the toxic effects inherent in the clerical model, the depersonalization of the elite clerical cast and the dependence and ultimate powerlessness of the "faithful" waiting always to be ministered to.

Thirdly, we must realize that no one faith community can survive in isolation. Faith communities need one another and must work toward interdependence. It is precisely in this context that the issue of universality is encountered.

Finally, one caution for any faith community is not to foster dependence in its members. Our goal must be continually to enhance the confidence of the members that they can in due time go off and help to establish other communities. Empowerment of the members, and not dependence, is a sign of health.

Clearly, it is this entire realm of expectations of membership that is the test of any faith community. This is the arena in which some form of compromise must be struggled for among all the differing expectations about sharing, cooperation, authority, leadership and so on. The community that is capable of ongoing, honest efforts at clarification of expectations, discernment of differing values, and constructive resolution of conflict will last into the future.

FUTURE

The question about the future of the faith community in higher education, then, is really a question about our present choices.

The faith community can stand as an antidote to social alienation (the sense of not connecting meaningfully with the systems in our lives) and to collectivism (control by multinationals and federal bureaucracy). The faith community can provide support for the religious values of our traditions and for the development of members through challenge. The faith community can be a refuge and a buffer against those contrary forces outside itself. The faith community can also provide a base for confronting issues in the future as they affect the individuals and the systems in our universities.

Formulating such programmatic strategies, studying the nature of organizational structures, and acquiring professional skills can help us work toward creating the robust faith communities so needed in the world of higher education in America. The future is not there for us to stumble upon; it is waiting for us to form in the spirit of the living God who created us for community.

NOTES

1. Rosemary Reuther, *The Theology of Experience*, Paramus, N.J., Newman Press, 1972, p. 34.
2. These considerations depend heavily on the nature of the group.
3. Evelyn Eaton Whitehead, "Clarifying the Meaning of Community" Volume 15, #3, Fall 1978, p. 385.
4. Whitehead, p. 376.

5. Gerard Egan, Michael A. Cowan, *People in Systems: A Model for Development in the Human-Service Professions and Education,* Monterey, California, Brooks/Cole Publishing Company, 1979.
6. Ibid, p. 189.
7. Ibid, pp. 175–76.

APPENDIX II

Roster of Participants

DIRECTORS

Reverend Myron B. Bloy, Jr., editor, NICM *Journal;* chaplain and professor of religion, Sweet Briar College, Sweet Briar, Virginia
Reverend Dr. David A. Hubbard, president, Fuller Theological Seminary, Pasadena, California
Dr. Parker J. Palmer, dean of studies, Pendle Hill, Quaker Study Center, Wallingford, Pennsylvania

WRITERS

Reverend Beverly A. Asbury, chaplain, Vanderbilt University, Nashville, Tennessee
Reverend Edwin E. Beers, United Ministries in Higher Education, University of Wisconsin, Madison
Rabbi Richard N. Levy, executive director, Los Angeles Hillel Council, Los Angeles, California
Sister Nancy Malone, O.S.U., director, The Beacon Retreat Center, Beacon, New York
Reverend Eric Payne, advisor to minority students, Gordon-Conwell Theological Seminary, South Hamilton, Massachusetts
Mrs. Rebecca Manley Pippert, national consultant on evangelism, Inter-Varsity Christian Fellowship, Washington, D.C.
Sister Elaine M. Prevallet, Sisters of Loretto, Nerinx, Kentucky
Dr. Lucien Roy, associate director, The Institute of Pastoral Studies at Loyola University, Chicago, Illinois; formerly director of campus ministry, St. Louis University, St. Louis, Missouri
Dr. Ronald J. Sider, associate professor of theology, Eastern Baptist Theological Seminary, Philadelphia, Pennsylvania
Rabbi Max D. Ticktin, professor of Jewish studies, George Washington University, Washington, D.C.
Sister Mary Luke Tobin, director, Merton Center for Social Change, Denver, Colorado

Reverend Joseph C. Williamson, pastor, Church of the Covenant, Boston, Massachusetts

Rabbi Arnold J. Wolf, director, Hillel Foundation, Yale University, New Haven, Connecticut

CONSULTANTS

Reverend Reuben Baerwald, director, Lutheran Council in the United States of America, Chicago, Illinois

Mrs. Virginia Suggs Brown, senior editor, McGraw-Hill, Webster Division, St. Louis, Missouri; member, Board of Trustees, Danforth Foundation.

Reverend Robert Bullock, pastor, Our Lady of Sorrows Church, Sharon, Massachusetts; formerly director of campus ministry, the Archdiocese of Boston

Dr. John Cantelon, provost, Central Michigan University; formerly chaplain, University of Southern California, Los Angeles, California

Dr. Corbin Carnell, professor of English, University of Florida, Gainsville, Florida

Dr. Gary Chamberlain, professor, department of theology and religious studies, Seattle University, Seattle, Washington

Rabbi James S. Diamond, director, B'nai B'rith Hillel Foundation, St. Louis, Missouri

Reverend Ralph G. Dunlop, formerly chaplain, Northwestern University, Evanston, Illinois

Mrs. Alice Frazer Evans, Hartford Seminary Foundation, Hartford, Connecticut

Dr. Robert Evans, Hartford Seminary Foundation, Hartford, Connecticut

Reverend Patricia E. Farris, United Campus Ministry, University of Delaware, Newark, New Jersey

Reverend Faith Ferré, United Ministries in Higher Education, Drake University, Des Moines, Iowa

Dr. James Fowler, Candler School of Theology, Emory University, Atlanta, Georgia

Monsignor Gerard N. Glynn, director, Newman Center, Washington University, St. Louis, Missouri

Reverend Douglas H. Gregg, chaplain, Occidental College, Los Angeles, California

Dr. Anne Harrison, coordinator for lay ministries and women, The Episcopal Church Center, New York, New York

Mrs. Marlene Hathaway, assistant to the dean of arts and sciences, University of Akron, Akron, Ohio

Reverend Richard Hicks, director, Wesley Foundation, The United Methodist Ministry at Howard University, Washington, D.C.; formerly director, Ministries to Blacks in Higher Education, Inc.

Reverend Henry H. Horn, pastor emeritus, University Lutheran Church, Cambridge, Massachusetts

Dr. Charles E. Hummel, director of faculty ministries, Inter-Varsity Christian Fellowship, Grafton, Massachusetts

Reverend Robert Johnson, president, National Institute for Campus Ministries, Newton Center, Massachusetts

Dr. George Jones, director of religious programs, Ball State University, Muncie, Indiana

Dr. Bernard LaFayette, professor, The Lindenwood College, St. Louis, Missouri; formerly director of central region, The National Institute for Campus Ministries

Dr. John McClusky, executive director, the Coro Foundation, St. Louis, Missouri

Sister Julia Mahoney, R.S.M., director of campus ministry, Carlow College, Pittsburgh, Pennsylvania

Reverend David Maitland, chaplain and professor of religion, Carleton College, Northfield, Minnesota

Dr. Sharon Parks, instructor, Harvard Divinity School, Cambridge, Massachusetts

Reverend Alfred C. Payne, counselor for religious affairs, Virginia Polytechnic Institute and State University, Blacksburg, Virginia

Reverend Phillip Schroeder, director, Center for the Study of Campus Ministry, Valparaiso University, Valparaiso, Indiana

Dr. Barbara Wheeler, president, Auburn Theological Seminary, New York, New York